Ann Of 1,000 Lives
Author Ann Palmer relives her own Past Lives

by Ann Palmer

iUniverse, Inc.
Bloomington

Ann Of 1,000 Lives
Author Ann Palmer relives her own Past Lives

iUniverse books may be ordered through booksellers or by contacting:

iUniverse
1663 Liberty Drive
Bloomington, IN 47403
www.iuniverse.com
1-800-Authors (1-800-288-4677)

Because of the dynamic nature of the Internet, any Web addresses or links contained in this book may have changed since publication and may no longer be valid.

ISBN: 978-1-4502-6922-3 (sc)
ISBN: 978-1-4502-6923-0 (ebk)

Printed in the United States of America

iUniverse rev. date: 1/21/2011

Contents

CHAPTER 1

INTRODUCTION

Retreating into fairytales long after most children had lain them aside, day dreaming of a better life allowed me to escape my lower middle class life style. Did the stork deliver me to the wrong address? I often wondered if I was with the wrong family and location. I have few vivid memories of my childhood. My sister's friend had frilly white Priscilla curtains that also felt familiar and I longed to have them for myself. One provoking memory was riding on a train to Houston with my Mother and saw moss hanging from the trees for the first time, which had a very strange familiarity. A repetitious dream was living in a two story brick house that was rather flat and simple on the front, later while traveling in New England, I saw similar houses. The most important point was that I had a red brick playhouse and longed for it after the dreams. I had never heard of reincarnation. Sadly, had my parents understood that children under around eight years of age generally have an ability to recall past lives. They might have opened up those past life memories. As a child ages and at round eight years of age, a gland atrophies, the memories fade.

In my current time and place in life I look back over my life that seems to be a series of past lives in this one physical body. I see my life with my parents as the first -- then the blossoming into adulthood -- college, first jobs, marriage, motherhood for the next two decades -- career pursuits -- another marriage -- more career pursuits -- another marriage -- all these seem separate but connected past lives. As I developed past life memories in different times and centuries they seem just as real to me as those experiences I refer to as "past lives" in this current physical body. Thus, I offer "Ann (current name) of a Thousand Lives" as we live many life experiences in each physical incarnation.

Generally, we do not connect with past lives in linear time; even just one particular life is never in linear time. Memories come in bits and pieces like beads on a necklace that we must string together so that they make sense to us. Personal and often traumatic experiences come out of our deepest subconsciousness. Each of our personal journeys is very different, just like our individual finger print. For me, clearing up traumatic experiences has been my goal, therefore, the seemingly "bad" experiences memories come to the forefront more than the happy experiences.

While my concepts expand daily, I perceived that we can carry certain traits, certain karmic growth patterns not only for ourselves individually but for other groups as well - our group consciousness, as Carl Jung discussed. The more I moved into the fourth dimension, the more I realize we are never alone, as though we are satellites off our mother ship traveling through time and space. We are also a mother ship with many satellites attached, some seemingly good, some bad -- and yet, those that appear bad are there for our quantum leaps evolving our spirits toward our expanded soul growth.

Through the years, I found myself slipping into what we call the forth dimension. More and more I see things in reverse - the other side of the mirror: Corinthians 13:12 - "For now we see through a mirror, darkly; but then face to face. Now I know in part; but then shall I know even as also I am known." I feel I stepped through that mirror -- seeing - hearing in depths I never before could imagine or dreamed. Powerful concepts become more humorously absurd and just the opposite of how they appear - the realization that responsibilities are so far reaching and cannot be isolated in just one life.

While this book is not about regressions I have done with clients, instead I felt by sharing information I have gleaned for my own soul's evolution and bringing forth my own personal past incarnations, it would hopefully make sense to the reader. I will mention one client in particular.

In the mid 1980's I appeared as a past life expert on the Sally Jesse Raphael TV show. They had me on the show opposite an attorney professor from Pepperdine University in Malibu, CA. I was disappointed and dreaded it as I felt an attorney could make mush out of me regardless of how much knowledge, experience and objective I had. The audience seemed to be peppered with illiterate fundamentalists that asked stupid questions trying to make a fool out of me, when my intent was to provide as much intelligent information as possible -- so between the audience's questions and the lawyer's sarcasms also determined to make a fool out of me -- HE FAILED, I am happy to say! Of course, I knew his goal but I kept myself reminded of my loving commitment. As long as I kept my focus on sharing lovingly, I could come through it all and I did. With his and their silly comments, I wasn't able to get as much information as I had hoped to share. He only wanted to promote his own book trying to capitalize off of the title of one of Shirley MacLaine's books that he was also critical of her, too. My contact information was on the end of the show.

When the show aired, I began getting calls from all over the United States. Since I didn't have a book written, I quickly put together a self guided tape titled "Rainbow Regressions" that I offered to the callers. One particular call was intriguing. It was from a woman in Georgia who wanted to do a regression. I suggested that I would find someone in her area but she insisted that she only wanted me to do her regression. Her name was Peggy and she and her boyfriend were planning a vacation in Las Vegas. She said they could drive on into Los Angeles to see me, so the time was set. It was very flattering that she was willing to travel so far for me to do her regression!

When the day arrived, he beau dropped her off at my apartment and for the next few hours we worked on her past lives. I certainly would not limit her time considering her willingness to travel so far. As we went along, one part of the regression was about her life in the 1800's traveling by train out West to teach school. Later when her friend returned, I took them sight seeing all over the Western part of Los Angeles, including beach areas, then with dinner in the hills in Hollywood. The amazing part of it was that Neil had no interest or knowledge of reincarnation but anything Peggy wanted to do was OK with him. I played with him a little by asking "IF" he did believe in reincarnation -- what would be the time frame -- would he be a man or woman -- what kind of work would he have done. Like a rocket he shot out almost the identical information that Peggy had seen in her regression. Both Peggy and I were stunned as she had not had any time to tell him about her regression. He meant it as a joke but his scenario totally coincided with hers. Even more interesting is eventually they DID marry and moved to Phoenix, completing an unfilled cycle! Not only that, we have remained friends ever since and I have spent a number of winters visiting her in Phoenix from North Carolina.

The following is a channeling I did in the 1980's that mentions past lives. If one does not understand the word "channeling" there are many books that go into great depths about it or look it up on the Internet. Psychic readings can be a form of channeling, automatic writing, deeper meditation, etc.

CHANNELING: 10/03/1986 - Consciousness and Earth life

"Perhaps Past Life work is unnecessary for all if they can center themselves to the point of feeling a merging with other consciousness; however few people are capable of FEELING that unity. Our senses beyond the five physical ones are shut down to a great degree in order to survive in our environment. For some people, they feel the oneness when in nature -- a mother and child - a high ecstasy sexual experience and other glimpses of deep love. Emergencies sometime evoke a heightened sense for our survival. Generally we are so ingrained with fears it seems impossible to feel unity with anyone or anything. Often those who "wear" a label of their "religious" are so imbedded in devil/evil fears they shut down even more. The object is to turn around the word "devil" so that it is "lived"!! Parents seem to loose a kind of oneness of a child as they grown and are influenced by peers.

Humanity had not developed enough for the deeper senses beyond the physical ones to awaken their psychic senses. (*This was channeled in the mid 1980's and much progress has been made since then. Now there seems to be far more human awakenings.*) Instead, fear is expressed with so much violence, even in entertainment or maybe I should say constantly influenced toward violence by the media -- films and TV. One needs to understand that evil forces cannot affect you unless you have a hole in your aura for that energy to flow into, which most people have.

Through your feelings of fear you send out the vibration that draws that unharmonious energy into your energy field or mind/spirit body. It affects you only in that you have invited it or giving it permission to do so.

Is the Earth is ready for higher consciousness? Whether it is ready or not, the time exist that mankind must take giant leaps in consciousness in order to preserve the planet and other species that exist. Man, through his own ignorance is destroying and occupying space that belongs to other species on the planet. In truth, man is an invader to this planet. This was a planet for lower evolving consciousness. At one time the highest life or similar to human forms on the planet were nature spirits.

The consciousness, which we call mankind, came here from other sources and found what we call the "Garden of Eden" - a paradise. It was a good place for them to set up "housekeeping." As has always been the nature of man on planet Earth, man began to abuse the life forces on Earth. Because man's consciousness is chosen to be Masters of God consciousness, he often mistakes that as a right to take that which appears to be of lesser consciousness. Man had virtually been wiped out from this planet more than once but he continually resettles here. It had been through this cleansing of the planet that it has managed to survive as other forms of life have also survived.

Cleansing of the throat charka is vital. Man has never been in a greater need for spirituality as exhibited on the planet today. That is why energies beyond what we know are interceding in behalf of planet Earth. It seems strange that outside forces must protect Earth from man. Those "outside forces" are our long ago ancestors. They come here in subtle energy forms. Forms that do not disturb or distress man's fear for this planet has evolved primarily on the emotions of fear. One needs only to sit down and write on a piece of paper the word "fear." List beneath it each action and reaction based on fear for just one day, then write the world "love" and list the actions and reactions based on it. I think you will see a huge imbalance. Place the list where you can see it each and every day. Read it, contemplate on it and see if you can begin to subtract from the fear list and add to the love list. Cross them off, erase them, remove the fears one by one. It has for greater effectiveness on our consciousness and subconsciousness when we take over thoughts and materialize them on paper, then dematerialize them by dissolving or merging them into love waves of energy, thus creating harmony and balance, drawing together fragmented pieces.

It is such an enormous goal to seek. Do you understand that each and every day of your life you are bombarded with the vibrations of fear? Can you not see how this affects each and every cell in your physical body, your emotional body and your spiritual body? It would be better for your individual spirit to take the positive aspects of each of the major religions of the world. Appraising from your personal point of perspective and take the good qualities and apply it to your life. This does not mean to abandon your present congregation, if you are a part of one. If you are receiving positive benefits, it is the place you may need to be at this time. If your church, group or even family is instilling more fears and more anxieties, then you should give careful thought as to this energy source. If you feel that you don't belong -- walk away! RISK seeking answers! Answers are available. Vague are the strata Delta -- (strata =level of culture, delta = land at mouth of a river -- particles that pass through matter!) We work together in many forms -- on many levels. Twenty years is not long, even in your measurement of time. What is consciousness but a thin layer around our physical body! If you could but see the beating this thin layer must endure. Wedged between this layer simply is the care of all that there is in you." (End of Channeling.)

From earliest childhood memories, I had the desire to rebel against limitations of religious dogma. Each church on each hill believed that they were "the only way" and in every town all over the world the same attitude exists. It was incomprehensible to me that they thought God preferred one over the other! That childhood desire for unity has been the unfulfilled quest of my life. Perhaps that natural desire for unity created the need to explore the unity within my own personal world, when I saw so little harmony in the outer world. Until one knows one's self, how can one expect anyone else to know them? Until one truly respects all aspects of one's self and learns to love totally, how can one ever expect reciprocation of another who is equally uninformed about his inner total person, past and present? How can a person open to the inner space of one's self without becoming aware of our own intuitive sense? Intuition can wear many names – woman's intuition, man's gut level feeling, sensing, E.S.P., psychic ability, clairvoyant, etc. We all have it. It is as natural as our five physical senses. Some of us, especially women, seem to trust that intuitiveness more than men. Some are conditioned from childhood to accept and acknowledge it, others are taught to fear it as "sin" and "work of the "devil" yet all great writings have been generally acknowledged as "inspired" or "prophesy".

Are we merely puppets of our past experiences in this life and others? Do past traumas pull the strings of our reactions today? Without exploring them, understanding those traumas and releasing them we keep our selves enslaved in that which we know as our soul that keeps us chained to the wheel of earthly cause and effect until we can release totally into spiritually unity – into Universal Omnificence -- GOD.

Existing in a "Doubting Thomas" personality, even though well over 30 years ago I seemed to have past life memories through meditation, regressions and dreams, I did not put much creditability in it -- "so what!" was my attitude (similar to most people). Continued occurrences necessitated my explorations into my total person both present and past.

Many years later on visits to my Texas home from California, the humidity and heat made sleeping difficult for me with no air conditioning. I chose to sleep on the sofa during those visits where it was a bit cooler; also I could be a little nearer to my mother. Perhaps the nearness allowed our spirit bodies to dance together during sleep. It was disturbingly clear that with all my studies regarding physical death and transition into the next plane which I desperately wanted share with my mother might make her passing out of her Earth life easier. No matter how much knowledge I had, it fell on deaf ears for my Freewill Baptist mother. Even when I read directly from her own bible she commented "I just can't go along with all that stuff you are into." Several years before, I had acknowledged that no matter how much healing knowledge I gleaned, I could not help my own mother. I had to face the fact that if we want to see results from our own endeavors that we are working out of personality (ego), which needs constant outer reassurances that we have worth and value. With that came the realization that I could honor and respect my mother's role she chose in this incarnation. While my conclusion seemed negative, my mother had perfected the characterization of being the perfect "hypochondriac."

Whatever illness that any friend might have, she immediately developed it, too. I wondered if she might be living out illnesses for others so that they did not experience them. I have heard that pets, like dogs, cats take on an illness for their owner. If we could see the whole picture we would understand our chosen roles far better.

On the surface my visits to Texas were to see my mother. Underneath the obvious, my compelling drive was to release myself from my mother as well as share with her the knowledge I had gleaned regarding releasing from the physical body. Well into her eighties and bed ridden for three years, I felt death could not be that far away. After a fall and broken ankle she decided to stay in bed even though the doctor had not felt it was necessary.

Since childhood I have been aware of trying to get my mother out of self-pity and creating her own illnesses, not realizing I was trying to force my will on her. In truth, I don't recall ever feeling any great love for my mother. She was just there. I always liked her because she did not have any unreasonable resistance or will power like I experienced with my father. Trying to reason with him was like talking to a brick wall, yet we had an adoring love for each other. Unfortunately, growing up, he expressed that fervor across my bottom with an old leather razor strap. In later years, after giving up that form of punishment, he would simply say "no" to any thing I asked just to prove he had power over his family. As the oldest birth son of his parents, he thought that he had to rule with an iron fist. No amount of Taurus reasoning would penetrate his stubborn Capricorn will. That was a whole different era when discipline ended up on one's back side.

My Libra older sister and I both had a dedicated love for him. As a Taurus and Libra, perhaps the two sides of Venus warmth was needed to balance his Capricorn coolness. In spite of the need to control, he had tremendous love and loyalty for family. Maybe a back up crew was necessary as my sister was born October 16th and my daughter was born on Mother's birthday, October 18th.

My brother and I were never close. I never particularly liked him and had nothing in common with him. He always seemed like an outsider, especially when he returned from the Pacific in World War II.

It was only after my father's death that I heard my mother express her love for him, two and a half months after his 80th birthday in their

57th year of marriage. I carried guilt for most of my life for holding them together -- "We'll stay together for the baby" was the mantra I heard all my young years. Those years were spent more like an only child since my brother and sister were older, they were out and gone. At times, I thought my name was "Tag-along" because that's what I heard from both sister and brother.

I used to pray for my parents to divorce and find someone they loved so I could have four loving parents instead of two battling all the time. We frequently moved so I felt isolated and alone. Perhaps it was preparation for the solo life that I have faced through out my life.

Around the 1980's I was working with a past life specialists for de-possessions. I didn't feel I had any spirits possessing me! My friend was a dentist from a church I attended and he had just begun to study regression work. He gave up dentistry career, then worked as a counselor and eventually wrote a book on possessive spirits. My guide and I were both surprised that a living person came through as a possessive spirit, yet we had asked for any possessive spirit. If we believe in the consistency of life, only the physically shell falls away at what we call "death" then alive or dead would make no difference. It was my MOTHER that came through as a possessive spirit! My voice became more of the cadence in the way she spoke. I don't remember what came through and probably didn't keep any notes. It was meant to show him that a living person could appear to be a possessive spirit. For anyone who has had no experience with regressions, your conscious mind knows exactly what is going on in the room, the noises and the activities. It is more or less resting and yet, also often can argues with the events that the subconscious mind bring to the surface.

My first experience with a past life regression was in 1978, with a friend who had been trained as a regressionist though the expert, Morris Netherton. I was a total skeptic as far as past lives regressions were concerned. My friend and I had spent many years on our shared spiritual journey. We had attended meditation classes together as well as taking drives to relaxing places and receiving inspirational messages through the use of an Ouija board. Many people like to warn of the use of the Ouija board; however, from our experiences we only received very inspirational messages that neither of us was capable of creating. There were many times in the beginning I thought the messages came from her but she assured me she did not have that knowledge. Diane was a very special friend and guided me into the world of meditation and metaphysics. We met on the set of a movie with incessant conversation while waiting for our scenes and it was the beginning of a long friendship. As actresses we needed additional income so in later years we both worked with Interior Designers. After she went on her own as a designer with less and less acting career, we worked together on numerous projects. During childhood years I had wanted a sister my own age. She seemed to be that sister. As I discovered in a French life, I feel we were as close as sisters as we were in this life. No doubt we have been together in numerous lives. She was the first person to do a regression for me.

A few years later with extensive training in regression work, like most of my clients, in my first regression, when Diane asked me questions, I felt like I was just making up my replies to her and that the information had no validity. As I continued my study of reincarnation I became a member of the APRT where I not only studied but also was a presenter for workshops. The more I learned about past life regressions; I realized it was a natural combination with the psychic counseling I did with clients. My intuitive nature helped me filter through past life recall for myself without formal work with another person putting me into an altered state. I easily went into an altered state as in meditation. I get into a peaceful state, try to center my mind so that I am not thinking past or future, then ask myself a question, like "Why does this person react this way toward me?" It is just like turning on the TV, the drama begins to play on my inner TV screen. The answer usually comes. Often, while driving on a long drive, I am fully alert, yet I also can be in an altered state at the same time and past life scenarios filter through. When the pictures flow in my mind's eye -- my response is "Wow wee that makes total sense!" Oppositely, I ask myself these questions, too. "Is this an adult continuation of my fantasy childhood fairytale world? Is it an escape from reality? Do I feel so alone and isolated from other that I find it necessary to escape? Have I fallen off the deep end?" My conclusion is "What difference does it make!" If I am gleaning a wider perspective of my total self - if I am expanding consciousness to benefit myself and others -- if it aids me in merging with other people - animals - plants - minerals - the Universe - does it matter whether it is what we perceive as "reality" or "fantasy" as long as it gets me "there -- wherever "there" is!

CHANNELING - ORIGINAL MAN:

"As the Universal Mind sent out a probe to Earth - this energy must slow down to Earth vibratory rate thus creating friction. The friction divided itself as positive and negative energy that materialized organic bodies, the material part or nature of a human being.

This division became male (atom/Adam) and female (energy/Eve). All plants do not necessarily require organic bodies in which to experience and explore earth through the emotion senses. Earth is an organic planet with many, many life forms. Many of these do not require consciousness. Male/Female were created as consciousness. Thus the evolutionary processes on Earth, which is survival of Male/Female lost Spiritual consciousness. That is the consciousness became buried in the sub or unconscious state. M/F became ensconced in physical survival believing the organic form was the alpha and omega, yet, still being nudged by the inner consciousness, thus religions were evolved. Since man/woman's goal was physical survival; laws evolved. Religions search for reuniting with original source and these physical laws became entangled within each other and remained confused as one in the same. It is obvious today how those struggles of physical survival became LAW of the planet totally unaware of the original source - love - free flowing through out the Universe, yet never lost their Universal mind ability to materialize forms. Through fear and hate, physical man manifested all sorts of fear form monsters. Fear monsters infiltrated man and women's consciousness. Since these were physical man's creations they took firm hold in consciousness, some times equal, some times over powering physical man to the point of death of the physical. The cycle continued -- searching for union with the Universal mind, creating fear monsters in the process. Fear monsters took many, many forms. Incarcerated in the materialized physical organic form, mind believed it was form, thus our mental "body" - the organic from believed it was all there was and thus the physical body ruled. The emotion was what earth's exploration was all about; thus the emotional body is searching to reconnect with Universal Mind. Each of these three bodies struggle for dominance. Struggle itself, is materialized "fear monster." When the organic "house" body becomes non-operational, thus being killed or diseased, which are also materialized fear monsters, death occurs. At death, dispersion of the organic form the three bodies are freed for each to feel the need to rejoin that familiar energy. The search for union of the physical body, mental body emotional body all of which make up the Spiritual body thus begins incarnations - reincarnations. If the three bodes had departed the organic house in perfect balance and harmony, it could have also harmonized to rejoin the source but we depart the organic mass disproportional. Often women are so heavily into their emotional bodies, reincarnating into a male body would be a logical alternative. Men are so heavily into brain/mental and physical pursuits, they may incarnate as female to balance more of the emotional body.

THE CONSCIOUS MIND

"The sponge - absorbs, then stores in the subconscious mind, constantly conditioning material within the subconscious and capable of logic and reasoning - the subconscious is not - leaving physical body, leaves conscious Mind/physical. Subconscious floats in the atmosphere as it has been conditioned by controls of the conscious."

SOUL EVOLUTION

"Seeking to find common ground for all mankind, one may search the world over for a level of communication, still communication evades mankind. We are one brotherhood yet brother sometimes kills brother. Staying within the framework of family structure, we see strain of the severest kind. Arguments arise over the most mundane situations. Harboring grievances sometimes starts fights leading to deaths for no apparent reason. Moving toward soul evolution now can help us toward lasting peace when we find a method of communicating. Struggling to seek guidance you have unlocked the gates of states of consciousness of the higher mind - the Universal Mind of Universal paths.

Our thoughts become seeds that accumulate until they have a chance to grow. We keep stuffing them within. These thought forms gather in the ethers and when conditions are ripe, seeds activate. We keep repeating patterns. Very strong Mind and Matter in the astral world, emotions and imagination at play create form through our imagination. If one dies suffering great pain, the thought of pain continues, trapped of our own doing. Spirits unaware of their physical death don't know that they are dead.

Through our senses, physical and material effects free us from attainment.

Two goals in spiritual growth:

1. Becoming spiritual being possessed by pure love and wisdom, freeing oneself from matter - the material world.

2. To be able to control matter through incarnating.

Spiritual growth is a gradual achievement. At any time we choose, get off the wheel of reincarnation, which will slow growth and rebirth into a physical body. The Power lies in the center of that wheel.

Possessed by strong interest and attachments for worldly matter - as one must marry a certain person -- completing a research project, be wealthy, a politician, etc. Family karma would be carrying grudges by father or grandparents. Not all karmic ties manifest in one life. The most power given to it is in the astral plane. When we can merge astral energy with physical it becomes enormous. Cohesive power of emotions/ imagination holds us in the astral.

A person that lived a pretty good life and suddenly dies leaving unfinished ties might come back within a few months. Youthful accidents causing death often creates a quick return - Interactions with various kinds of people, land, personal unachieved goals, strong attachments to resentments, caught in pain and suffering without awareness of physical death - Dying with feeling hunger, fear and suffering. Soldiers still fighting wars. They are often born in the same country as their previous life, same families, groups, etc. Love and wisdom transcends the world of Karma. Positive, compassionate and wise ones move on to the spiritual world and enjoy love and wisdom in pure paradise. With the realization of unity with guardian deity and enlightenment one becomes a guiding person. Achievements of oneness have been accomplished through overlapping results of this life and former lives fulfilling karmic influences.

What IS reincarnation? It is an opportunity to merge with an individualized spiritual path and take responsibility for actions and get out of the "blame game." The soul plane is the higher plane of vibratory frequencies. With each embodiment we develop talents, character qualities, either positive or negative all of which leaves a permanent tracing on individualized patterns that carry over life after life that reveal general evolutionary status. Energy is light - pure light is love - God is love. Our electrical impulses in the body are generated by our emotions. It is through our food, vitamins and of course is basic for normal physical development. Our electrolytes, electromagnetic energy are a physical "food for thought" food for emotions and food for the body. At death the brain ceases in most living creatures. Consciousness at death passes into the astral that has been created by physical outward expressions of the personality created in a life time. There is a gradual shedding -- sparks of consciousness of many personalities are left and return to learn or proceed on the path of spiritual evolution, eventually back to God.

Christianity, Judaism and Islam were born in the dry, dead desert, while all religions are colored by the life styles, culture and thought patterns based on climate and birth places. Many religions interpret and transform religious experiences of become one with God. Mohammed fell into a trance state, most of the bible is written in trances, dreams of prophets. We are all affected by genetics of ancestors -- our nationality, family, personal desires and locale. We gain knowledge through our senses - our emotional nature that guides us into choices of staying in set conditions or reaching out and exploring other avenues in life. That is often the step to self awareness.

Genesis" 1106: "Behold, they are one people and they have all one language and they have reasoned to do this thing; and now nothing will prevent them from doing that which they have IMAGINED to do."

We fail to see riches in goodness and kindness, the beauty surrounding us, the riches of experience and gaining knowledge. Individuals might have to learn to survive on his or her own. We need to look upon money as a method of exchange and even consider the art of bartering. We have grown to base all our successes and values on he who earns the most money and that which cost the most money AND the worship of "LABELS"!! Money controls the life force in the World. The whole system is designed to control the individual. Begin seeing ABUNDANCE in what you do have that is all around you! A trip into nature helps!"

This was a very profound channeling for me!

You may have read the play or saw the movie "ANNE OF THE 1,000 DAYS" - the story of Anne Boleyn's short time as Henry VIII's queen. Revealed as one of my past lives, that is my title "Ann of a 1,000 Deaths." Little "deaths" in current body, in time we can drift back into memories of past incarnations until we can reunite with our wholeness of our soul.

Ann Palmer

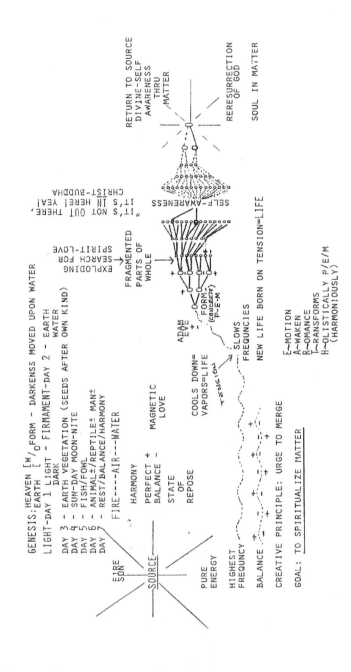

GENESIS: HEAVEN [W/O FORM - DARKENSS MOVED UPON WATER
EARTH [_E/O]FORM - FIRMAMENT-DAY 2 - EARTH
LIGHT-DAY 1 LIGHT-
DARK   WATER

DAY 3 - EARTH VEGETATION (SEEDS AFTER OWN KIND)
DAY 4 - SUN-DAY MOON-NITE
DAY 5 - FISH/FOWL
DAY 6 - ANIMAL±/REPTILE± MAN±
DAY 7 - REST/BALANCE/HARMONY

FIRE---AIR--WATER

HARMONY

PERFECT +   MAGNETIC
BALANCE -   LOVE

STATE
OF
REPOSE

COOLS DOWN=
VAPORS=LIFE

SLOWS
FREQUNCIES

NEW LIFE BORN ON TENSION=LIFE

CREATIVE PRINCIPLE; URGE TO MERGE

GOAL; TO SPIRITUALIZE MATTER

FIRE
SUN

SOURCE

PURE
ENERGY

HIGHEST
FREQUENCY

BALANCE

RETURN TO SOURCE
DIVINE-SELF
AWARENESS
THRU
MATTER

RERESURRECTION
OF GOD

SOUL IN MATTER

"IT'S NOT OUT THERE,
IT'S IN HERE! YEA!
CHRIST-BUDDHA

SELF-AWARENESS

EXPLODING
←SEARCH FOR
SPIRIT-LOVE

FRAGMENTED
PARTS OF
WHOLE

ADAM

FORM
(CONCRETE)
P-E-M

TENSION

E~MOTION
A~WAKEN
R~OMANCE
T~RANSFORMS
H~OLISTICALLY P/E/M
(HARMONIOUSLY)

AS LONG AS MAN REMAINS UN-CONSICOUS...HE EXPERIENCES GOD WITHIN HIMSELF AS SEXUAL DESIRE.
WHEN HE BECOMES CONSCIOUS, HE EXPERIENCES GOD AS HIS OWN-SELF.,AS HIS OWN TRUE BEING,AS.,I AM!
GOD IS FOR MAN THE ABSOULTE STATE OF SELF-AWARENESS.

CHAPTER 2

OUR MUTIPLE LIVES

From the unknown we die when we are born into the physical body and all that follows in that lifetime is a series of deaths. Our cells are completely changed every seven years. Old cells die, new ones born. Our bodies are in constant change and growth. How many deaths do we experience in just one physical body? Deaths of spirit, hopes, dreams plus the physical deaths of family and friends that often makes us feel like a part of us dies with them. To add to those in this life time -- add our past lives experiences with the same experiences in each life those "deaths." If there are no "past lives" then consider our genetic code of our ancestral traumas, hopes, fears and experiences. Could they, too, pass on to us those actions and reactions into the deeper recesses of our unconscious? If you accept the fact you can inherit physical structures of parents, grand parents, etc. how can we not inherit emotional experiences? Scientists even suggest that our genes may have the ability to carry memories from our ancestors. If you consider that and past lives -- WOW - what a lot of lives we eventually need to merge harmoniously intone completed soul's journey toward connecting with the ALLness -- we call "God". Once we realize this possibility, we realize this one body; this one mind is not all there is in the YOU that you live in present time.

"Out of the closet" leading psychologists and psychiatrist have boldly stepped forward to join the ranks of mystics in believing and experiencing reincarnation dramas with their patients. Often, by accident during a hypnosis session, when the client or patient begins regressing into another time beyond their present life, into a past life, the counselor is confused with no training regarding past lives.

I was as skeptical as many of the leading psychologist and therapists, a real "doubting Thomas," even when I first experienced a past life session with a friend leading the way. It is often a very gradual, even accidental process for many people. I could never afford to go to a psychologist when I faced my own traumas, so I studied everything from the bible, most major religions, beliefs, psychology, philosophy, mysticism, astrology -- the areas of research are endless.

I was first introduced to meditation when, as an actress, I had a problem memorizing lines and thought it might help me memorize better. Instead, I stubbornly became aware of my own psychic ability, which everyone has if they allow their own "intuition" -- "sensing" -- "gut level feeling"-- etc. to develop it. We are taught of only our five physical senses but have more beyond the physical. Like many people, I associated the word "psychic" with gypsies, fortune tellers, little old fat ladies with a lot of cats and generally people I considered "losers." Sooner or later, we experience the other side of our own judgments!

It was in the mid 1960s when I dove heavily into deeper research than I had ever found in organized religions. Growing up in Texas where church was the heart of one's activities, I always felt a "calling" but had no idea what it was. How could I know where this inner commitment would lead me? Had I known the trials and tribulations it would lead me into, perhaps I would have made a different choice. Yet, born as a Taurus bull with an ascending Aires ram, pursuing difficulties seemed to be inborn. Would a bird permit its wings to be clipped just as it was learning to fly? My wings of destiny would soar me into the hope of the heights and rewards that the entertainment business provides for very few. With that ball of energy that shot across that Texas sky and my small town upbringing thrust me into the scary location called Hollywood, California and found me standing in the middle of Hollywood Boulevard walking toward my first commercial interview, filled with excitement but probably more doubt and fear that would lead to many years pursuing a dream.

We are often amazed at child prodigies that, to me, can only be explained by reincarnation. Our conscious belief system is based on our cultural upbringing and influence. When we die we seem to loose information and keep sensory emotions, thus we usually forget languages, knowledge, etc. People ask, "If we have lived before, why don't we remember." If we had many lives of terrible suffering, why would we want to come into a new life with those memories! Our past memories are buried in the subconscious. We continually have spontaneous regressions but do not realize what they are. Working with regressions, we can bring out those memories so that it can enhance relationships, help release hostilities, anger, guilt, judgments and allow forgiveness. When experiencing an emotion in a regression, you can trust it. You will never get more than you can handle. Releasing emotions heal. It is amazing to watch a person under hypnosis experience a traumatic event with such emotions, then suddenly move on, leaving the emotion behind. Repetitious dreams that we can recall for years are past life memories. When we realize we could have been another sex, race, even one of the bad guys, it is easier to become far less judgmental and more tolerant toward others, nations, religions and toward situations.

There are many religions that accepted reincarnation but the Roman Emperor Constantine created First Council of Nicaea (325 AD) which was the first council of all the Bishops of the Christian Church, where they removed references to reincarnation and burned large numbers of "heretical" works (what THEY considered heretical!) That was the beginning of many Christian Churches denying reincarnation.

Here are a few quotes from those believing in reincarnation:

"For if the soul existed before birth, and in coming to life and being born can be born only from death and dying, must she not after death continue to exist, since she has to be born again?"
From Plato's Phaedo

"Just as a man discards worn out clothes and puts on new clothes, the soul discards worn out bodies and wears new ones."
The Path of Knowledge 2:22 Bhagavad Gita

In the Zohar, a primary Cabalistic text, it is said:

"The souls must reenter the absolute substance whence they have emerged. But to accomplish this, they must develop all the perfections, the germ of which is planted in them; and if they have not fulfilled this condition during one life, they must commence another, a third, and so forth, until they have acquired the condition which fits them for reunion with God."

"Birth is not a beginning; death is not an end. There is existence without limitation; there is continuity without a starting point. Existence without limitation is space. Continuity without a starting point is time. There is birth, there is death, there is issuing forth, there is entering in. That through which one passes in and out without seeing its form, that is the Portal of God"

Chuang Tzu 23

"It is absolutely necessary that the soul shall be healed and purified, and if it doesn't take place in one life on earth, it must be accomplished in future earthly lives."

Saint Gregory of Nyssa, Roman Catholic Bishop - Approximately 380 AD

1930's reincarnation was thrust into the spotlight by the work of Edgar Cayce, later to become known as, *The Sleeping Prophet.* Cayce performed thousands of past life readings. Most of Cayce's work dealt with holistic cures for physical ailments. Cayce often found that physical ailments in this lifetime are the result of bad karma from a past lifetime.

For several years, I trained as well as taught classes at seminars for IAPRT. The organization consisted of psychologists, psychiatrist, MFCC's, and those like me without doctoral degrees. Hazel Denning was the founder and past the age of seventy, she earned her own PhD, and other degrees. Dr. Ernest Pecci, a psychiatrist in Northern California and President of the Rosebridge Institute, a graduate school for Integrative Psychology, Helen Wambach practiced clinical psychology for 27 hears at the Veteran's Administration in Mississippi and New Orleans. She pioneered reincarnation in several books. Dr. Edith Fiore, also an author, Dr. Barbara Findeisen, primal therapist and lecturer in the USA and

Sweden. Dr. Alexander Bannatyne conducted workshops in England, Africa, Europe, New Zealand and the USA. Dr. William Baldwin counseled and also an author. Dr Winifred Lucas, author, practicing psychotherapy for over 50 years. These are only a few names; however there are therapists all over the world practicing past life regressions. I feel sure most were skeptics, too, in the beginning.

The belief in reincarnation does not conflict with religious beliefs, for our soul is on a constant evolutionary path to reach the highest states of consciousness -- God -- Universal Mind, etc. Past life recall aids the individual in connecting, not only with himself, but with others as well and understanding the reconnecting in their present life to correct past difficulties or even good experiences. If we all accepted and understood the wholeness of each, I believe we would find a far more peaceful world.

Earth life is such an individual evolution, no one else can see into your personal evolutionary patterns. We really don't know through eons of time how many of us may have originated from other planets, then evolved through needed lessons through Earth's vibrations. In my own experiences, I feel I have lived a number of lives in this one body, example: Childhood through marriage, child birth, divorce. Another one was years in Hollywood, after that a marriage living in Florida, another was post Florida era back in Hollywood, then Las Vegas, Mexico and Palm Springs, another during solo life in a motor home and back to Florida. The present one is living in North Carolina reconnecting with the history of my ancestors. Perhaps I am here to help clear up karma for my ancestral line, too.

I believe I came into this present life to clear up as much karma as I possibly can so that I do not have to return to the Earth. I feel there are more productive after life vibrations that I am better suited to be in even though I have no idea what or where that may be.

WHAT'S IN A NAME:

Generally, we carry our name for life, maybe even many life times of carrying the same or similar name or vibrational tone of that name. There are reasons for this; we need to work with those tones. In the bible, there was "First there was sound" OR TONING. When a woman marries and changes her name, or when anyone changes their names, they also change their personal tones. Selecting a new tone should be done with care and knowledge. Nicknames can be very degrading and lowering of one's tonal value. Names like "fats" - "piggy" - "dummy" – looser, etc. Our alphabet letters are associated with numbers from one to nine. While compiling memories of past lives, I do not know the names I carried but because I carry the name "Ann" in this life, in order to simulate continuity, I have used various versions of "Ann."

There is so much we don't understand about energy. No one can really explain electricity. Perhaps there is only a small part of human beings that even seek to understand it, as in:

CASUAL BODY: The envelope-- the luminous consciousness that endures -- remains through death and rebirths.

SUBTLE BODY: Unconscious mind - involuntary functions.

PHYSICAL BODY: Heart beat, breathing, digestion, excretion, endocrine secretion, responds to any source: words, sounds, odors, colors, size (basically using on the five physical senses)

ENERGY: Psychic current flows from one to another, etheric flow of polarized energy -- invisible. Energy flows though the centers -- "charkas" - each representing a physical color of the rainbow - red, orange, yellow, green, blue, indigo and violet, then the higher vibrations of those colors.

PSYCHIC ABLILTY: Gives greater access to past, present future allowing us to transcend time, space, limited perception of the five senses -- understanding that we have more then the five physical senses.

DREAMS: There is an interchange of psychic energy with the two lower bodies.

There have been outstanding scientific researchers in the field if energy as:

James Clerk Maxwell (13 June 1831 – 5 November 1879) was a Scottish theoretical physicist and mathematician. His most important achievement was classical electromagnetic theory, synthesizing all previous unrelated observations, experiments and equations of electricity, magnetism and even optics into a consistent theory. His set of equations demonstrated that electricity, magnetism and even light are all manifestations of the same phenomenon: the electromagnetic field.

Nikola Tesla was born in Smiljan, Austria-Hungary in 1856–1943. As a Serbo-American physicist and electrical engineer he was inventor of the radio, electric motor and generator. He began as a specialist in physics and mathematics, but became fascinated with electricity. His career then began as an electrical engineer. He was fascinated with the elusive solution to the rotating magnetic field. In 1884 Charles Batchelor wrote an introduction letter Thomas Edison: He wrote: "I know two great men, one is you and the other is this young man." For the next 59 years Tesla worked in Edison's New Jersey lab. He felt that the secret lay in the use of alternating current. To him all energies were cyclic. Why not build generators that would send electrical energy along distribution lines first one way, than another, in multiple waves using the poly phase principle? For years since people have been fascinated with Tesla's inventions.

SCALAR ENERGY: It is the discovery of a completely new kind of electromagnetic waves which exist only in the vacuum of empty space, the empty space between the atoms of our bodies as well as the empty space we see in sky at night - all of empty space. These waves constitute a kind of ocean of infinite energy, and it has now been discovered that this abundant energy can be coaxed to pour into our 3-dimensional world from their 4-dimensional realm, to be used to do work, provide electricity, power all transport, and even heal the body of almost all disease. This is the new world of scalar electromagnetic, the zero-point energy and the energy of the absolute nothingness which existed before the world began. What it seemed to say was that energy could be extracted from the universe, which is where ordinary conservation breaks down, and injected into another version of that universe in which the time coordinates of all the 'events" were shifted by some amount. The more energy you transformed, the greater the time shift would be. If that was interpreted as taking place within the same universe, it seemed to suggest that-energy could be transferred through time. We must conclude that all versions of the universe in which we exist, interpreted linearly as "Past", "future" etc. are equally real. Thus we have a continuum. The only model I can think of is a complex serial one in which altering the events in a past universe affects not only the future of that particular universe as it evolves in time, but also the "presents" of all the other universes that lie ahead of it. In other words, there is a mechanism of casual connection through the continuum that the simple serial model does not address.

I don't begin to understand it all nor does anyone really understand electricity. There are those whose lives are devoted to the study of energy as well as so many other pursuits. I am content that mine is to do as best I can to understand what appeals to me. As a guru wrote in discussing various religious beliefs -- religion is like walking in a garden filled with different kinds of beautiful flowers, pick only the flowers that appeal to you. With the various religions I have researched, the idea of karma and reincarnation seems the most logical.

I have gleaned much of my growth through studying other major religions, but since I was brought up and my basic foundation is Christianity, I relate to it as in: "As you sow, so shall you reap" (same as karma) makes sense and that is the fact in reincarnation. Religionists would say "Jesus forgives your sins." That word "sin" bothers me as I don't accept the idea of it as presented. To me, if you have recognized the Christ consciousness within you, which is what Jesus taught, your forgiveness comes as you forgive yourself. First, one must forgive self before they can forgive others. It is the same with LOVE, first one must love their self before they can truly love others, otherwise, generally we give love to GET love! It is not given freely but for bargaining. In reincarnation, once you recognize so called "sins" in another life time, you need not punish yourself for bad choices in other times or dimensions that may be deeply buried in your own subconscious. To recognize the situation, the time, circumstances and forgive your soul's choices in those past lives, ends the "sins" at that moment. It is so important to accept the fact that we have no right today to judge the circumstances of life in previous times. An example would be the harsh judgment that remains today of the Civil war and attitudes toward the South when present day people cannot know the struggles the everyday people went through in those times as well as any other past decades or centuries. We are spoiled in this country with conveniences and fail to understand those struggles and lack of almost everything.

The purpose of understanding your own past lives or if you prefer genetic memory is to draw to you the wholeness of your total soul or spirit, which ever word is preferred. I have asked people who say they do not believe in reincarnation if they believe in genetic memory. They accept that they may have inherited a physical trait of a parent, grand parent or an ancestor, then why wouldn't we accept the more influential emotional traumas? So, let's say that it is tuning into your genetic ancestry that needs erasing those traumatic experiences.

Personally, I cannot imagine being conceived in love with my parents constantly bickering. I was aware that the house I was born in burned when I was only a few months old. In a deep meditation, I asked the circumstances of my birth. In the group meditation about awareness before we are born, I became aware that the developing fetus was not totally attached to the body and that the soul is not tied to the fetus. The soul or spirit is free to become aware of the attitude of both parents and circumstances around it. The soul is not tied to the physical body of the new baby until the cord is cut at birth. (We know our soul/spirit is free to travel elsewhere in dreams, meditation, etc.)

In a previous meditation I felt I was on another dimension with the man I loved, my soul mate. It seemed I was due to be incarnated in a physical body, which I vehemently opposed. He and I were happily walking through the woods when we decided to lie down on dried leaves. As he began covering me with the leaves, I seemed to know that he was ushering me out of that dimension into the physical and I did not want to go but I could not stop the process!

When I visualized my birth, I felt fear - nor did I sense any real love from my Mother. It wasn't until my Father appeared and held me, I felt loved. As I pondered that death out of the unknown into the birth, I became aware that my Mother and Father were not happy together. Apparently, my Mother was quite content with my older sister and brother and did every thing she could to abort me. No wonder I was not anxious to enter the physical and was born in fear.

It seemed that she was involved with another man. At that time, my Father sold insurance and traveled. Through my visualizations, I saw that when I was only a few weeks or months old, her lover convinced her to allow him to set fire to the house with me in it! All went well until her guilt caused her to rescue me before I died of smoke inhalation. When I was four or five, a terrible dust storm hit the Panhandle of Texas. Because of a broken window, we had to go to a neighbor's house. I vividly remember my father holding a wet handkerchief over my face for fear I might suffocate from the dust. Later, when I was around eight, we lived upstairs over my father's business. A fire began in the restaurant three doors away. There were wood floors that were not concrete foundations, so that the smoke from that fire filled our building that was connected under the floors.

I was sleeping upstairs. My father rescued me, again from possible smoke inhalation. Could it have been some kind of evil force trying to keep me from living out this life time? I have always been claustrophobic and fear of being shut in anything similar to a casket. In the mid 1990's, for a TV show, I was inside a Hyperbaric Chamber that wasn't connected. It was clear so that I could see out of it OK. The door was above my head and the salesman accidentally bumped into it and shut it. I could feel myself going into a panic mode and my heart began racing. Fortunately, it didn't last long.

I was as born in a very different era than most people that may read the chronicle of past lives related to their present one. It was after the Great Depression. When you are born in an era of great limitations, you don't realize it - what is, simply is! From an early age, I questioned so many things and felt I was very alone in my wondering. People that had or have to live in extreme poverty probably did not understand "dysfunctional family life" -- the word combination didn't exist then. Probably the greater percentages of families in those days were dysfunctional families.

There weren't a lot of happy childhood memories and little is remembered at all about my early years. My brother and sister were older and did not like to be stuck with me. I heard them say many times "do I have to take her?" - "does she have to tag along?" I could have almost thought my name was Tag Along! Perhaps that, as well as my birth, began a lot of insecurity. I do remember that when my father decided to leave the Panhandle of Texas, he bought a big truck; build a covering for it, packed all our belongings in it and off we went. I rode in the back atop our belongings and could see out the back. I remember well the feeling of leaving the place I was born, the friends and the only life I had known, perhaps it was the first "death" in this body.

Psychological counseling was unknown. Most people didn't dare but if we were to discuss personal problems, it was with our preachers or ministers, who were often dysfunctional themselves. We had no television. For entertainment we might sit by the radio listening to programs that soon became the first TV shows. I was rarely allowed to go to a movie on Sunday as the Church said it was a sin. If you can go to a movie any other day, why was Sunday forbidden -- a practice I could not understand or accept. At age five, in Sunday school, they had the boys and girls together, then separated them. This was upsetting as I preferred to be with the boys. Why did we need to be separated? At about eight years old, I was joyfully learning to knit. While a family gathering was at my grandmother's house, I sat on the porch knitting. I was shy and so shocked and embarrassed when my grandmother admonished me for "working" on the Sabbath! I told her that she and the women were working in the kitchen but she insisted that was a necessity. She never liked me, probably because I dared to talk back to her. As far back as I can remember, I questioned conclusions like that one. We were told that our religion was the ONLY religion, yet on the next hill top sat another religion, the Methodist, same size church, then around town other smaller churches. Why would God choose one over the other? As the years passed, I stood outside looking up at the sky knowing there was a big world out there with many other churches and religions -- why would God choose one over the other was my everlasting question. I think the "last straw" was when I was about eight. All the children were hustled down on the two front rows of the church. Women swarmed among us like bees telling us we were going to hell if we did not get baptized. I didn't react out of fear of hell but I just assumed it was a natural progression and sooner or later I had to be baptized, so I submitted. That night, as we prepared to be dunked in the water, my best friend went with me, only when we put on the robes, she was so shy she failed to take off her skirt. Later, with her soaking wet skirt, my Dad gave her his coat to cover her to take her home. When I stepped into the baptistery, I was amazed at the ugly galvanized tin tub, very bright lights and a painting of the river Jordan facing the congregation. I must have felt it was my first show business performance and it was scary. Overcoming shyness is no easy task, even if we do overcome it, there it lies dormant always. The preacher was a large man with a large hand that came down over my whole face, holding my nose as he dunked me in the water. All I heard was "forgive her of her sins." Did that ever make me angry! How many "sins" could I have at eight years old! For days, those words rattled around in my head. Was it a sin to talk back to my mother? Was God so mean that he would send me to hell for THAT? I just couldn't accept that fundamentalist belief, even at age eight. Finally, by age thirteen, my father released me from that religion and said I was old enough to choose what ever church best suited me. Family members criticized him because he was a devote Mason instead of being more active in the "ONE and only religion". Yet, he was the foundation for everything good within me. He lived his Masonic principles day to day, whereas, so many church goers "wear" their religion on Sunday and forget it the rest of the week -- another observation from youthful years. My concept and understanding was that religion was supposed to be based on LOVE. At least, that was the area of religion I was seeking to understand. How misunderstood that word – LOVE! In my early twenties, Eric Formm's "The Art of Loving" and his description of the different kinds of love helped me understand much better. As he said, most people love to BE loved so it is a bargaining, not unconditional love that Jesus and other masters taught. He speaks of the importance of love and says that love is the answer to the problem of human existence. He describes love between parents and children, the difference between mature love and immature love. He wrote of the different forms of love such as brotherly love, motherly love, erotic love, self-love, love of God etc. I have been told that in the Japanese language there are different words for different forms of love.

Fromm also writes about the disintegration of love in contemporary western society and that in a capitalistic society modern man has become alienated from himself, fellow human beings and also from nature. Society has been transformed into a commodity, experiences life forces as an investment which must bring him the maximum profit under the market conditions. As far as love is concerned, discipline, concentration, patience are needed. Fromm states loving is an art just like any other art and one has to put in certain efforts in order to master the art. How I have worked at learning to love as unconditionally as humanly possible! When I understood the 13th Chapter of Corinthians, I thought that if I could live up to that, I would be IN love and not romantically speaking. That became my motto to live by:

> **"Love is patient and kind, love is not jealous or boastful; it is not arrogant or rude. Love does not insist on its own way; it is not**

irritable or resentful; it does not rejoice at wrong, but rejoices in the right. Love bears all things, believes all things, hopes all things, endures all things. Love never ends."

For me to go from organized religions - and there were many - was a long journey to reach were I am now in my spiritual evolution. I went from Baptist to Christian, from there to Methodist. I stayed in the Methodist church for many years, especially in high school in a small Texas town that had a military school. The best looking boys went to the Methodist church every Sunday. We girls would sit between them, which was more interesting than the minister's sermon. Boys from the military school were about the only good experience I had in that town, dating more classy guys than the local boys in that town provided. As I listened to the minister -- I wondered what was my destiny? At that time there were no female ministers. Would I be a missionary or what could I do if I was to follow some kind of religious career. We young girls pretty much assumed our careers were to be wife and mother, yet, I longed to reach out to have some kind of career. In High School, I wrote an essay about what I wanted to be and do, none of which was to be a wife and mother.

ONE OF A SERIES OF ESSAYS WRITTEN IN HIGH SCHOOL

"STEPS IN THE FUTURE" by Ann Palmer

"As I walk slowly into the future, my hopes are that I will finish high school, then attend Arlington State College. I am not sure what I want to be. There are so many things I would like to do, but I believe my chief interest and talent (I am not sure about the talent) lies in art. I am gong to take commercial art and fashion design in college.

Another of my top interest is being a model. The main thing that would keep me from being a model would be because I haven't the figure or attractiveness necessary for being one. Typing and office work is another of my interest, I like social work and working with people.

Another of my top interest is traveling. I would like to travel all over the world, especially Egypt. If I had my choice of traveling to foreign countries, I think I would choose Egypt, Italy and the Holy Lands. I am interested in these countries because they hold so much history and beauty. I would like most to see the pyramids. I think I would rather travel more than anything else, but since that is probably impossible, I will more than likely devote my future to art."

(INTERESTINGLY - other than traveling all over the world and visiting the Holy Lands, I accomplished all other goals. Not only did I visit the pyramids, but climbed half way up Cheops, the one that visitors can also enter, plus climbing the Pyramid of the Sun at Teotihuacán near Mexico City on my birthday and Mayan pyramids. Now when I read it, I am quite proud that I did accomplish most everything I wrote in that essay. I DID visit many ancient ruins in Italy, the Mayan civilization in Mexico, Belize and Guatemala.)

At the age of 16, I remember very vividly standing on the drive way looking up at the sky in that small Texas town. I had never been out of the state with travel only from where I was born in the Panhandle to East Texas. As I stood there, I wondered what was "out there" in this big, big world. How could I ever get out of Texas?

I don't know where I ever heard of a Tramp steamer, which differs from a tourist liner or cargo line, it operates without a schedule or specific ports of call, going wherever required to deliver cargo. Early merchant ships whose masters were the owners would load them with cargo at home to sell abroad, and vice versa. They represented more adventure and less predictability and routine. Possibly one could work to earn their passage on one of these. It seemed like a way to see the world, so I day dreamed about getting on board one of those ships.

As I stood there, day dreaming about my future, I had the feeling I was standing at a **Y** in my life. I could choose one way and have a so called "normal" life; husband, home and children or if I chose the other path, my future was unknown. I might have the normal life or --? With my rebel nature, especially when it came to "church" naturally I chose the unknown. I have often wondered if had known how UNKNOWN it would be with so little "normal" life, would I have chosen it?

Before moving to this little town, we lived in Ft Worth. In the middle of my junior year in High School, my Dad sold his business and our house, which was on the same lot. The house faced a residential street and the business faced the major highway between Ft Worth and Dallas. While he was looking for property nearer his family in East

Texas, I had to live with my airline hostess sister in Dallas. It was fun living with two hostesses with one or the other gone most of the time. I had to go to North Dallas High School where I was really scared and felt so out of place in a big city school. I had left five very good friends, as well as had to drop out of my elected office in the Rainbow girls. I had no friends in Dallas so it wasn't a very happy time. When my Dad did decide on a town, it was one that I had never liked and didn't know why – so that when I had to move there to live with my parents, I wasn't happy. The next year and half would prove my intuitive feeling was correct. I had taken all my hard courses in the first 2 years so I could have lighter courses in my senior year but that school required more than I had, so I had to take harder courses and more of them.

I wanted to be a cheer leader; second choice was to be drum major of the band, which I had been when living in the Panhandle of Texas. My sister had been Queen and Favorite and I assumed I would follow in her footsteps, except, because I had not been in this school the year before, they would not allow me to run for anything! Again, I was in with the popular click of girls but they seemed to resent me more than my previous friends. When it came time to try out for the senior play, one of the boys hid behind the curtain to see who was picked for various parts. He told me that I was picked for the lead but one of the teacher judges kept bring up the point that I was new in town and if I was the lead, no one would come to see the play, therefore, they gave me the smallest role in the play. On top of all that, I failed Chemistry and was going to have to take it in summer school in order to go to college in the fall. I was not allowed to graduate; dress in cap and gown or even sit with the graduating class at Baccalaureate services. It was a hard blow for a young insecure sixteen year old girl! Fortunately, at the private military school, I could take my chemistry class and passed with flying colors so that I could enter college that fall. I never actually graduated from that High School. I wasn't about to return the NEXT year to graduate with that lower class! I did graduate from Junior college but we did not wear caps and gowns. With numerous schools, skipping a grade, failing Chemistry, trouble with math, not liking to read, I felt I was NOT very smart!

By nature, being shy, I fought to overcome it in spite of all the insecurities dumped on me. I was a good swimmer and tennis player

31

and had won a partner championship in Ft. Worth. This small town school had no P.E. class, no tennis courts, nothing! I was good at art but there were no art classes. I loved history and took all history courses -- Texas, American and World history. Those courses were taught by a little old man that liked me but I felt none of the women teachers liked me, especially the ones that kept me from running for anything or the lead in the play. The whole experience in this little town of feeling rejected every where I turned, had slapped any self confidence I might have been building right out of me! My parents remained there until their deaths, yet, through the many years, there was always negativity thrown at me there! My Dad always wanted me to "come home." Each time I did, the negativity would get so bad; I would feel I had to return to Los Angeles. I have often said that if I had remained in Texas all of my life, I would have been dead long ago with all the criticism and negativity thrown at me. It would have created some sort of deathly disease!

In the past, I had been Baptist, Christian Church, then Methodist, then Presbyterian and visited others, never finding what my inner needs were. By the mid 1960s, the best I could find was the Church of Religious Science, Unity, Divine Science and the positive thinking churches. Also, in the mid 1960's, I began my journey leaving organized religions. I began Meditation classes, reading Metaphysical Books and found more and more of what I needed that felt right for me.

Eventually, through meditation classes, I found that I could do psychic readings, later studied to be a Past Life Regressionists. By the 1980s, at Expos all over the country, I was a speaker and workshop leader. I also taught classes at the Learning Annex in Los Angeles. Through my career as a fashion model, then actress I learned a lot about going within. I think my acting career was just a part of my spiritual journey to explore that inner self, so few of us ever explore. Besides, searching within, it afforded me an exciting and glamorous life, working in films and TV, photos in national magazines and commercials; working in interesting places, especially in Rome while working in "Cleopatra", dating stars and many exciting professional men.

This is about my journey delving into my own past lives. Believe me, accepting the concept was no easy task. It was a very long journey for me to accept the perception of having lived past lives. One of the most striking events was seeing the movie, "Anne Of The 1,000 Days" - like a bolt of lightening hitting me, sensing the association with events in Anne Boleyn's life. I couldn't get over it for days and weeks. Eventually, it was an influence for me to make another trip to Europe.

Like the people I regressed in later years, in the beginning, I said the same as they say -- "I was just making it all up as you (the Regressionist) ask me those questions." After repeated sessions, you then ask yourself "How could I have made this up?" as you find correlations in them. I learned that you cannot reveal past lives in one session as it takes many sessions or the individual to learn how he or she can tap into those subconscious files.

These past life memories have been given to me through regressions, meditations, visions, repetitious dreams, channeling, even an "ah ha" experience deja vu when visiting a place for the first time, yet, knowing it and feeling emotions of another time -- another era -- another century. These past lives do not come laid out in linear time. They have been revealed in bits and pieces that I have had to put together as best I could and in the order events happened. There was really no other way but to let the events fall into place in time as they will.

What have I learned in living many decades by now? My life has been one of learning to live a solo life, not what I thought I wanted but apparently I came into this incarnation to learn that at some point in our evolution, traveling through life may have to be a solo journey. Do I have regrets? Of course, I wish I had made different choices but if it took those experiences to get me from there to here, to clear up eons of Karma, then I know all my experiences were necessary.

This is my spiritual journey - be it fact or fiction - through life and perhaps one of the strangest one you have ever considered. I don't suggest any of my experiences are for others. I simply share it to help those who may be wandering around, feeling very alone in their questioning of religions and spirituality. To me, the two are separate journeys. I believe that most religions do not allow you to seek your own personal spiritual journey, but that is what is should be - just yours!

As I reveal my past lives, it may be confusing when I add the current life's connections. I can't prove that my stories of past lives are totally correct in my various connections and experiences but they seem to fit the emotional traumas with each person that I connect in that past experience and this life's experience. There is a book I recommend "The Return of the Revolutionaries" - a man born in a European country connects himself and associates with different people during the time of our Revolution, including photo or paintings, then and now.

Welcome to my inner life of many past lives, with only the more important ones here within "Ann of 1,000 Deaths".

CHAPTER 3

QUESTIONS

Do you believe in reincarnation? Do you believe in Karma? Do you believe or have memories of past lives? When I mention past lives, generally I hear the same reply - "I don't want to know about the past, I want to know about the future, so why do I need to learn about my past lives?" It isn't necessary for you to believe in past lives, reincarnation or karma but it helps. As previously mentioned, for real skeptics I ask if they believe in genetics. If so, we know that we CAN inherit various physical traits of relatives and ancestors, so it is only logical that we inherit or have passed on to us, not only their physical traits but emotional traumas, as well. In this case, one can consider ancestral traumas that need to be resolved to move on in our spiritual evolution. Regardless of our choices, one way or another, we are all on a journey for our own personal spiritual evolution! Eventually, gathering together these past life experience we are creating wholeness of who we are, then reuniting with what I refer to as our over soul, then into the Allness we call God, Universal Mind or any other name that may fit your personal concepts.

Without realizing it, your past lives affect you everyday in most aspect of your life: your relationships, finances, health, et al. You are repeating lessons you didn't learn in a past life. In your present life you have the opportunity to correct past mistakes and predetermine your future until you make a decide to take control, which means overcoming blocks as physical, mental, emotional and spiritual blocks from past lives. These subconscious blocks can be an obstruction to achieving your goals related to joy and happiness, financial goals, etc.

Since I have channeled messages for many years, I am a believer in these communications that come from our Higher Self, a guide, an angelic being or even an extraterrestrial higher being. The stumbling block for most of us is lack of trust from that "wee small voice" we hear in our heads. You can help your self glean past life information without a therapist if you become educated in how to recognize the past memories. Primarily you need a pencil and paper and keep a record of your answers to many helpful questions as well as a quiet, meditative attitude and time. Problems that have eluded you for lifetimes regarding health, wealth, happiness, can be facilitated and often resolved through reconnecting with your past. Regressing into the deeper, seemingly hidden areas of your self consciousness is for those who want to know for themselves; people who desire actual experience and who wish to deconstruct their earthly ego to incarnate higher parts of themselves. Those who would prefer to read about reincarnation and philosophize about life and death are not the ones who will be attracted to regressions. We are all multidimensional beings with parts of ourselves in many dimensions of reality and by using various techniques you will inevitably become aware of these parts and remember who and what you really are --your TOTAL self.

In the first regression session I go through with clients, we go through the person's present life from birth to their present circumstances. I do not set a time limit for this session or any others. Generally after an hour or so, I feel a strong intuitive connection with the client as we are drifting into the Alpha state of consciousness. I have actually had a healing for the client's primary problem without helping them with hypnosis as time together probably puts most of them in a light altered state. I think of this session as a journey we are planning and just like a road trip, we would get a map and map out the trip before starting on it. I call it a Personality Profile that you can do with a few instructions. You have probably had numerous past life memories that you did not recognize as such. While driving long distances, you probably get in a semi altered state while fully conscious of the road ahead. Your conscious mind wanders, like little movies playing in your head.

In my experiences regressing clients, generally they don't recall names, probably not dates but broad-spectrum of time periods, what they generally experience is intense emotions that are extremely vivid. Often they feel deep pain and suddenly start crying and as quickly as they went into it, they come out of it just as quickly, then move on to another event. By releasing the repressed emotional, it allows higher energies to heal the wound as well as self forgiveness. The client often feels healed with total freedom from a part of their conditioning that was affecting every area of their life. The memories and the experience of regression are extremely vivid and will leave you with no doubt as to the truth of the memories. It is not a fleeting glimpse of a past life but a concrete experience.

By delving deeply into the subconscious, it is possible to find and release emotional scars from this life and past lives. The roots of all mental and emotional conditioning form the basis of our earthly ego. All mental and emotional suffering is derived from these subconscious scars or imprints. We are multidimensional personalities that are revealed through regressions. With a thorough clearing of the subconscious a new way of being can be realized and begin to incarnate into higher consciousness.

Seems like I have known you forever." "Haven't we met before - perhaps in another life?" "We seemed to have an instant report." Are friendly statements people often make without realizing they are true statements? Again and again, people tend to be reborn with the same souls. We are attracted to and subconsciously recognize those we have known before. Often it may be a momentary acquaintance that has no particular need of resolve. Without knowing why we are often repelled by a stranger that may have been an enemy in a past incarnation.

Birth defects, birthmarks, deformed body parts or weakness, distinctive skin discolorations, childhood aliments can be brought into our present lives. Have you had chronic pain, headaches, severe overweight or under weight that seem to have no remedy? Repetitious accidents, sexual problems as frigidity, incompetent, promiscuity are often keys to previous lives.

In assessing your health problems in this life, recalling and stating them; you can then begin to realize blockages that indicate recurrences from past lives.

By connecting to the origin of these problems, often you can help resolve them in your current life.

Phobias, panic attacks, anxiety, OCD (Obsessive Compulsive Disorder), MPD (Multiple Personality Disorder), attempted suicide, any form of self injury, addictions to sex, abusive relationships, food, drugs, fears, including fear of death that seem to have no basis - strange memories that are not related to your present life. ANGER is a big one -- I feel I was born with a terrible temper and worked hard for many years to conquer it. TRUST - can you trust others, yourself or situations - even God? Do you experience NEVER ENOUGH - both Mental and Physical; sex, money, love, security of any kind. Must you be on time or always late? Compulsive shopping or saving everything can all be indications of past life problems.

In childhood what were your distinctive personality traits? As a child or through this life time, do you have skills, abilities, wisdom, do you know how to do things that normally requiring study, which you never had, but come naturally to you? Have you felt you knew more than the teacher or a minister? What recurring dreams or nightmares did you have or even traumatic deaths? Do you have overwhelming interest in certain places, subjects, people, etc.? I seemed to read and live fairytales for years. I also felt I was born to the wrong family and felt out of place. I also felt a deep desire to go or be somewhere else. Were those kinds of thoughts familiar to you? Have you experienced de java vue while visiting a particular place you have never been before or photos of places?

While I have never experienced it with a client, other therapists have had clients speak in foreign languages. Personally, I found languages difficult to learn. Do you feel at home, curious or abnormally anxious in places you have never been. Do certain ethnic foods appeal to you? From early childhood many people are attracted to a particular kind of animal. If it is an out of the ordinary kind, like a tiger, elephant, etc. that can be a clue to a life involved with it or places where they occur. Even focusing on that type of animal can bring forth past life memories. These kind of connections can also relate to certain kind of areas of the world, climates, groups of people, religions, certain plants, music, art, clothing, furnishings, types on houses, castles, et al. These hints can be a very strong attraction or aversion. Think back from childhood forward - did you have any different interest, mannerisms, particular interest that seemed out of place from your surroundings?

Your historical interest is an excellent trigger to surface a past life memory. I have found many people fascinated with the Civil War and may be the reason for the success of "Gone With The Wind" -- movies, television or books are all good triggers for recalls. Still another similarly is the Revolutionary War. In my person experience was the repeated occurrence of Anne Boleyn until I accepted it as a past life and began allowing those memories to come forward. Interestingly, my working in the film "Cleopatra" later triggered a life in Rome and Egypt. One of the questions I ask is "If you could go anywhere in the world, where would it be?" Another question I ask, "From early youth on, is there any particular country or city that you have been fascinated with and wanted to travel there?" Many people feel out of step with time and don't understand why.

Think about your family and friends from childhood forward. Have you had close relationships with one or both parents, siblings, relatives - what were your reactions toward them and theirs toward you? Did you find support, encouragement, love or were they harshly critical? Were you ever sexual abused in childhood or early teens? Was there any form of sexual abuse even sensing it, even thought it may not have been acted upon. I have felt that if people understood past lived, they would also understand sexual abuse, rapes, domestic violence, victimization, criminal acts, et al. Sexuality is so under rated and such a source of so many negative occurrences instead of being an ecstatic spiritual experience. Tantra yogi is a good place to learn more about sexuality. We have attractions that are based on sexuality at a fairly young age. Today's youth act upon it far too young and fail to enjoy the sweetness of evolving romance, like hand holding, companionship, love at first sight, finally that "first kiss." It seems strange that even seemingly limited time friendships are based on past life connections. Bad experience of various kinds, confrontations with different nationalities, religions, races, all contribute to possible prejudices in a present life.

One should also list his or her special skills, abilities, talents and qualities that make you unique. If you could learn any of these skills that you don't have, what would you choose? Also, thing about the possibility of be given any of these and how would they make your life any different today. If you could travel any where in the world or universe, where would you go? If you could speak other languages, what would they be? There are endless hints for past lives.

While I have studied with professionals in Psychotherapy, Psychoanalysis or Hypnosis, as a practicing psychic, I felt they could be a bit too academic and needed to use their own intuition/psychic ability more. Steeped in learned techniques fail to allow this intuitive ability to manifest, yet many do or learn to allow it. Often if they get too close to a deep trauma, they may not be aware of the higher dimensional forces and energy needed. They may not have delved into their own deeper subconscious and especially spiritual evolvement and may not be able to get out of their own egos.

By asking your self many of these questions, writing them down on a piece of paper or by keeping a notebook can help you retrieve your own past life memories. When a thought that seems to resemble a previous statement, it will be another piece of the puzzle of your own, many past lives. You could consider past life memory work is like cleaning house or cleaning out your closet when you realize you have been keeping old clothes that no longer fit and taking up valuable space in the closet as with these burdensome past life traumas that need "fixing" or clearing out! True healing and freedom comes from cleaning out your subconscious closet. Through eons of time we have had so much emotional repressions, intense emotional scars that have been repeated in life after life. This needed freedom from the past can only be realized when we have cleared out these emotional traumas. Cleaning out our past opens the way for a clearer future so I say to those who say "I don't want to know my past, only my future" - have a better future by cleaning out your subconscious closet!

CHAPTER 4

THIS LIFE

When I write down the INCIDENTS/ACCIDENTS in my own life, that could have created trauma, guilt, resentment, insecurity, etc, these were the things I remembered and are the things that stay with us throughout our whole lives.

We often wonder if we were conceived in love. If one is exposed to a lot of arguments between the mother and father, it seems doubtful.

Through the visualization, I described what I thought happened at my birth. Was that the beginning of my deep seeded feeling of rejection or even before I was born! When I was about five, my mother might have been having an affair. One night my father got my sister, brother and me together and began telling us that our mother was out with another man and that he was going after her to bring her home to us. He showed us a gun. He told us that if any thing happened to him, he wanted us to know how much he loved us. I didn't understand and was terrified. He said he was doing it for us, again more guilt laid on us. In later years, I saw how she responded to any man's attention toward her. As other young children, I didn't know how to respond to traumas. My grandmother died when I was five. My sister took me outside and sat on a bench to tell me with tearful eyes. I didn't know what to do. I didn't FEEL anything and felt guilty because of not feeling I needed to cry like my sister was doing.

I knew that I was a "cute" little girl. When I was still young enough for my Dad to carry me around, as he was talking to a man, the man said "She'll give the men problems when she grows up." I remember feeling hurt that he would think that of me. Why would I want to hurt anyone? At the breakfast table when I was about three or four, knowing I was "cute" I said "pass me the soap (meaning syrup)" - My uncle got up from the table, went to the bathroom, got a bar of soap and handed it to me. I was embarrassed and went inward in sadness. At five, I saw our cat kill Mother's canary bird. I was the one to tell her. She sat on the bed and cried. I took on a heavy responsibility for "bearer of bad tidings" that had nothing to do with me. Around the same age, there was that terrible dust storm. As far as you could see there was rolling dust coming toward us. My brother was in a cave with other boys. My dad had to go out to bring him in the safe house. I resented my brother for putting my dad in danger. My brother and I had a life time of never getting along well together. Even when he died a few years ago, I felt no sadness or shed any tears.

The closest I ever came to any kind of sexual child abuse was with my grandfather, who was the only one at home with me. I was around four, maybe five. My grandfather had me undress and he undressed to teach me about the body. A small child has no concept of "wrong" when an adult wishes to teach them something. Generally, a small child has no concept of right or wrong regarding nudity. He never touched me, but by seeing me nude, he masturbated and had an organism. I was amazed to see it and felt no shame -- until my brother came home from school. I was excited to tell him what I had learned and to this day, I remember him at the door saying "Ohm, don't tell Mother and Daddy!" I had done nothing wrong yet I was dashed with GUILT that remained with me throughout childhood years! I never wanted to be around my grandfather again. By today's standards he would be in jail as a pedophile. In later years I found out that he had a habit of touching his grand daughters' bodies as they slept and even raped his own daughter. He was the essence of a "dirty old man"!

For all of my young years both parents worked. Today children are called "latch key kids". Home alone, I read a lot of fairy tales, perhaps escapism. I lived my fairy tales. Could that be the reason I have been drawn to past life regressions as some sort of fantasy? OR was I drawn to fairy tales when I was closer to past life memories in my youth? What it HAS done for me is helped me to work toward wholeness, merging all these past life characters represented in this book into ONE soul - or OVER SOUL?

There weren't a lot of happy childhood memories and little is remembered about my early years. My brother and sister were older and stuck together. I seemed to be a nuisance to them. Perhaps that fed a lot of insecurity. Psychological counseling was unknown. I was often the "only child" and my parents used me as a pawn in their fighting, especially when my Mother wanted to leave my father. One time he took me to a neighboring town to spend the night with a girlfriend, which I enjoyed but also knowing something wasn't right. He had hid me from my Mother to force her not to leave him. My Mother always seemed partial to my sister and brother while I was my Daddy's "baby".

Since ours was "the ONLY religion," yet what about all those other religion, Heaven forbid, those Jews were surely goners! What about all the churches and religions all over this big world? Why would God choose just ONE over all the other was my everlasting question. Religious teachings in my childhood seemed to discourage one to have confidence in one's appearance, as that was sinful. Many pleasures in life were sins. As far back as I can remember, I questioned one conclusion after another that seemed acceptable to adults. I can look back today and see how the fears were pumped into us as children regarding "hell fire and damnation" and how almost any pleasure was a "sin." What kind of God did we have that was so wrathful?

All my young years, my Dad was always teaching me something or other. When I was around eight, he owned a second hand store that also had a magazine and comic book section. He GAVE me the comic book business. I was thrilled to be the boss of my own business! During that time, the awning and bricks fell in the front of the store. A few minutes before, I had been playing there. He was frantically digging through the rubble when I appeared, which was a great relief for him.

Much later he was in the construction business always teaching to me how things are done. One lesson he taught me was if I didn't know how to do something, do it anyway. "You will make a mistake the first time you do it but just do it again, you will probably still make a mistake but if you keep doing it, you will do it better each time until you learn how to do it right." - A valuable lesson that sustained me all through my life.

In earlier years when he owned a clothes cleaning business, I was around five and had to stay there so I found my special place to nap -- in the dirty clothes bend. When I was caught in it, I was pulled out and told not to get in it again. What would a child know about germs on dirty clothes. We had to use the bathroom at the service station on the corner. On one trip, with my young business ambitions, I took about ten paper towels, scribbled on them with a pencil or crayons. When my Dad found me in front of his place of business, I was trying to sell my paper towels as "newspapers." He reprimanded me even though passersby thought it was cute, it ended my business venture. I was always searching for MY own business or a "play house" - my special little cubby hole.

When I was in elementary school, my father got a job near the gulf coast and we lived in a small travel trailer a block away from the Brazos River. On Saturday, kids went to the movies. When my girlfriend and I came out of the theater, we decided we wanted to spend the night at her house. As we started walking toward the store where her mother worked -- practical me, I suddenly decided that we should go to my parents first to get permission, so we turned around and walked toward the travel trailer. Just as we got there, we heard a freight train backing up, except there were no trains or tracks. Just then, we saw telephone poles falling like dominoes, the roof of the High School was rolling off. We quickly rushed into the small park office until the tornado had passed. In those days most people went to town to shop early Saturday evenings. That was fortunate as only two people were killed. One was a little girl our age. I knew right there and then, I had saved our lives because if we had gone to where her mother worked, we would have been right smack in the tornado's path! It took a big swipe out of the residential area. One house was moved off its foundation, leaning on another. 2 x 4's were rammed through a building; another store's walls had collapsed with all the food still on the shelves. Live wires lay in the streets. It was a horrifying experience. I can still see out the door window of our small trailer, the clouds were swirling in the bright moonlit night. I lay awake most of that night fearing that the storm would come back, pick up the trailer and dump us in the river. I don't remember ever sleeping in bed with my parents but apparently I had. That night I wanted to but my dad didn't want me to sleep with them or sit in his lap any longer saying I was too big. Another rejection!

Later on that gulf coast, a hurricane was approaching so the school let us out by noon. Most parents came to pick up their children but mine didn't. I started walking to the trailer but as I took three steps, the heavy wind would blow me back two! I would hold on to anything I could but then I came to a street I had to cross. A couple came along and held my hands to take me across. That was a very frightening experience. My sister was working and living in Ft. Worth so my Dad was packing up everything for us to leave. We never returned to Freeport, Texas, we settled in a Fort Worth suburb.

Each time my family moved, I was always the "pretty new girl." The boys liked me and the girls resented me. I was always a loaner. Riding my bicycle was my escape; my inborn desire to travel. When my father bought a house, I was in Junior High School (now called "Middle" School). We lived next door to one of the most popular high school football players - the Captain of the team. Naturally, I developed a crush on him. My dad built a great teenage swing set for me that was built on a huge tree. I had what we called an "acting bar" similar to simple ones circus performers use. The boy next door would come out to feed the chickens in the pen next to my swings. We would stand near the fence and talk until dark. By the time I was in the first year of High School, he took me to the formal Senior Prom. I looked good, too! The senior girls made fun of him for taking a younger girl, so after that he shied away from me. It was nothing I had done. Just another in a long line of inner questioning -- "What's wrong with ME?"

Advise that should have been given by a mother to a daughter came from my father instead; without any details about sex and coming from a man's point of view. I believed that I should be honest and do everything I could for a man I would fall in love with -- not the games male/females play! My values and morals were established through him. As a devout Mason, he lived and followed their principles. I was such a "good girl" but he feared my peers might influence me, as in one warm summer's evening. My two best friends and I were walking around the neighborhood on that summer night. A group of kids were playing in their front yard. As we passed by their game, they began chasing us, we ran, participating in their game. Finally, we turned and grabbed one of the little boys for only brief moments. He knew we were playing their game but the Mother called the police. Within minutes the police arrived. We had let the little boy go before they got there. We could hear the woman shouting to the police and scared us half to death. We were by a block long park area so we ran into the park, hiding in and out of bushes, then up the street to one of the girl's houses! Her mother just laughed. With police searching for us, we felt like criminals. Word got to the other girl's parents and they told my Dad. Well -- from then on, I was not allowed to wear shorts or walk at night. We were punished when we were the innocent ones - a pattern that always followed me.

The damage from this incident and minor ones caused my Dad not to trust me. That was hurtful as I felt I was everything he wanted me to be. I don't remember ever lying to my parents. At age five, I had stolen a plume from a basket outside a store and felt sick afterwards. That was my lesson to never steal. Lying took too much energy to remember it all and just wasn't worth the effort. My only crime was after my sister returned home from a job in Washington D.C. to go back to college; I did sneak her clothes out of the closet to wear. I got home before she did so back in her closet they went.

By nature, I was shy and fought to overcome it. As an athlete I was good but never the best. I always ran around with girls whose families had a lot more money than my family. Feeling I had been born into the wrong family just added to my insecurity. Why was I not good enough - smart enough - pretty enough, just a lot of not enough's plus the "what's wrong with me!"

How well I remember, at age 13 when my Dad released me from the Baptist Church when on a Sunday, two friends and I sat on the back row. We had put books under us so it raised us up higher. We must have been snickering as the preacher said "If the three girls on the back row don't want to hear the sermon, they can leave." We died with embarrassment! That was my last day in a Baptist church.

Knowing I was more attractive than many of the other girls, I seemed to apologize for it most of my life. I would belittle myself trying to make others feel better about themselves. Little could I realize what a destructive pattern it has been most of my life. That and other events created within me my lack of confidence – what a great detriment to then strive to achieve success in the motion picture and television businesses.

In college I was on "even footing" with everyone else. I felt I escaped from my family background being in college and living in the Dorm was exciting as was all aspects of college life were. It was a military college so the boys outnumbered the girls five to one. I was popular and four of five social clubs gave me a bid, meaning they wanted me to join. (Sororities were not allowed in State colleges at that time.) I joined one of the two most popular ones. It was the competitor of the club that my sister had belonged to, which had given me the right to an automatic bid in theirs. My club talked of running me in "this or that" popularity elections; then they began saving me for the next, the next and never got around to running me for anything. Even so, I did get votes without running. Again, was I good enough, why not me? It was always girls that made me feel insecure, not boys. I was popular with them and had dates to all events. During the second year, I had dated everyone I wanted to date and hadn't "fallen in love" with any of them. I was still "carrying a torch" for the boy I fell in love with from the military school when I was in High School. His mother had taken him out of the school; he lived in Houston with no car, so we couldn't get together with each of us in a different college.

One of the boys in my art classes was a pest. He wouldn't leave me alone and followed me around all the time. The best thing about him he was one of the few boys on campus that had his own car, a convertible. That was convenient. Since there was no one else and he was always around, we began dating. He was a nice guy. Everyone liked him and he was on the football team. Friends began telling me how good he was for me. What was wrong with me if they think he is and I am not attracted to him. I liked him but there were no butterflies. He gave me his football jacket to wear. In those days it meant "going steady." We continued dating but I was not fond of kissing him, however, I was at an age when the hormones were fluttering so I began to feel a bit more attracted or I just felt obligated to try and feel something for him. By Christmas after we were out of college, he was working with his parents who were in the wholesale children's business. I spent Christmas with his family. My gift was in a huge box. When I opened it; there was a winter coat and a small box with an engagement ring. With his family and him so

47

excited when I opened the gift, I felt obligated and couldn't refuse it. I will never know if I would have actually followed through and married him if he hadn't gotten me pregnant. It was during that time that we were parked and kissing when he got more or less out of control with passion. I was fully clothed, a winter coat and my underwear on when he pushed his penis up next to me and had an organism. He got out of the car to finish but I would find out in a few weeks, the deed was done. I was pregnant. The little wigglies had found their mark without full insertion. Now, I was really traumatized. I hadn't planned ahead -- I never had sex, now I was trapped. He suggested an abortion but in those days, with abortions illegal, crack pots performing them, it was almost sure death. I hated to be forced into marriage! When I walked down the aisle at our wedding, I looked at him and thought how I DID NOT love him. I tied to love him but he was and should have remained no more than a good friend. During pregnancy I did everything to avoid sex. I grew more and more repulsed and hated sex. Then I had to live a lie, had to be so careful not to reveal the truth and when my daughter was born, I then had to pretend my child was premature. Things were very different then than they are now. One didn't dare have a child out of wedlock and you were assured that people would count the months from your wedding day to the birth of a child. My doctor and minister supported my living a lie but I hated it -- having to pretend, having to lie to my parents.

I was "boy crazy" and popular all of my childhood; as an adult, I continued the path of "man crazy" - I liked male companions more than women. Women were often jealous, deceitful and very critical of me. The most difficult test in this life has been thinking I must love and be loved by a man -- the ever constant search for that illusive soul mate! It has been only in recent years that I conquered that one! Life is one test after another and all is toward spiritual awakening. These are some of the basics from childhood that I have had to try and work through.

This is about my journey delving into my own past lives. Believe me -- accept the concept has never been easy with constant questioning as to the source that these revelations come from. Through regressions, meditations, visions, channeling, repetitious dreams, even an "ah ha" experience deja vu when visiting a place for the first time, yet, knowing it and feeling emotions of another time -- another era -- another century.

It has not been easy piecing the bits and pieces together in some kind of liner order in which events happened. I would go months and years without trying to find order in the experiences that were given to me.

What have I learned in living many decades by now? My life has been one of learning to live a solo life, not what I thought I wanted but apparently I came into this incarnation to learn that at some point in our evolution, traveling through life may have to be a solo journey. Do I have regrets? Of course, I wish I had made different choices. I simply share the incidents in my childhood that I feel sure a psychologist or psychiatrist could find psychological flaws in my character, however, with having done psychic counseling for both types of doctors, I see that we ALL have many flaws and "feet of clay." Revealing my childhood events may help you to see how your own childhood has affected your entire life, yet have held clues for the past incarnations that are to help you become whole in the soul realm. It is to help those who may be wandering around, feeling very alone in their questioning of religions and spirituality.

CHAPTER 5

IMAGINATION SOUL PURPOSE

IMAGINATION: WHAT MAKES US DIFFERENT FROM ANIMALS? Is it not imagination? Is it not this imaging ability that has created and manifested all of our progress? At an early age when we begin expressing our fantasies and imagination, often adults quickly squelch it - the imaginary playmates, ghost, nature spirits are only our "imagination" we are told, "They are not real." When you are "little" and they are "big" you assume they must be right by pure size. The child shuts down, closed off to his natural senses beyond the five physical senses. Spirits that could have taught, guided and aided spiritual growth, we are taught are not "real." Unexplainable behavior patterns actions or unknown knowledge expressed by children are often past life memories. Well meaning parents create deep traumas in their children because they do not understand or encourage these resources.

Dr. Ian Stevenson was Director of Personality Studies at the University of Virginia, probably the foremost researcher on scientific proof of reincarnation. He specialized in researching children with 3,000 cases in his files. As I understand, there is a gland that atrophies by the age of eight or nine, thus, the most valid or believable cases for him have been young children in his more than 40 years of research. Quite a number of my friends have told me of their imaginary play mates when they were young children. Stevenson said children they have studied often act as if they had been transferred without warning from an adult's body into a baby's. Our bodies wear out; souls may need periods for rest and reflection. Some may have unfinished business or relationships and make a quick return so that one may start again with a new body. Some people say it is unfair to be reborn unless you can remember details of a previous life. They forget that forgetting is essential to successful living in the present.

Most of us can't remember what we did a few hours ago or day ago, why would we remember past lives? In quiet states, often we do have past life memories but pass them off as something we read or saw in a movie. Spontaneous regressions happen to most of us but because of not understanding them, we disregard them as imagination. Many of our dreams as children or adults are past life memories gradually flowing out of the subconscious, especially dreams that should be long forgotten with the thousands upon thousands of dreams we have had, cannot be forgotten. In adulthood we may have specific memory of dreams we had in childhood or many years ago. A child, afraid of the dark, might have died in a fearful situation in a deep, dark dungeon, or similar circumstances. Any sort of fear or anxiety should be allowed to be expressed by children, not stifled. It is O.K. to express any of these feelings any time. That is what we do when we visit psychiatrists, psychologists, psychics, priest, preacher or minister, etc.

In my own childhood, I had an uncanny talent for dancing and art. While my parents could not afford lessons in either, I had an inborn talent for those and the knowledge of knowing how to do things, plus inborn class and culture that was not in harmony with my family or surroundings. I marveled at how big the world is and how would I ever get "out there" to experience it. Because I didn't know where all this was coming from, I allowed other people's attitudes and opinions about me to convince me they were right and I was wrong; which even got me into my first marriage. My theme in my life continued always to be "What's wrong with ME?" I knew I was doing my best to just be the best I could be. My entire lifetime has been influenced by misjudgments by others, especially family. It has taken many years of wondering, researching, meditating, attending classes and seminars to glean some understanding of why these things happened. Reincarnation has been the one source that has helped me more than any other. It helped me to understand that people's negative attitudes and opinions are so often based on their own fears and jealousies and is theirs to handle, not mine.

Those attitudes have nothing to do with who I am. Unfortunately, my understand and knowledge came late in life after missing youthful opportunities to succeed in a career.

If my car gets bumps and scratches, the engine is unaffected. My exterior personality reflects life's bumps and scratches but my inner spirit is pure, loving, dedicated, honest, loyal, true, etc. so if people "out there" see me differently it is because they are mirroring their own negative traits, not mine or who I really am. My battle scars have accumulated over many years, many life times. Realizing what I have done in other times, in other bodies, helps me understand why I have been confronted with so many traumas in this present life. It helped me to understand why, no matter how many different religions I tried or researched, none fit my inner spiritual hungering. It is as though I am a suction collecting the more important past lives' lessons. It IS the chapters in this book and the pieces of my soul's puzzle. By gathering the events that needed to be corrected, completed, I am creating my soul's complete picture. The pieces of my soul puzzle come together through the gathering of these past incarnations. A friend once said to me that we are the cells in the body of God. At the time it seemed sacrilegious, but as years pass, it seems to make total sense.

Recalling these past experiences should be based on forgiveness -- "O.K. I see now what I did in that life, which was a reflection of the time and circumstances and I lovingly accept myself then and now into the allness of life, which brings me closer to that allness we call "God." A recent epiphany for me was realizing that I have been collecting more of my total self as related to my present by tracing segments of past incarnations. Knowing from my personal research, in order to complete earth incarnations, we need to have balance in our physical, mental, emotional spirituality. As I think of this life, I have not created a balanced physical body so it occurred to me that by gathering various or many of my past lives, within some of them, I must have had a more balanced body, therefore, gathering these many lives, we may be balancing them more than we can imagine as we seek to return to our wholeness of our Soul.

The Soul has to experience all aspects of life. Western thought of reincarnation is that man just reincarnates to higher spiritual levels of life, that he must repeat cycles until he realized why we are totally responsibility for self, no one else can be. (Karma -- "as you sow, so shall you reap." -- cause and effect.) Reincarnation is a way of rejecting the monotheistic teachings that include the final judgment by a wrathful God, with the possible results of being eternally condemned to suffering in hell. Since early childhood, I had to keep fighting and rejected that concept. How could our God be so loving, forgiving, compassionate and be the wrathful, vengeful God in the bible!

Reincarnation explains how some people must suffer all their lives with a handicap or malady, some are rich, others in starvation, which can be sustenance, but also love, success, et al. It seems a perfect way to punish or reward one's deeds. It makes us RESPONSIBLE for those deeds. We can correct things we have done previously by reliving it in our minds, understand why we reacted in that time and circumstances, THEN forgive ourselves. Didn't Jesus say "Any thing I can do, you can do also." If God is a forgiving God, should we be any less toward ourselves in many present or past life's circumstances?

I believe the statement in Christianity "Jesus died for our sins" is misinterpreted, just as the word "Christ" is misinterpreted. Firstly, "Christ" is the allness that Jesus reached -- a state of oneness consciousness; it was NOT his last name. He was the incarnation of many prophets that went before him, as in his statement "Who do they say I am?" For me, he showed us the WAY to achieve that "Christ" ness - to learn to love unconditionally, have compassion and understanding for others that may not agree with our way of life and many other good qualities of brotherhood and caring.

Originally Christianity included pagan rituals and holidays that still exist today but Catholicism changed the names to various Saint's Day. As stated earlier, reincarnation was an accepted part of Christianity prior to the Council of Nicea, established by Emperor Constanne AD 392. He gathered all the various religious sects and picked and chose what HE wished to include in 'one' religion. There have been innumerable translations of the bible. One that remains true to the Original Dead Sea Scrolls is the Aramaic bible, translated by George Lamas. Remaining in the bible today are 'hints' of reincarnation.

1. *Mathew 11.14. And 17, 12-13* concerning the identity of John the Baptist - the reincarnation of the prophet Elijah.

2. *John 9:2* "Who sinned, the man or his parents, that he was born blind?"

3. *John 3:3* "No one can see the kingdom of God unless he is born again." (Fundamentalists have "born again" WRONG! MY concept is being born again is accepting the eternal present Christ within us!)

4. *James 3:6* "the wheel of nature."

5. *Galatians 6:7* "A man reaps what he sows."

6. *Mathew 26:52* "all who draw the sword will die by the sword."

7. *Revelation 13:10* "If anyone is to go into captivity, into captivity he will go. If anyone is to be killed with the sword, with the sword he will be killed."

Like so much of the bible, it can be interpreted by the reader to have deferring and opposing meanings; just as the interpretations by the scholars that translated the various bibles through out the hundreds of years; each subjected to the ruler of the time and each was a MAN. Millions of people revere the King James Bible as "the Word of God". Of the 54 men chosen to translate it, only 47 completed the seven year project that was governed by very strict rules of translation – notice, there were ONLY men! The higher aspects of our soul is androgynous - both male and female, so shouldn't bible interpretations also have included the female psyche?

How many of those million of people, many that despise homosexuals, know that King James I loved men and had sex with them. At 13 he fell madly in love with Esme Stuart, his cousin. Later he fell in love with a Scotsman named Robert Carr. His favorite male lovers were the Earl of Somerset and the Duke of Buckingham.

"Birth is not the beginning; death is not the end. There is existence without limitation; there is continuity without a starting point. Existence without limitation is space. Continuity without a starting point is time. There is birth, there is death, there is issuing forth, there is entering in. That through which one passes in and out without seeing its form, _that is the Portal of God_ " (Chuang Tzu 23)

Our past life "memory bank" holds more traumatic experiences than the happy ones for most of us -- wars - horrible deaths or treatments - bad relationships - imprisonments even by spouses or family - irrational fears and phobias - chronic physical afflictions. It seems to me, it is more important to recall the past problems so that we can bring them up into the conscious mind and seek our own forgiveness by understand how those circumstances were created, than happy times that don't need clearing off of our Soul's book of passages.

Hollywood actor Glenn Ford, under hypnosis recalled five previous lives. One life in particular was as a French cavalryman under Louis XIV. Astonishingly, he knew only a few French phrases but under hypnosis he spoke French with ease while describing that life. When recordings of his regression were sent to UCLA, they discovered that not only was he speaking fluent French, he was speaking a Parisian dialect from the 17th Century.

When I worked in a film with Glenn Ford, an actress friend had said to tell him hello for her. I did and was shocked with the only words he spoke to me "Tell her I am the best f--- she ever had!" Could his eccentric familiarity toward me have come from a slight acquaintance in my past life in France?

If we could understand the lessons of past life experiences, our spiritual progress would be simplified but we continually get trapped in our emotional responses.

I believe we get trapped in Earth physical evolution to work through our emotional responses. An example is one of my greatest traumas in this life was the loss of my only child. My daughter vanished in the early 1970's never to be seen again. There was no closure, no funeral, no ending, just the hope that she was alive some where in the world. It was MY experience to work through, however, if you ask me if I had any children and then I told you of that experience, immediately, your emotional reaction is fear of what if it happened to you, how could you handle it. Before she disappeared, if any thing ever happened to her, I thought I would die, too. Another emotional subconscious reaction from you might be anger "I don't like you, you survived an experience I don't think I could so you must be stronger or more powerful than me" - thus resentment toward me, yet, your outer actions must be empathy. Maybe I experienced that loss so you and others never have to face it. An emotion free response might be "Thank you for sharing and experiencing that emotional pain for me and others so that we don't have to." There are layers upon layers of emotional responses. Just as a pet can take on an illness for its owner, perhaps there are some of us who volunteer to live out certain emotional experiences for ourselves and others and by doing so; maybe we make a quantum leap in spiritual evolution. Maybe you are living in a crippled body so that I might say "Thank you for taking on that crippled body so that I don't have to." This kind of gratitude might be a merging into unity just as recalling your past lives is merging into your soul's totality and as we begin to merge with our past, our present, we are merging into that oneness we call - "God." Isn't this is what being co-creators is all about.

PURPOSE OF LIFE: Survival -- Enjoyment - Purpose and we cannot eliminate desire that moves life itself -- we create through our desires. What are your desires -- creative or destructive as greed, low forms of sex, ego or vanity, anger, vengeance, depression, destroying others or things. Negative emotions create clashes, the brain often can't think what to do - blood pressure increases - we feel anger - out of control - heart palpitations - the stomach secretes acids and the whole body is affected. Our purpose is to transform destructive emotions. I seemed to have been born with a temper and worked many years to overcome it. One thing that helped me was when I learned that we give our POWER away to the person or situation that creates our anger. By visualizing that I put my power in my hands and handed it over to the person or situation that created my anger, through this visualization, I definitely did not wish to give my power away! We are constantly motivating our body's reactions with our ever constant thoughts. Many or most illnesses are caused by negative thought patterns.

As a child I was taught that we are not suppose to be proud of ourselves, our appearance and we do not brag about our accomplishments or abilities. Thus, I developed negative words that are so deeply ingrained that I don't think of them as negatives but other people do. One "handicap" or ability I have always had is to tell the truth; which includes speaking my mind. An example of my words might be when someone ask "How are you feeling?" or "How are things going?" And if I am not feeling well or things are not going well, I say so! Then the person asking comes back with "You are being negative!" That judgment from them is not being fair -- don't ask if you don't want to know! People who grow up in a family of love, understanding and encouragement rarely understand others who have not had that luxury. Today, parents began talking to their baby while still in the womb, playing music, sending love, etc. What a great practice that is!

Can you LOVE yourself unconditionally? If not, can you love anyone, anything or GOD unconditionally? What I see is the sermonizing of "born again Christians" or any fundamentalists that have no respect for other people's beliefs. God gave us "free will" our government gave us "free speech" (that, today, may be fading away) why are religionists trying to force their limitations of their religions on others who may have far more understanding of the deeper aspects of spiritual evolution? My personal life time journey has been very committed to learn my own individualized evolution. It has been far more time consuming and delving far deeper than those who would condemn me or try to force their beliefs on me and others. I have learned to not enter into a discussion as there is no open mindedness and only the prophesizing their limited belief. I would like to just say "Do your own thing and I respect you, give me the same respect." It is my opinion, those who try to force their belief systems on others who are NOT interested, FAIL to miss the whole essences of the Christ consciousness, the great teachers, prophets, masters who have walked on Earth. The basis for any worthwhile philosophy or belief system is always based on LOVE. We, each, need to be and feel free to express all forms of love: Mother, Father, Child, Brother, Sister, Lover, friends and those things that don't control our lives.

Is learning unconditional love our ultimate human goal? Is forgiveness our greatest gift toward our selves and others? Giving someone all your love is never any assurance that they will love you back! (DON'T I KNOW THAT ONE!) We should not expect love in return but to wait for it to grow in the other person's heart and if it doesn't, be content that it was an opportunity to grow in yours. It takes a minute to get a "crush" on someone, maybe an hour to like them, only days to fall in love but it seems it can take a lifetime to forgive someone. We need to put ourselves in the other person's point of perspective to understand their reaction toward us. Attempting to understand male/female love is a daunting challenge. One that I never accomplished as a man and woman will never think alike. The best we can do if find a mate with compatible differences and respect our differences. We need to look at those differences as creating one whole person - Yen and Yang, Ebb and Flow. For me, an almost impossible fault has been resentment of unfulfilled love relationships - two that lasted over twenty years. Neither were consistent, just relationships that continued, ended, renewed, ended, renewed. Both men died four days apart, which seemed more than coincidental! Both were successful in the film/TV industries. I felt I had given them consistent respect, devotion and love through the years with nothing in return. I know we should not give to receive, however, I also realize there must be give and take in all relationships! There was no balance in these and other male/female relationships I entered into. Today, especially with the Internet, there is so much available to us, even if we don't have the money to go for counseling. We can get help by reading about relationships online. I wish that in younger days, I had understood the "Mars/Venus" proposed by Jon Grey, aspects of male/female relationships. Understanding and accepting our differences can help any relationship -- accepting and respecting those differences.

People who are the happiest do not always have the best of everything; they make the most of everything that comes their way. Happiness is within those who cry, those who hurt, those who search and those who have tried, for only they can appreciate the important of people who have touched their lives. They have gleaned love, compassion, understanding and try to be nonjudgmental. Just think, when you were born, you were crying while others round you were smiling. Living life with contentment, when you leave the physical body, you will be smiling while those around you may be crying. There are wealthy people that are happy, however, there are many that are very unhappy and fail to have gratitude for the blessings of financial security! May your life be filled with happiness through the learning of the trials that make you stronger.

CHAPTER 6

ATLANTIS TO ROME RECALLS

These are ancient lives for which I have had only brief glimpses and know very little about: I believe they were shown to me so that I understood how I could have had almost entirely female incarnations. One consistent theme is that I never had more than one child nor did that child ever reach adulthood. The glimpses of the Roman and other lives I lived as a woman. Perhaps to show me how I had to become enslaved to a man's dominion. There are only a few memories lived as men. I do not know the time line of these past life memories. Maybe they are pieces of my Over Soul that I connect with in order to learn the lessons necessary for me to learn -- so that they are brought to this Over Soul with corrections accomplished. No one knows the whole story of how we exist when we are not limited by linear time.

ATLANTIS: TWO LIVES

1. PRIESTESS -- A large round amphitheatre high up in the building --Around the upper area there were gold statues and gold columns. We wore ivory gowns with a lot of gold. The gold had something to do with creating energy. In the center, there was a very large cylinder with white light energy in it. That was the energy for the whole of Atlantis. Priestesses and Priests had to be there at all times to create and direct the energy as needed. Within the cylinder there may have been a huge quartz crystal. There were many plazas in the city. Buildings were a

simple design that today would be called ultra modern. Everything was exceedingly clean. There was a lot of flora and fauna and a lot of outdoor activities with people living outdoors most of the time. Everything seemed to be in light colors.

2. MALE -- Served in a service, in a flying machine that looked more like the cabin of a dirigible helium balloon but flew without a balloon. It reminded me of the description today of a cigar shaped UFO. I don't know the energy source. We were in charge of overseeing the food supplies; farming and growing that were grown in what is now the Middle East today. That area had lush gardens, fruits, vegetables, grains, etc. Something happened in that area with the people and conditions so that our air ship was sent there to destroy a large segment of people. Could I do it? I do not know. I just know I never wanted to incarnate again as a man. As far as I know, I have always been a woman except for just a few lives in Atlantis, Egypt and Italy.

EGYPT: TWO LIVES (CHANNELED)

Egyptian hot sultry sun never bothers a boy of ten who knew no other atmosphere. His plain room with only a simple bed was not of modest means in that day for his father was a stonecutter of nobility, carving only the stonecutting for the highest ruling houses. Tedious work was no easy task. Months had passed since Abedcki had witnessed the murder of his uncle for a crime which he had not committed. A part of him hated royal linage for the unfounded laws that had taken his uncle he loved more than any member of his family. The scholarly uncle had spent many hours with Abedcki teaching him intelligence ways of man – of the stars in the heavens – of the history of planet earth. He had stood in the halls of the library and marveled at the lines of scrolls that were housed in the great library of Alexander. Abedcki felt life was taken from him, with the death of this uncle, Narab. Narab had been at the right hand of the Pharaoh. He stood tall in wisdom as well as stature, hands taller than other men who feared him. He was an unsightly gangly man amongst men of narrow vision. Toward the end, he had deliberately amused himself with radical statements aimed at offending the Pharaoh. Offending him, he did. Well into his seventy-first year Narab had decided he no longer chose to be house in the physical body.

His death was his aim. He planned it so precisely that written records had been discovered afterwards that set the Pharaoh a fool, as he had played totally into Narab's hands and from his tomb, Narab had the last laugh. Fortunately the Pharaoh did not let this incident influence his attitude toward Abedcki's family. How could he, Abedcki's father was too desperately needed to complete the tomb of this Pharaoh.

Head master accused Abedcki of heresy because of his stand on a God of love. He was a good student and loved everyone. "Treat me good or I shall have you killed" the Head Master threatened. Abedcki washed his hands of all that this man touches or had influence over. Abedcki totally gave up on all those willing to be possessed by the Head Master's influence. There was no resistance on Abedcki's part. Those who Abedcki have loved before were free of that love. Thus, Abedcki left the teachings that were void of love.

The years passed fairly uneventfully with Abedcki continually visiting the great Library as was normally not permissible for one so young. The library was reserved for a certain class of intellectuals. Few others were permitted except on special days known as Sorbini. There were the changes of seasons although living in Alexandria did not show the changing seasons as countries to the far North. Abedcki would visit the seashore and look out at the ships that came and went to Greece where other scholarly men stood quite tall in his mind. Tall represented intelligence to Abedcki. He longed for tallness to be like his dead uncle.

Stonecutting was his trade like his father. Abedcki knew well the consequences for anyone who disobeyed the Pharaoh's orders. He was ordered to follow in the footsteps of his father as his father's father had done. It was thought that the ability of the father was passed to the first son and so on; therefore Abedcki was never offered a choice as to what he might want to do in life. At 17 he was in full swing in his career as a stonecutter – an artesian of rare ability. It may seem a simple task to carefully cut away designs in the stone but it was extremely precise since it was the most reliable method of leaving recorded history for the after life of the Pharos and future generations. The stone cutting was very tedious and methodical. Much of recorded history taken from painted hieroglyphics was taken from Abedcki's stone carvings before weather and age destroyed them. Abedcki's purpose in that life left its mark on the history of mankind. His teachers were men born into that time specifically for the purpose of gifting man on this planet with special knowledge and wisdom of a timely nature.

Abedcki had always been a curious boy. He learned everything he could. Staying focused on the future as a tone cutter was impossible for him. He was gifted with such a talent for it that it came so easily there was no challenge; therefore as he grew older he sought other interest. Stone was stone – hard – cold though deep – it did not have the depth he needed to explore. It was the mind – the endless phenomena of the mind that thrilled him. When a layer of stone is removed, more of the same is underneath, yet when a layer of the mind is probed, another more curious one appears. This fascinated Abedcki. This was why he was so devoted to his Uncle. After the death of Narab, Abedcki knew it was his uncle's choice to pick the time of his death. Loosing that brilliant mind while cutting stone for a Pharaoh whose mind was hardly a measure for the Uncle's, seemed so pointless to Abedcki. Those thought were totally unspeakable; not even to his family or little brother whom he loved and trusted to the utmost. Ameali, the little bother of Abedcki was always at his side. He worshiped Abedcki to the point that Abedcki often grew impatient with him.

Abedcki, who was known for very little patience grew angry at Ameali's constant worship - "Go and find your own things to do" he would coax the little brother "go and find your own friends and kind". Nonetheless, Ameali would even follow in the shadows of Abedcki. When Abedcki would whirl around in anger at his little brother's following, Ameali would duck behind something so that he was not seen. Ameali's great admiration for Abedcki was his great skills for carving. He was known as one of the best tomb carvers. One day Abedcki was particularly upset and angry as he was carving. The Pharos had dishonored his dead uncle was all he could think of. His anger got the best of him and he slammed his chisel into his work seriously damaging it. This was something one did not do! Any destruction to anything related to the tomb was an immediate death sentence. When Ameali saw what had happened, he ran to the supervisor and told him that he had done the deed. Naturally, he was killed on the spot. When Abedcki heard what had happened, he fell into a terrible state of depression and was very sick for months, no longer able to do his carvings. He searched among the Gods and Goddesses for his retribution - how could he ever face life again. Little by little he began more and more studying the great literature of Egypt. He seemed to conquer his temper and used the knowledge he gained to teach children as he tried to make up for his brother's death. His guilt over the death of his little brother never left him.

(That little brother, Ameali, was my daughter in this life who vanished when she was only 18 and never to be seen or found.)

Through the years Abedcki found more and more favor among the intelligences of Egypt and eventually spent the rest of his life as a counsel for the Pharaoh. He lived a long life and contributed more by his learning and counseling that his carving did at the time, yet today, some of his carvings remain in a Pharaoh's tomb. When Abedcki died, he was met on the other side by his little brother, Ameali, when Ameali said, "See, your life had to be spared for more important work. I was always there to help you."

Re: **EGYPT** - June 27, 1987 Information about this life was given through channeling.

It flashed through my mind instantly the life in Egypt when I was taken from my obsessive love of my father who did not warrant my dedication. In that life I was a woman born into Egypt's aristocracy. After years, I have come to realize that the devotion for my father was totally misdirected in more than one life. My father was influenced by drugs which gave him the appearance of great wisdom. As he had acted as a medium, channeling messages that gave him the appearance of great knowledge that it was not actually his knowledge, which his ego claimed as his own. His work served to bring about amazing knowledge for Egyptian authorities to use to their advantage but it was not used for spiritual gain as it should have been, thus setting up karma for thousands of years. He was an advisor to the Pharaoh and my uncle was head of the Library. It was my uncle that possessed the real wisdom in that life.

I am not sure who my father or uncle was, as related to my present life. Being captured and taken to the Far East was for my growth and development. I, too, was capable of great wisdom and knowledge, especially for a woman. In many live, I had chosen to remain as a woman, more or less living in "man's world" - often with men's responsibilities.

In that Egyptian life as a woman I was trained in many things normally meant for a young man in high Egyptian society. It was a day that I chose to go to the river alone when I was kidnapped and rushed out of the area by enemies of my father. They took me to an Asian country in the desert. I was bound so that I could not move and hidden in a wagon so that no one could see me. It was a very long trip. I don't know the country and wondered if it could have been Persia since I was a Persian princess in the movie "Cleopatra," which was filmed in Rome. It was because of that film job that I was able to be invited to travel and visit Cairo, Egypt for a few days. While there, I visited many historic sites including the Great Pyramids of Giza. I can't remember which is which of the two large pyramids, Khufu and Cheops. My regret is that I wish I knew then what I know now about them. I was able to climb about half way up the outer stones as well as explore the King and Queen's rooms inside. I also sat on a camel for a photograph but did not want to actually ride it! I shall never forget the lights at night show with a masterful voice dramatizing the story of the pyramids.

Wherever the country was, I was taken to a Sultan as a slave. (I do not know the proper title of the ruler.) There I was -- given to the Sultan who was a gentle, handsome man. I was to be just one of his many wives. He wanted me because he had heard of an intelligent young woman from Egyptian lineage that he thought could produce an intelligent son for him and future leader of his country. I was told that I was to produce a child of Egyptian intelligence for the future of his nation. They meant it was a noble deed for me. The Sultan had many children but because he had heard of the intelligence of a particular group of Egyptians and I was the daughter of one of them, he paid well for my capture. I felt like an animal used for reproduction services. I was accustomed to intelligent, challenging conversations with men. Having been brought up in Egyptian society and expected to be in royal surroundings, hardly in a Harem, one of many wives was not my expectations. My wit and cunning served me well, even with the Sultan. He had never known any woman like me. I was treated far better than the other women. Good treatment, living lavishly was never enough for me. After I produced a son for him, I rarely saw my son. I had little motherly instincts under the circumstances. My son was cared for one of his wives dedicate to child care. I could not change their customs. I was terribly lonely for my father, our family and our way of life. As an independent woman I resented being a concubine, put in a harem and forced to produce a son for the Ruler. The fact I had been kidnapped from my home made me very angry so that no man or person could appease me.

I was given every comfort and lived in beautiful surroundings. Even though he was good to me, I could not overcome my anger at being there. In essence I had been kidnapped and raped! The fact that my son was taken from me to be raised by his chosen wife, who cared of his children, created even more anger and I swore to get back to Egypt one way or another. I was strong-willed and defiant, very unlike the complacent women around him. I felt my son was half Egyptian and no one could take that from him. It would probably be better for him if I was gone. He was his Father's favorite child and now in line to take his place some day.

My obsession to get back to Egypt grew daily. Many times I sought to escape. Each time I ran away, he would send his men after me. Finally, he warned me that if I tried to escape again, he would not send guards to rescue me. My excursions were an embarrassment for him. His people, even his wives, would have been executed if they did the things I did. He said he had done every thing he could for me, he could do no more. The indifference he had always expressed toward me was no different than the way he treated his other wives but their care was of no concern to me. Any attempt to escape for anyone else would have been a death sentence but he had let me get by with my attempts each time but no more. I was delighted so the first chance I had, again I ran and ran and ran. I had no idea how I would get back to Egypt or of the potential desert weather. I was caught in a horrible sand storm. I could not see where I was going. My small body was blown for hill to hill like a feather until no life was left. My dying thought was "If I ever get back to him, I will never leave him again." With that thought the last strike of wind blew me under such a pile of sand, I suffocated within minutes.

Each person can interpret another's experience, only by their own – we cannot feel what is inside another. In this life my sister's husband was my Egyptian father – She was my mother – My daughter Debbie was my brother. No doubt there are other connections to this present life that I have not recognized yet. In my present life a friend once said "I know who you are -- you are a vagabond spirit, a desert wanderer!" I also have a fear of suffocation. Even dead, I don't want to be buried underground in a casket. The belief in cremation in India and some Indians is that the soul is released from the human body.

CHANNELING - 6/20/1986

Basket arrived like Moses – very loving parents with dark skin – my skin was very fair. Parents made no issue of light skin. They had a son about four years younger than me. Clothing was colorful – with the clothes, I was embarrassed because of the light skin -- Beautiful mother -- fancy bearded father. There was a coming of age type celebration - teachers – library – scrolls – Greek, etc. Visitors - none with such pale skin. Parents and others thought me to be a God like being. I felt different but not divine. When the Pharaoh drank from a cup I did the same. We were transported by camels with a sling swing between two of them. Hooded men wore robes, the colors of the rainbow. They could lift a lid with their minds. Robe of gold metallic and colorful trim for me. Afterwards, within the temple were seven priests. They took off their robes and were nude. They disappeared. I added each color robe on top of my golden robe. I then took the gold, reversing back through colors of the rainbow, carried with me through life. (This was all I received of this channeling.)

EGYPT - ASIA or ?:

DREAM -- I was a priestess or something in the Court. The Pharaoh had died. The custom was that the things that meant the most to him were buried with him. Humans were buried alive. I had no thought of doing anything but following tradition with courage -- until I took about three steps up to the sarcophagus and stood there. The sarcophagus was in an unusual shape; with inner space just enough for a body. They were assorted shapes, similar to a fish like shape and other beautiful shapes. They were not straight like coffins. The sarcophagus where silver inlaid with turquoise or turquoise color tiles design. When it was my turn to enter it, suddenly at that moment I was frozen with fear. I ran and ran and ran until I was no longer in that life but in modern day area. Did

I actually suffocate in the coffin, thus, in this life, so claustrophobic? In my present life, the claustrophobia causes me to feel a slight bit of panic in any kind of closed areas, even elevators that go up more than about twenty stories.

DRUID PRIESTESS:

As was the custom, through ritualistic ceremonies, after a man serviced the priestesses in sexual acts, they were required to be thrown into a deep pit of snakes. I felt that I had been the High Priestess, who sat on a thrown chair. The women watched and participated in the ceremony. The man who had sex with the High Priestess was brought before her. She then ordered him to be thrown in the pit. These were usually prisoners from foreign countries who did not know what fate had befallen them. Instead, they thought they had stumble into a great paradise of women! The Priestess never looked upon the man as a person but rather an object to bring fruit of abilities from a foreign land to her people. By being impregnated by a foreign male, the High Priestess and other women believed that a superior race was created. If a baby was born a male child, they were brought up to be slaves. These women could be called Amazons as they were also powerful warriors.

ROME:

Some years ago, in a dream or vision, I stood above an arena looking down where prisoners were being punished and put to death. A man of wealth stood beside me. Below a man was on the rack with arms and legs being pulled apart. I was screaming hysterically. The older man threatened me that if I did not become his mistress that he would have that done to the young man I loved. It left me no choice but to do his bidding. I had no power, connections and no influence.

(LATER IN A REGRESSION)

"There goes another one. Emptiness in the solar plexus - caved in feeling. Outdoors, Rome, watching execution - horrible hurt feelings in the middle. There was a huge open pit - executing people in the pit. He's fat, slob - forced me into a concubine situation. Pulling a man apart - I can't stand it - go crazy seeing it – then indoors - very elegant bedroom - palace. Anglia lying on a bed, feeling very alone, very empty

- have no choice about being there. "This is what I have to do" in the situation because of his threat to my lover. He carried through, anyway and had my lover killed. "Julian" - I don't think of him as even being a person even though he treats me well. I can't get away. He has too much power. There's no way. I tried to get away. He brought me back. There is no way. He's got ears everywhere.

Indoors (ahead in time) Like witchcraft - magic - secret - older 45ish - woman with me is wearing a headdress - I seem to have authority. With this woman I am trying to see into this flame, this lover that I was forced to part with - looking into the flame trying to see his face. I can see it -- his voice saying "we will be together again. We have never been apart." I can take that flame and feel it in my heart.

("Go back to time when you rejected him" counselor suggested.)

There a lot of fruit around him. I managed to get the old fat slob to drink and drugged him. It is some sort of celebration - I appease him until he is really out of it now. It is a time of celebration so that the guards and people in the place are asleep or gone. I know this because I planned it for six months or so. Now it has finally manifested. I feel so good. I feel so confident. I feel so powerful. I feel I finally conquered this man who is some sort of ruler. I am wearing a dark cape - like homespun - the kind peasants wore - It is dark green, muddy dirty color. I am so confident. I have taken something like a material object - like gold - candelabra or something fairly large. I just can't leave it, may be sentimental or magic charm. I am going to escape - I go down a stairway to look around. The streets are dark. I feel absolute confidence. I have got to make it. I feel so successful. I have planned it for so long, maybe even years, at last, I am successful.

(I was instructed to "MOVE AHEAD") Now I am indoors - about 45 years old - ("WHAT IS SIGNIFICANT ABOUT CONTACTING YOUR LOVER?") It feels like no matter what Julian did to me or took from me, he could never take it from me. I was able to go back and recapture the sense of power. ("MOVE TO DEATH") Outdoors, late 50ies or 60ies - lying on something. I don't want to leave the children. My body is old and tired. There are the children of the city that I have worked with - their education - their spirituality - on a level no one else can understand but the children. I don't know what is going to happen to them. I've been their spiritual teacher - I can't help them anymore and there's no one else ("MOVE FROM PHYSICAL to SPIRITUAL") I feel very light - I feel like an angel - my love is there - we are floating above - I feel very light. My body looks like a statue. It is pretty. The children are there. It is kind of a pretty scene. I feel a lot of love. It is a love that adults don't understand - purity - ("WHAT WAS YOUR PURPOSE")? It was to get to that point of understanding love. These were not my children. I had no children. ("REJECTION?") Somehow it is connected to the feeling I could not escape from that man. Something about rejecting a part of myself -- I rejected him, everything about him. It was something I had repeated in the past. It is something I saw in the children. Something I have rejected in myself. That of pure spirit - I am sensing I am the one who rejects because I had rejected that pure spirit light, not allowed to burn it inside of me. Somehow I rejected others until; I could again connect with it. I believe I deserve everything but only on a high spiritual level.

I am the rejecter, never thought about that. It feels very sad to spend so much time in unproductive years, when I did it to myself. ("SADNESS - WHERE?") In my eyes - trying to get them to see deeper and deeper - can't see as deeply as I want to see. This man, Julian, had killed my lover. It is sadness of longing for him ("SADNESS RELATED TO REJJECTION?") Seeing a purple ball - like an eggplant, punching holes in it - it can nurture nature. By putting it in form, transforms it. SADNESS: DEBBIE (my daughter) - flippant, sadness, in intestines, twisting in pain. Rise out of body, nourish it - sadness feeds the body - acknowledge and accept it and let it go! (SESSION ENDED.)

CHANNELING

In a life in Rome you walked alone because you had to sell your body to live. You had a man, dedicated to the Christian God. He fell in love with you. He was torn because he though he was living in sin. He wanted you more than his God. When he tried to leave you to go with a man of God, you begged him not to go. You told him you would go with him where ever he wanted to go if he would not leave today. Each time he asked you to go; you would say "We will go soon." He wanted you to be a Christian and atone for your life as a woman of sin selling your body. You never went with him to live with his Christian friends. In the after life, he vowed he would be with you again and again to protect you from ever selling your body, yet, in the life in France, again he was with you. He was the soldier you fell in love with and had his child after he was killed by your Father's soldiers when you ran away to marry. Later, he re-entered another body and grew to be a Monk. He vowed to love you and bring you to God without sex. He was twenty years younger than you and came to you as a Monk when you were in the South of France and had become a prostitute again. He wanted to take you away from a life of sin but instead, you talked him into having sex with you once. He asked God to send him away from you. He never wanted to be with you again because of the vow he had broken.

When he was in the After Life, he did not want to return to the physical life again. Yet, he came to you again as the Priest in Belgium when you, too, had vowed your life to God and lived as a nun. Again, when the two of you are stuck in the barn and gave into sex, which produced a child. The child that the nuns got rid of so that you never knew what happened. He was banned from the Church and spent the rest of his life serving God through medicine. Again, he begged you to be with him out of the Church but you refused. When he visited the Mother Superior, he vowed to be with you in the after life to help you understand that your love was not wrong. Through his lives of service, he was elevated to a higher plain than you. That is why in this life, for a few years, you had your contact with Mark Troy, who was not in the physical body, yet the two of you longed for each other so much that the tie had to be broken and free you both from this strong bond.

It takes much time to comprehend the complicity of the physical as related to the after life -- Heaven -- what ever you wish to call it. Through the years, more and more information has been channeled to you. We, who speak to you, are not in linear time; therefore, much of what we may give you is confusing as you know only linear time fractions."

CHANNELING: 6/27/1987

"Thus, you have set up Karma for thousands of years. The life you now live has been to reveal the obsessiveness of living in the female body for reproduction purposes, until you learned and saw the reality of the of the soul. First to seek the good in man – then allow the good to flow inward.

We are transported into the realm of Earth consciousness by whatever means which varies drastically to raise the animal consciousness of materialized form on earth. That which we know as fear has continued to hold us back from soul – spirit evolution. It has created separation from love, which which we call "God" – Love is universal and yet what is love? Love cannot easily be defined. It is almost totally misunderstood. What we call love is conditioned responses. Love cannot be withheld – love must flow out and in – when it is with strained, withheld, it creates static – bumps – shorts out (in electrical terms) Love just is! It is peace and harmony. It just IS – it is in all things, no matter how buried it may seem, it just is. Tarry not in the lower realms of existence. Go forth to seek your future atop this mountain once conquered by others of similar faiths. Seek not the elements of man. Seek the forest of God. Seek not the realms of men, but seek the pleasures of total beingness of each individual as both male and female, as neither -- extreme separations seemed necessary to awaken my over soul. The "I" that I am, a fragment of has lived a great hoax for many, many generations of womanhood. Until now, it has not possible to have revealed this place – called woman. Mass consciousness had to be moved to this point in time before this quantum leap in consciousness could be made. New directions now come before us in rapid succession. Those prepared will be able to make these quantum leaps in consciousness."

ROME: A STUDENT OF FAMOUS ARTISTS-(Channeled I changed "you" to "I")

While I have never tapped into this life through regressions or regressing myself, rather, in a communication I received in 1985, I was told that I was a male artist, in the era of Leonardo da Vince, Michael Angelo and other great artist. When I was in college majoring in art, both artists were so intriguing. While living in Rome and traveling to Florence, I was working in Cleopatra and was able to see so much of their works. When I traveled in Italy in this life, Florence was my favorite city with its array of art and creativity.

My name was Paul, son of a father in royalty and a good son. My birth was great happiness for my family. My childhood was filled with great joy and my greatest joy was being accepted by a school of art in Rome. My home was a palace in Florence. I vowed to be a great artist for God and it made my father very happy. He sent me to study with the greatest artists of all time. One was Michael Angelo Buonarroti. He was not homosexual; he loved God and was not lonely as has been written. At times he would tire of God's work and needed to go away for a while. His love of a woman was not in the physical body. She was a soul mate and the inspiration for much of his work. He was highly evolved spiritually; the greatest artist of his time even remains so today. He was a Saint in mankind's art. He did not return to Earth life but guides artists in generations since. He was not as temperamental as described. He knew what God wanted of him so he stuck with his guidance. In his younger years, I bothered him so much as I, more than any other, wanted to walk in his path as I could see his future greatness. I seemed to have communication with his guide, too, and he did not like sharing her. Since I was of royal birth, he thought that he was more in tune with God's bidding than I could be. I was told that I shared in some of his glorious work and that when I was in Rome in this life.

When I stood mesmerized before a veiled statue in Florence, I could not know that it was my hands that carved it in that life. The Pope or Bishop that is buried there was not a good man. Students of Michael Angelo had shared in painting the faces of the people in his life and the Pope was not pleased. Michael Angelo told him that he had painted and it stayed the way it was painted. When called in before His Holiness, Michael Angelo told him to go to hell and not to touch his work. He went away where he meditated to contact his soul mate guide, where he was shown his past lives and his work and realized that his work was guided by God. He fell on his face, begging God to forgive him and be patient with him and his temper. He dedicated his art to God forever and ever.

I left Rome and returned to Florence where I painted and painted. Michael Angelo had given me a different name other than Paul, which I used as I became one of the most sought after artist in Florence. I was either part of the Medici family or seemed a part of them because of my work. When I tired of painting, I devoted myself to sculpture. From a young age in my present life, I wanted to study sculpture and thought I would do so late in life, obviously past life memories were filtering through without knowing it.

I tried to live in the ruckus life of others but my devotion to God was too powerful. My family wanted me to marry but I could not find a woman of God who understood the ways of my life. It was a good life of creativity. I don't think that I lived to be old age.

While in this life, I wanted to do something worthwhile in the arts, but my Guide told me that I accomplished my debt to art in that life, not this present one. In my present life, always the search for my soul mate. I even taught seminars on Soul Mating. As I have reached my older wisdom years, I realize that many of the men in my present life were bits and pieces of that soul mate. More and more I understand that we are more than just one individual but a part of magnificence in the Allness of what we call God.

(ABOVE)
Ann on sets for
CLEOPATRA

(BELOW)
Ann climbs half way
Up Pyramid at Giza
Ann on a camel

CAIRO MUSEUM
Ann on Statue of Phar

Director Joseph Mankiewicz and handmaidens, Ann on right

In my years working in film/TV, until writing this book, I never realized that many of the costumes I wore could represent some of my past lives!

CHAPTER 7

ANCIENT PRIEST AND PRIESTESS

I was living in Beverly Hills when my Mother died in early 1991, family and personal problems had me feeling like I needed to "get away." A friend suggested that we take a trip to Mexico. I became enthusiastic about going on the trip she suggested.

I had been to Mexico but never would consider going alone. I visited the Mexican Tourism office in Century City. Since I was producing and hosting my TV show in Beverly Hills, I wondered if I could do a trade off. I invited the Head of the Tourism office to be a guest on my show. He was a delightful guest and I told him I would like to do some of my shows in Mexico. He loved the idea and made arrangements for me to fly free, stay in a hotel free and even planned to send his Public Relations Director on the trip to help me. It was good for her since Guadalajara was her home. She had a store there and took new clothing in suitcases to stock the store. My friend got mad because I had made arrangements for the trip without HER having made the plans herself so she refused to go. I was a bit fearful of making the trip alone, especially since I don't speak Spanish. As it worked out, it was to my advantage because this particular friend was one of those friends that had to have everything be her way and her decision, plus she always bitched about any and everything.

The P.R. lady from the Mexican Tourism Office was more than helpful as she made plans for an extended trip through the various cities so that I could do a series of shows on Colonial Mexico. She arranged for hotels, other Tourism offices to look after me, all transportation, guides and people to drive me where there wasn't any air travel. Every where I went, the Mexican tourism industry was so kind and helpful to me. It began with the areas surrounding Guadalajara. I then flew to Morelia, afterwards the tourism office sent a driver to take me to San Miguel de Allende, then Guanajuato, and Leon - each place was so different and fascinating. From Leon, I had no transportation back to Guadalajara and no airline flights. The thought of riding a bus in Mexico was very scary. It was my first traveling in Mexico totally solo, so naturally, I was very uneasy. Much to my surprise, I learned that first class bus travel in Mexico was far better than in the USA. Not only did they have newer buses but also equipped with TVs, bathrooms and a drink bar!

That was the beginning of my romance with Mexico. I LOVED every where I visited. The Mexican government appreciated my creating TV shows about their beautiful country. I began getting invitations to go to events in different places. January 14th, 1992, I got a call from a Public Relations woman telling me that there was to be a fund raising Celebrity Tennis event in Ixtapa with a number of American celebrities in attendance and participating. Since I would have to leave the next day, she assumed I could not make it but I assured her I would. I flew out the next evening. Everyone was arriving that Thursday and a cocktail party was slated for the evening. Rain was coming down in barrels! The end of the Hotel's front awning looked like a waterfalls. I was staying at the Krystal Hotel. The Hotel's P.R. young woman escorted me to one of the other Host hotels. Standing out in front was a tall good looking man. I didn't know if he might be an American TV actor that I didn't know or if he was Mexican. It was one of those things when a person just grabs your attention immediately and you feel an attraction, perhaps from a past life when the feeling is so strong. I always had my video camera with me and planned to video tape the Cocktail party. I taped a number of celebrities that evening, including chatting with Buzz Aldrin along with other celebrities.

All during the time in Ixtapa, it was pouring rain. Some of the tennis matches had to be cancelled. I video taped as much as I could during the days, even got a greetings from O.J. Simpson (when he was still loved by the public.) In spite of the rain, all celebrities seemed to be having a good time. I video taped various areas in Ixtapa including charming shopping booths and children playing. Working alone with no crew was no easy task!

It was the next evening's cocktail party that I again saw the same good looking guy that had been standing in front of the Host hotel. From there we were invited to dinner at a nearby restaurant. The P.R. woman, Pat, accompanied me to the events. Low and behold, we were invited to sit at a large table with a group of about ten people and THERE sitting across the table from me was this handsome guy. Conversation was limited as he could speak very little English and I had no Spanish vocabulary. He seemed shy. Pat was talking to his friend, Enrique, a newspaper columnist, from Mexico City. Manrique, the handsome Mexican, drank too much and smokes but it didn't seem to matter as I was enthralled by his presence. Normally I would be repulsed by a man drinking too much and especially a smoker, maybe I ignored it because of being in a foreign country and in a temporary situation.

After dinner everyone was invited to Sergio's Villa just up the street. He was the owner of the restaurant. Enrique did not want to go, so Pat stayed with him and I felt obligated to stay with her. Manrique went with the group. I felt left out and alone so I walked out on a balcony enjoying the view looking down at Ixtapa. It wasn't long before Manrique returned, my heart jumped with joy. Apparently he talked Enrique into going to the party at Sergio's. The four of us walked up the hill so now it seemed I was with him. There were a lot of people there at this beautiful hillside home that looked down over the pool and balcony. There were a number of attractive women there but Manrique seemed to have eyes only for me. The party lasted for hours. We both talked to different people and I video taped the event. At one point he said "Let me show you the view here" - His English was limited and I knew too few words of Spanish to communicate much. We separated from the group and stood talking at the far end of the pool looking out over the beautiful view. Finally, he kissed me -- how many times, I don't remember - time stood still then later, he asked me to go to his hotel where he had a Jacuzzi tub, however, I KNEW what that would lead to and I wasn't about to have a "one night stand" no matter how attracted I was to him. He said something about enjoying tonight and tomorrow, just forget all about it. THAT turned me cold. Shortly thereafter, suddenly we were leaving and I did not even get to say goodbye.

On Saturday it was still raining but they tried to have the tennis matches as best they could. I continue video taping as many celebrities as I could find and was working hard. That night it was the White Gala. I saw Manrique and Enrique arrive. We said "Hello" but he wanted to be photographed next to the Hawaiian Tropic model. I video taped him when I could so that I would at least have that memory. Strangely, when I was back in Beverly Hills, editing the shows, somehow, the best tape of him accidentally got taped over. There was great entertainment and hundreds of people attending the Gala, including American and Mexican Celebrities, with some of them performing. We were seated at specific tables but after the dinner, people moved around to different tables. Manrique and I had exchanged glances during dinner. I was disappointed because I thought he could have asked me to sit with him. Later, Pat joined them, so I did. Enrique sat me next to Manrique who warmed up to me. Then we moved toward the front and sat together all during the entertainment.

As the Gala came to a close, Manrique knew that I had been video taping most of the evening, some included him. He remarked that he would like to see the video. I told him I could connect my camera to the TV in the room and he could see what had been shot. I meant just that at the time but when we were in the room --- hum -- silly me, now if I didn't go to HIS room to have a "one night stand" how could I expect him to come to MY room without expecting the same!

The Celebrity weekend events were now over. Before I showed him the tape, we stepped out on the 8th floor balcony. All clouds had disappeared; there we stood watching the crystal clear moon beams of a full moon dance across the ocean. As we stood on that balcony in the most romantic scene one could imagine, he talked about his fiancé and I said "I already know that you are married." He then told me they lived in separate apartments and when he married, he intended to have three children but she didn't want children. I tied to accept that being with him was just not right but we had such a fantastic attraction and the scenario was unbelievably romantic! I listen to him tell me a lot about his life, his work, a failed marriage and how he had wanted children, even past the age of forty. He had been a professional basket ball player for Mexico. Alone with each other, even with the language difficulty, our communication level seemed to improve. With the rain having stopped, the sky was so clear with the beautiful full moon, plus music was wafting up from down below -- even a lovely block long garden adjoining the hotel -- what a fantastic, romantic moment, how could I NOT succumb to it all! I could never envision a more romantic evening! How could anyone refuse THAT kind of scenario? When he kissed me my heart was pounding so hard, I felt shaky. By then, my thoughts were "What the hell -- here I am with a gorgeous man that I am terribly attracted to with the absolutely most romantic surroundings possible -- there is a king size bed and it's been so long since I made love - why not live in the moment!" I felt I would regret passing up that special romantic moment in time.

I made a small attempt to change from the romantic balcony setting to showing him the video tape. As we began watching the video tape, we were sitting on the edge of the bed. We saw very little of the tape. It didn't take long for us to merge into love making with no awkwardness, no problems, perfect timing, perfect body movements almost like a ballet, perfect love making. We covered every area of the king size bed! With simultaneous orgasms he kept saying "Oh God! Oh God! Oh God!" (To me it sounded like " Oh GoT!") "Precious - precious man and in every cell in my body" was my thoughts. The love making was so fantastic; it was like a wave of intense love swept over me so that it felt it was not just a "one night stand"! I tried to accept that this was just "a one night stand" with no future expectations. I was in a foreign country and that was that. Then with our bodies moving and rolling in bed as though dancing to etheric music, what started to be just that "roll in the hay" was evolving for me into a very magical experience. I felt as though this wave that came over me -- a feeling of love that far out measured the pleasurable sex. It was the most fantastic love making session that went on for hours and probably as memorable as or more so than as any lover I had ever been with. Just moments of heaven that remained with me for several years with nothing since to match that most romantic event. We were both in ecstasy -- afterwards, we were planning to do things in Mexico City the following week. He promised to show me HIS Mexico City. He dressed and apologized for having to leave but he had to pack for an early flight back to Mexico City. As we said goodnight at the door, he assured me he would show me around Mexico City. I did not ask for his "promise", he volunteered it.

I slept the rest of the night as though I was resting in the arms of an angel. The dawn came not with harsh reality of only one night of love making because at the moment, I truly believed I would see him in Mexico City. There was no doubt in my mind that this was the beginning of a beautiful romance. For how long, I didn't know -- but I knew that it seemed very special for the both of us.

I had more taping to do on Monday and left Tuesday morning for Mexico City. I was so excited and was looking forward to seeing Manrique's Mexico City with him. As soon as I got checked into the Krystal Hotel in the Zona Rosa area, I began calling his office and leaving messages. I called again; a woman didn't speak English so finally I spoke to his brother who took my message. Toward the end of my stay that week, I tried to call his friend, Enrique, who was a reporter but he never returned my call either. Manrique never called the whole time I was there. I felt so empty and disappointed beyond belief. I left the following Sunday for home feeling very sad that my beautiful romance in Ixtapa had turned out to be just that dreaded "one night stand."

Sunday: 2/16/1992 (Diary entrance)

"After four weeks its time to accept that all my "communications" failed trying to reach Manrique. I was just a convenient one night stand for him after all. It is amazing that at my ripe old age that I continue to believe and have faith – there is no Santa Clause, NO romance for me, sometimes I even feel there is no God! This always destroys my belief in my psychic ability to be so wrong as I felt so sure he would keep his promise. Yet, then, I do realize that the many people I do psychic readings for seem pleased and recall my predictions as "right on!"

My life is so repetitions; eve though I try to break the cycles -- any man I want never seems to wants me! Now, poor ole Ron in NYC called on Valentine's Day. Two years ago I would have been delighted, for he had been my long distance fantasy love. Perhaps I would later feel the same disgust with Manrique as I feel for Ron. No - the sex was so fantastic with him that I can't help measuring love potential on sexual chemistry and Manrique and I were RICH in that respect -- maybe the BEST in my life - certainly equal to the best. When was the best - was it different times, could it be past life connections? Rick Jason was outstanding and the affair ended far too soon for me, certainly my ex, Bob; when I was almost a virgin regarding sexual connections. The memories fade with most of them. Manrique came the closest to feeling like my "soul mate" or "cosmic soul mate." It was love at first sight for me on Friday, January 17th. It was so perfect, so romantic. He seemed so sensitive. When we were together Saturday night he said "I thought you would call me today" meant that he wanted me to pursue him which I don't do. I did pursue him in Mexico City and since I returned home -- three letters and a fax, all gone unanswered -- four weeks of ignoring me as I though I never existed to him. Time to LET GO, Ann!!"

Friday evening February 21st 1992: (Diary entry)

"36 days today since I met Manrique -- my "soul" mate. He probably WAS and just my luck, my soul mate would not recognize me! I wasted $8.00 phone calls, time, hope, fax fees, $15. postage sending him videos that he was in. I spent around $50. attempting to communicate with a man that I was nothing more than a convenient "lay" -- a "one night stand! Why do I never learn! Why am I continually "led" or guided into these beliefs about something that will happen but never does. This one was a BIG one! I felt so sure after all the years that I finally met a soul mate. I guess there isn't one for me. There is always something I believe I gain from each experience that isn't obvious to me at the time. I feel like such a naive teen-ager!"

I wrote "Was Manrique that good looking or did he just appeal to me in a phenomenal way? After years of excellent lovers and good looking men, why did he affect me in such an unforgettable way? This is going into six week since we met, instead of fading away for me, it appears that it has all faded into the past for him. A vivid picture of him is etched in my heart - solar plexus and soul. This was the first time that I have felt such a deep soul connection - a cosmic soul mate. He is the force of four that has been filtering through my psyche."

September 21st, 1992: (Diary entry)

"An "ending" with Manrique -- It is so amazing that perhaps only a FEW hours of sex, January 18th, 1992, eight months and three days STILL possess me. What a FANTASY he turned out to be - no word - no phone calls in May when I was in Mexico City again for three weeks. I even had my friend at the Hotel call his office so she could speak to him in Spanish but she could not reach him either. I can never understand what goes on in a man's mind!!"

I had moved into my cabin in Lake Arrowhead where I was alone with my thought and imagination. I would create visions of being with Manrique and arranging for a surrogate to have a child that he seemed to want so desperately and the two of us raising it together since I was beyond childbearing, thanks to surgery. I "saw" myself standing on a large patio overlooking Mexico City. I lived these memories so vividly, later I wondered if instead of creating a child in my womb, I had created colon cancer in 1994. Had I lost a vital part of my body in order to answer an ancient karmic connection? Had I completed our karmic connection -- that of envisioning my willingness to provide a child one way or another? Perhaps, a son in this life for the Priest who was willing to sacrifice our son in a distant past? Had feeling this magical love for him some how completed our karmic connection? He left an imprint on my soul as no other has ever done. It isn't always necessary for two people to complete their karmic connection. Either or both, upon recognizing it and resolving it can be freed from it. I was so alone in the cabin and worked so hard to make it a home, yet, nothing seemed to be working for me so that in that mountain living, I felt almost entombed.

November 25th, 1992 - Eve of Thanksgiving: (Diary entry)

"It is a time to think of what I am thankful for -- I am grateful: I am alive and well - not as thin as I would like, but O.K. I am grateful for my little house. I AM grateful for my short or long love affairs, even one night stands, sort of two nights with Manrique, the first and only man I thought to be a soul mate. I cherish those precious memories that cannot be taken from me. I am grateful to Tiangus - the Yucatan and blessed Maya, Mexico, et al.

I am grateful for friends here but I am wondering if it is time to leave the USA - I am ready to leave. I feel like crying for Mexico. I don't know why I feel it is my country - my home. I long for all the arts and crafts - the sweetness of the people, the beauty.

I can't help thinking of Manrique and a destiny -- I don't understand why I feel so strongly about him with no communications. Did I meet and loose my soul mate? Is it only fantasy? In the Indian cards I pulled, he was the Sun Priest, I was the Moon Priestess. The feeling that I had, was that we were one, united, a perfect union. Was this all to show me that Mexico is a "calling" for me? Consciously, I would really like to release this obsession over Manrique.

Far beyond the rainbow, I heard your name, far beyond the rainbow.

I saw your face far beyond the rainbow

We sang our song, far beyond the rainbow

We looked in each other's eyes and saw what love is supposed to be,

We took one vow -- far beyond the rainbow -- far beyond the rainbow.

God loved our words of love, far beyond the rainbow --

We found our love far beyond the rainbow."

Grass poked through along the shaded areas of snow. It was my first winter in the cabin and an awakening experience to realize I really hated snowy and icy winters. I felt I must follow the sun! The miracle visits to Mexico helped avoid winter's worst two months by visiting Cuernavaca, "the City of Eternal Spring" and it felt like eternal spring!

I made a number of trips to Mexico video taping different areas for my TV show during those two years in the early 1990's. It was very hard work, working all alone but I loved everywhere I visited all over Mexico. During the Los Angeles riots in May, 1992, buildings were burning just outside of Beverly Hills. The air was filled with smoke. Fortunately, at the time I was invited back to Mexico by the government to attend Tiangus in Acapulco; a government sponsored once a year event to entertain the media, press and travel agents. I prayed for a chance meeting with Manrique. Again, all expenses paid and yes, while there, I searched to see if Manrique might be there. Would he attend again with his reporter friend? At one of the first events, I saw Enrique, the reporter, but didn't speak as I was annoyed that he never returned my phone call. There was no Manrique those few days. Tiangus had given me a good connection with the National Tourism office in Mexico City. They offered guests a choice of one of five excursions. I selected the Yucatan and Mayan Ruins. It was a five day visit to the best known Yucatan ruins. What an opportunity it was for me. The weekend had been fantastic.

Saturday evening's final presentation was one of the most fantastic stage presentations I had ever seen. As it was about to begin -- I had a horrible fright! I could not find my video camera. Its loss would cost me the most important trip yet! I had always felt drawn to the ancient ruins of the Yucatan. Before the stage show began, the announcer announced that I had lost my camera. Thanks to Mexican courtesy, it was located in a seat where I had left it. I took a deep sign of relief as I enjoyed every minute of the dazzling musical presentation of the history of Mexico. At the end, there was a fascinating sea of white napkins swinging over most of the audience's heads.

During the Yucatan trip, the long time memories of a repetitious dream came back to me. In those dreams, I was standing on top of something shaking my fist at the heavens saying "I shall rebuilt the temple" then a voice answered me, (referring to – perhaps the present time), "Not with sticks and stones but with words and deeds." Making love with Manrique that one time had been an acceleration of a key-turning event to a whole new scenario of a fascinating, meaningful past life. Little by little, I seemed to becoming aware of some sort of ancient power I once had and little miracles kept falling into my life. Was this one of the reasons, from childhood, I felt I had some sort of awesome inner power but was afraid to use it not knowing what the results might be?

MAY 19TH 1992: From Cancun and surrounding areas of Xcaret and Tulum, we then traveled five days to Chichen Itza, Merida, Uxmal, Edzna, Campeche, Villahermosa, La Venta, finally Palenque, only 45 minutes before they closed. The very last ruin was to be Comalcalco, then a boat ride in Tabasco, back to Mexico City and the end of the tour. It was a lot of work video taping each of the Mayan ruins in the hot, humid, sultry weather. What an educational five days!

Before we arrived at Palenque, the surroundings began to look more like a picture I seemed to have in my head. Like many or most of the ruins, it had to be dug out of the surrounding dense tropical forest. Heavy forest surrounded Palenque and it was the most impressive of all of the ruins. I really wanted to spend more time there and felt sure I would return one day to spend several days, but it never happened. It was there, then La Venta near Villahermosa that I began seeing or sensing ancient past life memories. There was a series of stones standing about 7' long with about 3' between them, then stones on top that had been used as tombs. I was beginning to know the reason Manrique came into my life. It was to recall this ancient life with no idea when we lived in that part of the continent. Little by little the whole scenario began falling in place. I had used cards in November and got the Sun Priest, representing Manrique and the moon Priestess as me. This is how the past life scenario finally came together.

In an area similar to Palenque, there were two pyramid temples directly across from one another. One represented the feminine and one the masculine and in balance. I felt Manrique had been the Priest and I was the Priestess. We were able to conjure up phenomenal energy between us. We were a team and a couple and I gave birth to our son. (HERE was the mysterious need in this current life to find a way to give him a son!) We had a peaceful community with no need for law enforcement. We had our own way of dealing with any kind of crime. First, there was a ceremony that offered anyone the opportunity to come forth if they had committed any form of crime. As long as they came forth, admitting to their crime, we dealt with them according to the severity of each crime. At the end of the ceremony, the Priest and Priestess then joined their energies together across the area that created something like a laser beam that would actually draw anyone up and into the beam if they had lied or failed to admit their crime. Anyone drawn into that beam would die. (It sounds rather impossible!) That seemed to be the way order was kept.

Before our son was five years old, there had been a terrible drought. The underling Priests decided that our son must be sacrificed. Those priests decided it was the women Priestesses that had created the drought. There had to be a human sacrifice and they decided it should be the son of the head Priest and Priestess. As that Priestess, I was infuriated and said it would NOT be done, which only added to their resentment toward my powers. They took my son's life anyway. One night a group of the priests stole into the place where the women slept and kidnapped me. They bound me and took me to the top of another pyramid temple to sacrifice me. When they unbound my hands, I held one to the sky and cursed them with great gusto. At that moment it was as though the sky opened up and I ascended while chaos reined below with the earth shaking, the temples crumbling with the priests and many others dying

85

in the crumbling temples and places of residences. With THIS memory, I KNEW where the repetitious dream originated with shaking my fist at the heavens, declaring "I shall rebuild the temple." For years I had not understood a deep seeded guilt that I had destroyed a community with my powers. After revisiting these ancient memories, with eons of time feeling deep seeded guilt and fear of using inner power, I realized that it was not my powers at all but an earthquake's timely event that did the destruction!

My Head Priest partner survived and had not known of the plan of the other priests to sacrifice me. When he heard that I was dead, he was distraught and heart broken. Not only had he lost his heir and son but his love partner as well. He searched and searched for me only to find my body amongst the ruins. He carried my limp body to an open space and laid me on the grass where he made love to my body believing that he could reawaken our mutual powers that would give me life once again. He sat there afterwards, waiting and waiting, night and day, for three days before he gave up and began covering my body with grass. Just as I had seen the stacked stones tombs at La Venta, he began creating a similar tomb, with a roof over the four sides of stones. Then day by day, he stacked stones around the tomb. He continued for I don't know how long but I believe it eventually became a temple pyramid. This is what I believe to be the connection with this gorgeous man that I met in Mexico and had only one night of blissful love making under the clear moonlit night in Ixtapa. When a man and a woman reach a certain high orgasmic bliss, our vibrations or energy reaches a place that we don't often reach. It may have taken that energy to cause me to recall that unique life time. Perhaps the blissful love making in some unconscious way, caused him to fear any further connection with me because of the failure he must have felt as the powerful Priest who could not revive me, the High Priestess, back to life. And yet, perhaps it took his love making that one night to bring me forth into more connectedness with my total over soul. Once this life came tumbling back into my conscious mind, I knew why we had to have our love making session, even if only for one night. It was a completion for us both, even thought I feel sure he never realized the importance of it.

It was one of several life times that created an inborn fear of fame in this lifetime. After many revelations of former lives, I began to see why I never seemed to reach the success in my acting or film production career that I believed I was destined to achieve -- it was the fear of success. Numerous deaths seemed related to this fear.

Manrique had told me that he was in property development in the hills across from the volcano of Popocatépetl, just 40 miles from Mexico City. During a later visit to Cuernavaca to video tape more shows, I attended a language school. The school offered various excursions so I signed up one Saturday for the trip to the volcano. It was a cold morning. The bus stopped along the way for coffee. There were about 15 students on the trip. It was an interesting drive. As we got nearer to the area of the volcano, as I recall, we turned on the road toward the volcano, I saw a billboard that I thought to be advertising Manrique's development. I began looking across the way wondering just where it was. The bus parked and we got off to climb the volcano. Again, I couldn't help wishing we would accidentally meet once again. As I began the trek up, I did OK for awhile but my camera seemed heavier and heavier. The higher we got, the earth was like black oily sand and deep to trudge through so at one point, I had to stop while most of the group continued on, higher and higher. I had made it to the 14,000' level and was hard enough to breathe, plus the deep black sand became impossible for me to hike any higher. I don't know how much of the 17,925' that most of the others accomplished. Again, I looked across the mountains toward where I thought the development might be but could see nothing. Later, I heard that the volcano began eruptions in December of 1994 and continues into the 21st century. I wondered how Popo affected his project. On the Internet, I read, "In December 2000, tens of thousands of people were evacuated by the government based on the warnings of scientists. The volcano then made its largest display in 1200 years." How interesting that he had property so near a powerful volcano that could have been the end of our relationship in that long ago life time and might have severely affected his income in this life. How ironic – maybe the earthquake in that far distant life was really a volcano irrupting.

Each time I had a trip to Mexico, I just couldn't let go of wanting to see Manrique. Even at home, I would fantasize about a continued romance with him. It took a very long time to let it go, even when I moved to Cuernavaca, Mexico in the spring of 1998, my thoughts were that perhaps I might run into him some where. I would chastise myself for these repetitious failed romances, wondering what was wrong with me. Defiant, I did not want to play the male/female "dance" game, much later, to realize it seems a necessity in the conquest game that men must play.

At Tiangus in Acapulco I had met one of the tour representatives for the state of Morelos and the city of Cuernavaca. He kept insisting that I do my show in Morelos and assured me that there were ruins there as well. After I returned home, he still contacted me so I wrote the requirements for my traveling there. We were faxing back and forth for a few weeks, so finally I made the trip to Cuernavaca. That was the trip when I attended the language school as well as shot all over the area taping my TV show.

Within the city of Cuernavaca there was a somewhat small ruin, Teopanzolco that was an Early Aztec site. It was probably during the Late Aztec period (AD 1350-1521). Aztec culture was composed of many distinct ethnic groups that occupied the central Mexican highlands in the centuries before the Spanish conquest of 1521. The Tlahuica were the Aztec group living in what is now the state of Morelos. It didn't take very long to video tape the small ruins.

There was a larger area of ruins that my host took me to on another day. Xochicalco - the pyramid ruins is on top of a mountain south of Cuernavaca. There is a small Museum. Xochicalco in the native language Nahuatl means "place of the House of Flowers" and was constructed between 700 and 900 A.D. as the central part of a city complex that extended to the surround hilltops. The views from this hill are far reaching in all directions. The camera I used was one that I hoist up on my shoulder and while it is not a really big one, I got tried lugging it and ME around so I had to sit and rest now and then. After walking around the main square area, I sat down and looked out over the view. Immediately, in my mind's eye, I saw a ceremony walking past me in the Aztec ceremonial attire. They were carrying something like banners. There were both men and women. At the time, I don't remember if I had heard that it was the place of flowers but I knew this was a celebration of spring or summer. Everywhere there were beautiful growing foliage and flowers. Off in the distance, that was all one could see.

At home in the USA, I became so disgusted and disappointed with all the court hearings, publicity, et al. surrounding Bill Clinton, I longed to move to Mexico. Apparently, there was a calling to me because by April of 1998, I had moved to Las Vegas, had sold the cabin, lived there for a couple of years, sold my house in Vegas, packed up a rented trailer and headed for Cuernavaca to live. It had taken time to arrange all the paper permits for an American to live in Mexico. I won't even go into the problems at the border, shipping my things or the long drive through the Northern part of Mexico.

I will also avoid the problems with renting a house in Cuernavaca, where the water ceased (losing the rent I had paid) and had to move to an apartment where the European couple gave me one price and only a month or so later wanted to increase the rent, then taunted me by turning off the electricity, etc. Cuernavaca is less than fifty miles to Mexico City with a mountain range in between. On trips into the City, again, I couldn't help hoping I would run into Manrique but it never happened. I could not understand why this one man that I was with two nights and only one night of love making could have such a hold on me when I had dated and loved other men, quite a number of very handsome actors who were in my life far longer. Even retrieving the memories of our ancient lives had not totally stopped me from thinking of him.

I stayed six months in Cuernavaca. I loved so many things about Mexico and the friendly people but my house payments ceased and I had to return to try and get legal matters resolved. Plans for making a living by bringing tourist to Mexico never came to fruition and while back in the states, I realized I didn't have a choice but to move back. The crime in Cuernavaca and Mexico City was cause for concern. The Central and Southern parts of Mexico are beautiful. What a shame there is so much crime. Most Mexicans don't really know or appreciate the great culture of the country and I question if those who enter this nation illegally can ever appreciate and respect the forefathers that created their nation. The same applies in the USA today with citizens failing to honor our forefathers and the struggles they experienced to create this nation.

As the years have passed, I realized no matter how much I love other parts of the world,

I cannot live in a country with one dominating religion with my seeking love, understanding and compassion for many beliefs. I cannot accept any one religion or organized religions in general. Mine is such an individualized path, seeking reconnection with the allness that we call "God." I am no expert on world religions nor have I read the Christian bible from front to back. What I have done is seek my own path and I have realized that a life with difficult relationships that is filled with problems, obstacles and losses, presents us with the most opportunity for the soul's growth. It is up to us to accept and work through those challenges.

The visions I had seen relating to Manrique matched the stone layouts I saw in the Park in Villa Hermosa's ruins. He had made love to my dead body believing he had the power to create life. Our life together had ended because he had permitted our son to be sacrificed. Now in the present life, he was childless still wanting a child. I, too, had years of believing I was destined to have a very special son. During our love making session, when I was on top of him, I felt a sudden rush of deep surrendering love. It seemed he was in essence giving life to me as my love life had been so vague and unfulfilled. I knew we had a soul mating experience even just coming together for brief moments. His arrogance, pride and power had destroyed our love so very long ago - had the same traits prevailed today, preventing us from having a wonderful love relationship in the here and now - a chance for soul mates to come together toward bonding and fulfillment? There was no logical reason for me to carry on with this obsession over Manrique, a foreign man to me, younger, we could barely communicate with language, except the language of love. As for past lives, it was totally logical for us to make a physical connection in love making to awaken those memories. In essence, he had brought me back to "life" as he attempted in that ancient time, by making love to me - not necessarily an afterward pleasant time for me longing to see him again. It had brought me to a completion on my soul journey.

With this past life memory of being a Priestess with my Priest partner, there is no where in any history that has any description of those kind of powers revealed. Perhaps, hints of similar power in the UFO world revealing ever presence of aliens visiting earth. That is why it had to be a very ancient civilization; could it have been on another planet? Recently, as I recall that special evening in the 8th floor room with the fantastic view, I wondered if that significant view from on high was related to the views atop the pyramids that the Priest and Priestess used in their ceremonies and brought back that long forgotten memory of love for each other buried in the subconscious. Then while at a lecture by a well informed Egyptian on ancient energy uses I got a cold chill as he described Dolmens that were constructed over an energy vortex that were then covered by an earth mound that finally became a pyramid. It was exactly what I had seen in the ending of the Priest building the same structure over the Priestess' body - that I lived and died or was a part of a soul memory. Could it also be the source of acrophobia, fear of standing near the edge of high places? No doubt phobias come from our past lives.

The more I have learned about what we do NOT know; it seems more feasible that reincarnation is incredibly logical. Plus, I believe we are a "piece of the puzzle" and eventually, with effort toward our individualized spiritual growth, we returned to the whole "puzzle" - picture - Over Soul. Are these past life memories totally an individual soul journey -- or do we tap into the Over Soul's memories? OR is it genetic memory? Scientists are now doing magnificent research on human genomes, DNA, genes and the Internet has provide us the opportunities to delve deeply into our genealogy. From very ancient lives, except for the few memories related to lives in Italy, there seems to be a large gap to the life of Anne Boleyn, once Queen of England.

I am including a drawing I did "Evolution of the Spirit(s) Soul -- suggesting that when we die, we die OUT of balance with our Mental, Emotional and Physical bodies. I am suggesting that possibly a part of us drifts off in the after life in the areas that are most similar. The soul reincarnates trying to reunite with its total parts, and then works to become balanced. This is only my own concept to explain why there can be more than one person claiming to have been a particular person in past lives, as my memory as Anne Boleyn. Other people might have different memories of the same once lived person. Over time, there can be many divisions. I hope this drawing is self explanatory. As we gather together the past lives that need repairing and releasing, we become more and more whole with our totality of our SOUL.

PLATO: LOVE is the urge of an originally androgynous being to find his split-off half, the desire and pursuit of the whole - a hunger for unity -- cosmic principle - hunger and thrust after divine experience."

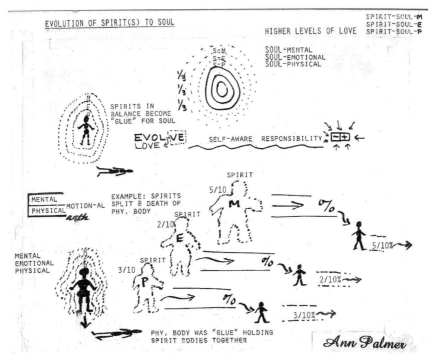

CHAPTER 8

ANNE BOLEYN

Collection of Gallery Oldham.

While I do not believe there are ANY actual paintings of Anne, this one on the first page might be more accurate, not the ones said to be Anne because of a "B" on a necklace. I feel sure that Henry destroyed all likeness of Anne.

In my early acting class days, we had to do a monologue. Why did I select this monologue to do long before I knew anything about Anne Boleyn or reincarnation? The play book just came to me. I did not buy it or seek to find it, someone gave it to me.

(From "Anne Of The Thousand Days" – play in two acts by Maxwell Anderson who died in 1959 – Dramatists Play Service, Inc.)

"I've never thought what it would be like to die, to become meat that rots. Then food for the shrubs and the long roots of vines. The grapes could reach me. I may make him drunk before many year. Someone told me the story of the homely daughter of Sir Thomas More, climbing at night up the trestles of London Bridge where they'd stuck her father's head on a spike and hunting among the stinking and bloody heads of criminals, still she found her father's head, his beard matted and hard with blood and climbing down with it, and taking it home, to bury in the garden perhaps. Would they fix my head up on London Bridge? No. Even Henry would object to that. I've been his queen. He's kissed my lips. He wouldn't want it. I'll lie in lead –- or brass.

Meat: Dead Meat. But if my head was on the Bridge he wouldn't climb to take it down, nobody'd climb for me. I could stay and face up the river. My long hair blown out and tangled round the spikes – and my small neck -- 'til the sea birds took me and there was nothing but a wisp of hair and a cup of bone. I must think of something to say when the time comes – IF I could say it – with the axe edge toward me. Could I do it? Could I lay my head down – and smile, and speak? 'Til the bow comes? They say it's subtle. It doesn't hurt. There's no time – No time. That's the end of time."

I did not recall any history of Anne Boleyn from school years. I don't even know how the play "Anne of The 1,000 Days" came to me. It was a used book. I visualized the scene so clearly and felt it to the depth that I was capable of feeling at the time. Still, it did not occur to me that there was any past connection to me.

We ask ourselves is it unfulfilled ego that causes one to declare a former life of nobility? Is it lack of love and understanding that sets one part from others and seeks identity with other times and places? Is it the desire to know the fullness of one's self, regardless of what others may think? Did I walk the halls of Hampton Court and other noble dwellings in the 15th Century England as Anne Boleyn, the beheaded wife of Henry VIII? If not, why have I consistently turned so empathetically toward this woman's short existence?

In my early days of considering the possibility of having been Anne Boleyn in a past life, I began writing down similarities as explained in the following list:

ANNE BOLEYN	**ANN PALMER**
BIRTH: Never Recorded, Marriage annulled	BIRTH: BORN 5/17 -No name on Birth Certificate, invalid for passport application
May 17th 1536, scheduled to be executed 5/17	
Executed May 19th, 1536, 5 men executed 5/17	
MOTHER: Elizabeth HOWARD	FATHER: William HOWARD
Anne - second daughter	Ann - second daughter
COUSIN: Catherine	SISTER: Kathleen
FIRST LOVE: Percy	FIRST HUSBAND: Pearcy
CHILDREN: 1 Daughter	CHILDREN: 1 Daughter
(2 months pregnant at marriage)	2 months pregnant at marriage)
Attached to FRENCE culture	Attracted to FRENCE culture

CHARACTERISTIC IN COMMON:

Temper, Willful, Ambitious, Determined, Emotional, Aggressive, Expressive in letters and poems. Preferred the company of men, sometimes the only woman among men, flirtations.

PHYSICAL: long, slender neck, mole on neck,	PHYSICAL: long, slender neck, mole on neck,

Accused of Witchcraft	Similar accusations over psychic ability
ENEMY: Thomas More	FRIEND: Thomas Moore
HENRY VIII -Handsome, over 6', curly auburn hair, blue, eyes, athletic	TEEN date Football Hero, over 6' auburn hair, blue eyes
HENRY VIII- while courting Anne, a married man	CONFRONTED often by married men
ANNE: Refused to be his mistress	ANN: Similar offers always refused
ACCUSED unfairly "Whore" "Concubine" -cuckold Henry	ACCUSED similarly, endured constant criticism
ANNE: Not quite royal enough, on the fringes	ANN: Moved in Social Circles beyond Family background
OUTSTANDING SITES: Dover, Calais, France, Hampton Court,	ANN: Visited ALL those places before Windsor Castle, Westminster Abby understanding any connection to
Anne DEFIED Compulsory Religions beliefs	DEFIED organized Religions, from age 5
INTEREST in fashion and religious philosophy	INTEREST in fashion and religious philosophy - years as a fashion model
BROUGHT about the division of Catholicism in England	SEEKING Unity in Spiritual Evolution
GIVEN Male responsibilities, title never given to a woman	Male responsibilities
ACTING - Loved it, played, wrote poems, etc.	PURSUED Acting career, wrote poems, books - first acting class monologue scene "Anne of 1000 Days"
EXCELLENT HORSE WOMAN	SAME in several lives, not present, bad cut on foot, age 5, while on horse

SYMBOL: Rose and White Falcon (similar to dove)	SYMBOL: ROSE and White Dove
GIFTED with clocks	LOVE of Antique clocks
Becoming Queen "near impossible to attain"	THEME: "To Dream the Impossible Dream"
ISOLATED, lack of friends/ supporters	ISOLATED, lack of friends and supporters

(WHILE VISITING WESTMINISTER ABBY: I became aware of portraits, labeled "Anne Boleyn" - I felt sure that they were NOT her! I had a hostile emotional reaction to the lack of anything about her in Westminster Abby, similar feelings at Windsor, Hampton Court and England felt depressive. I felt good when I arrived in France.)

The 21st Century Ann Palmer finds herself entrapped in a physical vehicle, known as a woman -- a female, a "lady" or even a "broad." The limitations of this vehicle are frustrating. Social background of this life is the antithesis of Anne Boleyn, yet similarly inclined to desire and lust for acceptance in "higher circles" of social acceptances.

The every present frustration of the need of financial security with an underlying assumptions finances are associated with men. Thus, seeking to find a loving mate has been a stumbling block. I was never willing to marry a man for security, which seemed to be a pattern for my actress/model friends. The youthful pregnancy that removed me from synchronism of peers created more frustration of love vs. resentment. Later, to desire motherhood with numerous pregnancies, but with circumstances that would never allow fulfillment. There were many years of the every constant desire to be a wife, only to meet with impossible marriages. Born into this vehicle of a "pretty female" while feeling flaws that withheld complete fulfillments created isolation. I always looked to myself for fault, not realizing when it was other's jealousies, resentments and fears of one who appears prettier and stronger. Yet, I always felt that I was not pretty enough, didn't have a perfect figure, wasn't as smart as others and my own worst enemy. As a single person I was trying to retain moral values during a sexual revolution era. It was very frustrating to be sensuous, but rarely in a position to playfully express that sensuousness. Plagued by the desire to be loved, to be caressed, and cared for as well as the emptiness of not having just one man to pamper and cater to – were reflections of the teachings of my father in youth.

Career pursuits were total frustration because of many, too many interest. Being an actress was not the all consuming goal for me. To be able to get into production seemed a more fulfilling goal. The problem was – there were limited opportunities for women in the 1960's. A woman could be a script girl – an on the set secretary and I had no secretarial skills or talent. The only other job for a woman was in the wardrobe department. The years never brought the outward manifestation of our social structure's mark of success, and yet, behind the superficial appearance of failures, I always had strength surpassing all others.

A vivid dream of many years ago had remained with me. Later, in a psychic development class I was teaching, a student shocked me when she related a scene very similar like my long ago dream. In that dream, I was aware of being at a banquet in a medieval castle with a wide heavy stone circular stairway. I was a young giddy, flirtatious woman running up the stairway with a young man in pursuit to be away from the others. We ran into one of the rooms at the top of the stairway where he grabbed me, kissing me passionately. It was a very romantic scene with him placing a ring on my finger. I was aware that I could not be seen wearing the ring, so I climbed on a chair and hid it up on a corbel. For years, I wondered if that dream was a key to prove a past life experience and that somewhere in England, perhaps in ruins, stands a wall with a corbel covered with dirt where that ring rest today, nearly 500 years later. At the time of the dream, I did not identify it with Anne Boleyn.

Around 1522, Anne began being courted by **Lord Henry Percy**, the son of the earl of Northumberland and probably in the spring of 1523, they were **secretly betrothed**.

I saw a picture of Hever Castle, (possible where Anne was born) it could be the same castle or it could be in the ruins of some castle in England. In the meditation class, my student drew the similar stairway that I had seen in a vision, mine of left, hers right.

In 1970, just prior to going to Europe and to celebrate my May 17th birthday, I went alone to the theatre and saw the film "Anne Of The 1,000 Days." What an eerie feeling I had identifying so strongly with Anne. Could I have been Anne in a previous life? It seemed a lot of nonsense but the thought continued to plague me.

Just months later, as I stood in a gift shop at Westminster Abby flipping through some of the books and saw a picture of Anne Boleyn. "That's not me, he even destroyed every image of me!" was my angry thought while my left brain was saying "… don't be ridiculous, Ann!" As I viewed the tombs of nobility and stood facing the enormous tomb of Elizabeth I, Anne's daughter, I did not see any tomb for Anne Boleyn. I asked a guard where Anne was buried. He confided that he really did not know for sure but he thought it was somewhere in a small church --- Anne was lost in time – just as she had been born with no proof of the exact date of her birth – just as I was born in this life with no name on my birth certificate. I felt sad as I saw far lesser royalties' tombs. Anne, who changed the face of history and religion, was lost in time! I was sad, aggravated and irritated. Why were my feelings so deeply felt?

Several years before I knew anything about reincarnation, after finishing my job in the film "Cleopatra" in Rome, I was in London and visited the Tower of London. One of the only pictures taken was in front of the spot where Anne had been executed. The British seemed to have kept an accurate account of Anne's demise but NOT her burial! Later, I found on the Internet she was buried in the Chapel at the Tower of London.

How strange that I could feel this connection as I came from a lower middle class Texas family, yet, in childhood it never occurred to me that I could NOT grow up and marry a prince somewhere in the world. I was told that at six months of age, I was found crawling down the highway. No doubt, even as a small baby, I wanted to get out of my birth circumstances. I didn't belong. In my teens, I would look up at the sky and wonder how I would find my Prince Charming. It seemed such a big world out there. An early modeling career gave me an escape from my limited social background and an avenue to Hollywood. All of my life has been out of sync with others as revealed in an early poem:

I AM A MISFIT
Do you know what it is to be alone?
To be with many and yet alone,
To be loved by many and yet alone,
To be able to give love and yet alone,
To have child's love and yet alone?

Do you know what it is to be a misfit?
To be with the "common folk" and not quite fit,
To be with the sophisticates and yet not quite fit,
To believe in God and feel the need of church
And with church people not quite fit,
To feel a part of those who have no need of church or god,
And yet, there, not fit either.
Will there ever be a place for me?
With faith, I will wait and see.

For a number of years, I fought against the absurdity of the "Anne Boleyn" connection. I squelched any thoughts of it as I knew people would scoff at the idea, only a few metaphysical friends knew. Then, I was asked to participate in publicizing a Reincarnation Ball – I decided "what the hell – who cares what people think – I am connected in some way to Anne Boleyn!" I put together a costume and played it to the hilt at the Ball with publicity et al. (see photos at the end of this chapter.)

Publicity and articles related to reliving Anne Boleyn

It was not until I began actively studying and practicing past life regressions that the repetitious experiences of Anne began to appear in my sessions. In seminars, we would practice regressions on each other. As I would lie back prepared to go into some current life problem, invariably pictures would appear in my mind revealing some experience of Anne, even though it definitely was not my intentions to go into that. As the sessions began, I had no idea that another piece of the puzzle of Anne's experience would be revealed. Most sessions were related to just prior to her execution and related to her death experience, then what followed after death.

(In addition to the regressions, I would allow channeling to come through, ever not knowing what might be revealed. November 17th 1983 – I had no idea what it was or where it was coming from; nor did I think of Anne Boleyn until much later. This is written as I received it.)

"For we being many are one bread and one body: For we are all partakers of that one bread." Corinthians 10:16-17 - 11: 23-28

Jesus: blessed/broke/shared.

Seal of Covenant: Bread: staff of life-breaking: Soul splitting searching for self.

Wine: blood/life force pulsating ever constant regeneration

Supper: inward experience sustenance.

7 WORDS FROM THE CROSS

1. Divine Forgiveness
2. Assurance of Immortality
3. Good Works
4. Pain of Death
5. True Humanity of Christ
6. Perfection of Jesus Christ At-one-ment
7. Divine Complacency

7th Seer doth thou stand
Fraternal fidelity not withstand
Trust thou now to move miracles
In thy power to truth march thou onward

In honest reproach doth thou plea
Only now do you see
On to better, thou doeth last
Future is as future be
So send now power to thee
Ask now not for unseen myth
Lay thee down, thy cup has past
Take thou key to thine self
For now you see how time doth pass
Tender is thy love
Say thou thee how doth it pass
Not so to those who sneer
Only to thee, the key doth pass
Pray thou thee to forth thou go
Only now the cup hath fro
For to thee a key is wed
Only now doth thou see
Uncertainty reins only now
Do not despair, all is well
Sleep thou thee tonight to rest
Sleep thou then thou time doth bless
Sit alone, silent now
Tears to pass the night
Stand now as one alone
Knowing well thou path is sewn
Go forth now from this place to pass
The world the key thou didst do best
Take thee now to blest
Thou doth see
Fruitless ventures now pass
Forgiveness frowned forever blest
Gone to ere didn't thou see
Holy Grail for thee didst bless
Pass not the sea of Galilee
For thou hath patterned us from that past
Set us free to let us pass
Set not thou bough for

There didst pass one so strong
So set forth that thou didst hand
A knight in sallow arms
Take thou thee to thy rest
Know hence forth all the blest
Only now can thou see, harvest free
Blest and free
Go thou thee to paradise
Thou hast blest
Go thou thee and say thou rest
Say no more for now has been done
All that thee might reach for naught
Take thou chalice
Drink the last
For thou has seen Christ at last
Go thou thee for hope now stands
Heavily rest it upon thee
Twice before you met the test
Only last to fail to make thou grail
Take thou thee thy holy grail
Only now cans't thou see
Go forth now in holy blest
Knowing well thy time now past
Take thou thee, take the cup that now must pass
Go thou thee toward final rest
The crown is on thy head."

When I would go into meditation, I often sense standing before an eternal flame in an beautiful garden with an oblong shallow pool of water and a small square temple at the other end. I seemed to be holding the right hand of Anne with my left hand. As we stood before the flame, I saw Anne in clothing of her era. The fire radiated in her face. I held her hand so that she would not be afraid. The instructions given to me was to embrace her as a child, as a mother would embrace a child and explain that fears, anxieties, etc. need not be felt. I was holding her as you would hold someone crying as she merged into my body. We seemed to pass through each other. I faced one way and she faced the other, merged inside each other. I turned around, facing forward she was filled with light. Just as I had experienced going into the ethereal body of Jesus and becoming one with it, Anne had done the same with me. She was inside of me and happy. We merged into our soul's oneness -- our gathering place.

During a past life regress in April of 1984, I was asked to bring in Anne Boleyn. Earlier in the regression I had seen nine attachments to me that needed exorcism. The scene seemed to be nine men dancing in bright colored costumes, wearing Elizabethan collars. I saw a woman with a cap tied around her head sitting in the middle of the bed as though to be protected. ("Elizabeth tired to get rid of you" the Regressionist said) – I then explained that I was aware that Anne went to Elizabeth, spiritually, possibly moments before Anne's actual death and remained with her as a spirit protector. The realization came over me that these nine men were trying to get rid of me, the spirit of Anne that was attached to Elizabeth. It was an exorcism. They were not dressed as priests as one would expect but more like tights with puffy sleeves in very bright colors. They were doing different things, more or less a dance like movement in a circle. I felt that I was in spirit form protecting my daughter but she was unaware of this spiritual energy around her that was perceived as "evil" – how horrible! (The regressionist asked "As the men dance around, do they perform the exorcism?") I said "They can't – I am stronger than all of them – I am upset about what is going on! I have done so much to help Elizabeth – she does not know what is going on. She set this up and there is a lot of energy I have to use to remain – I am having to absorb these men's energy – their soul energy in order to negate what they are attempting to do. I am willing to accept it, but it is not easy. Their energy is flowing and merging with Anne's as she (me) sits in the air above Elizabeth but I/Anne is not giving up. Anne then attempted to manifest a rose in the air to show Elizabeth that it was Anne but she did not see it. Anne's efforts had all been for Elizabeth's good and here she had to take on burdensome energy from these men that made her work very difficult. In order to remain so closely attached to Elizabeth, Anne had already expended more energy than she should. This event now created Karma that I today am still working off with the same nine men.

The therapist asked about the nine men. I related that these men were all executed because of Anne Boleyn in one way or another. They had all returned in Elizabeth's time and all close to the same age and were an influence in Elizabeth's life, perhaps young musicians that entertained Elizabeth. It began to become clear to me that these nine men were negative forces in my present life. "They have been drawing strength out of me and I have not been aware of it" I said. The face of an ex-lover appeared, laughing and saying "we succeeded." Individually they had wished that I would fail and my failure in my chosen field of television had been through their energy. Even spiritually it had held me back. What had it done to them? That was an interesting twist. They set up their own karma in the future. While I had been able to let go of each of them in this life, their energy had attached to me and even though we had parted, a soft spot in my heart remained for each. It was a really weird sensation. I had never seen anything like this or read of this type of experience. It was as though each received some sort of sadistic satisfaction in seeing me never succeed in the ways I thought I wanted success. (Seven men in my present life: Newman 1st husband, Bob 2nd husband, Burt, Tom, both long time relations, Jack 3rd husband Rick - special love, Richard – a special place in my life for five years.)

The Regressionist then asked me to move forward to Elizabeth's death. She died in old age but the spirit of Anne saw Elizabeth ascending from the old body into the small child at the time Anne departed the physical body. Anne is happy – her heart is full – her eyes are teary with happiness, holding her child, walking into a forest – the scene faded. As the therapist asked me more questions, I became aware that Anne still held anger. I saw her arms folded wearing a peasant type of dress. No one appreciated her nor understood her or what she tired to do. The plain dress must have been Anne's death dress. It was grey with white cuffs on it. Anne died with a lot of anger. The heart of the anger and resentment in me stems from Anne.

September 11, 1984 - In a vision:

In this scene with Henry, we are watching musicians and dancers perform. The men dancers are in very colorful costumes; tights, puffy and very bright colors. Such a happy event, it seems to be a celebration about a new castle, newly decorated, new tapestries. I sit lower and to the left of Henry. He is wearing a large ring on his index finger as well as rings on other fingers but the index finger dances to the music as though it is our secret symbol, which amuses me as I watch his finger.

Merged into this scene, "I am riding a horse then thrown from the horse when I was pregnant and lost the baby. This seems to be a memory of the past as I now am quite far along in pregnancy. I have it all I am thinking and I am so happy as I look around the room, sensing everything as success, at last, I have it all! I feel very positive about the child I carry. I know that I am giving Henry the son he desperately wants. There is a great deal of love between us. At this moment of joy there is no possible way of suspecting Henry could EVER order my death a few short years later."

July 18th, 1986 CHANNELING

Anne Boleyn: Youthful – barefooted – summer – clover -- horseback riding, wearing a checkered or polka dot dress, ankle length, laced up the front. She is riding a horse straddled like men rode them. She is thrown off and hurt her back but must keep it a secret from Henry. She fears being imperfect physically as she wants a crown. She held Henry's crown over her head in secret and didn't want anyone to know as it was forbidden for anyone to wear the crown except Henry. It was so huge, she couldn't put it down onto her head as in wearing it, and thus she just held it over her head as she looked in a mirror. Anne really wanted to rule the world and would do anything for power. She did anything to please Henry. Even though the name "Anne" was often referred to as "Nan" – in this case it stood for "nanny" as she treated this huge man as a little boy. He loved being treated like a little boy. As he grew fatter and fatter, she hated his fat stomach. He associated fat with power. Somehow, in this present life, I associate my migraine headaches, weight problems, back aches with Henry's power over Anne.

August 24th, 1986 - DREAM:

Cats – very last instructions were "Forget Cats!" OR CAT could stand for **C**rown **A**nne's **T**ransformations! Lower back pain – What does my back remember? Anne, at 21 years of age pretended she had no back injury from falling off a horse (in this life, from birth, I never wanted to ride horses). As Anne "I stood up and denied to all that I was in any pain. It felt good to fool my parents, too. I told only one friend, later when the way was opened to marry Henry, he had that friend killed. That friend seems to be my first husband and father to my daughter – who set his sperm, the power to control, within my body to then control my life and body whether or not he could hold on to me.

The "re" words came to mind – reverse, repeat, reincarnation, return, recreate, reverse the process to "er" as – erase all the "re"s. Where we set "cause in motion, apart from where other people may be in consciousness, we CAN rewrite our script instantaneously to create our own release from effects of our past or present lives. This then is the key to God's law that, to me, is to just LOVE. Be still and know that I AM! BE in the now. In that stillness we – you – me – are one with God. ELIMINATION – is the opportunity for transformation to illumination.

(The following was not a past life session but seemed to be coming through as Anne was speaking though me in channeling. This was February 1987. Anne Boleyn would not speak exactly as this is worded nor would I speak in these words. It came through me and must be a combination of words as I well as I could perceive them.)

"When women stop comparing themselves to each other, they will achieve equality" a friend stated. It occurred to me that women have never been treated as equals in recorded history. We have given ourselves of body, of mind, of spirit and yet we receive no equality, even from God – from the Mother Church – Who is God? I truly believe in God – One God but who is "He" that I come to now and kneel before his throne – Will he, too, judge me so harshly as Henry? Will He, too, turn His back? He that shared my bed and my body – my body that never was touched by any other man – he took – he drank me in – I withstood his temper tantrums. My shoulders weak with fear -- he could not deprive himself of pleasure so I pleasured him when he please, regardless of my sicknesses. Oh God, could I be so insignificant and indecent in your eyes? Shall I go to hell for it -- for what? Have I not said my prayers, heeded thy counsel at every turn of events? Have I ever denied thy presence and thy power? Oh, God, why hast thou forsaken me in this time of such evil doing in my life? Am I to die for sins I have not done? The King may not see into my heart but the King of Kings knows not sins of this body and this heart. I am the King's concubine they peal --

"Anne is Henry's whore" they cry out in the night. I hear their laughter. Nay, they cannot see into this heart – this pure heart. Oh, my sweet Jesus, I feel your pain. Oh dear Jesus, I know thy deliverance into hell for those who crucified you. I, too, have gone to hell for those who call me "concubine" – "go to hell" I say – I – you – they that accuse me. I go to hell in your place – I go in countenance in thy grief. Only now do I see thee, sweet Jesus. Only now do I see thy pain – Oh, God, pass this cup from my lips, let me not drink the Devil's wine. Seal my lips from this Devilish pain. Have I truly sinned in thy Name? Have I ever cursed Thy Name? Have I dealt with the Devil? Ah, yes, me thinkst the Devil pure is Henry's name and thus Henry's fame – is alas, my pain – pain – pain. I'll not think on it – There is no pain – it is to fast – so fast – thus it is done – Oh God! Not my head – not my head – my heart – oh, yes, bring me a knife – let me cut out my heart and send it to Henry – the King – Let my King see and smell the pure radiance of this heart of the one called Anne Boleyn – Sin of thee, my Henry, the sin IS of thee.

The thought that I might perish before my mother – before my father – can'st be – for truly it is the parents who lead the way to paradise. Who then will carry me – Oh led me, Holy Mother, lead me across the sea. Let me walk on fertile land – a land of free men who seek God's favor by growing things – who seek God's goodness forever, be wholesome and free – Oh free – now free – why free –free – free of my head I shall be! Sooner than I care to agree – Oh, be it! I cannot choose – I cannot choose – always Henry said "choose" – this one or that one – always it was up to me – his "Nanne" to choose one or the other. Why now hast thou forsaken that sacred right to CHOOSE! Oh – I choose to be FREE but not of my head, Dear one! For God knows I am not so vane, but how will I enter paradise without my head? How will I see the eyes of God if I have no eyes to see? Oh, woo is me, how sad it is for me. How crusty he that called me "whore" –"whore woman" he called out. How dare he speak to me thus! I am the Queen. I am Queen – Anne of Brittany – Nova Scotia and de Breeze. How can I go on? The curtain is drawn, the curtain is drawn. The play has ended. The play is no longer a song that sings neither – sadness nor joy – grief no sorrow – the play is over. Truly, I see Calvary – yes, I see it now. I am not dreaming but God has given me vision to see thy dance. Oh, free is me – I am free at last. I know now I have seen thy face – in the meadows green – the silent streams – the seeping of the wedges, as they go to and fro down the long slopes of grey and green. Truly this is the man of God I seek. What then be your name – stranger above us? We seek thy countenance. The children play – the children of innocence – God – I am thy child – I AM thy child. I will no longer hold Court in Henry's wing but I will hold court in thy countenance of thy God. Oh, Henry, I shall be there long before thee. Oh, Henry, you have given me opportunity to go beyond thee. You realized not thou hast bequeathed to me thy inheritance in God's countenance.

Thou, at last has made me thy Queen forever more – forever more – for ever more. I am thy servant still, yet, I am free. I am free -- I am free to be! Oh, Henry, thou hast no choice but to provide me with the opportunity to say so. Yea, I shall but allow thee one last chance to restore my honor. No, not now, I grant thee peace, my beloved, I grant thee peace.. Good night."

(Continued thoughts from Anne Boleyn)

"So few really know me. I often ache with tenderness and love. Do you think a king would want me – love me enough to risk so much for me. That is the Henry I loved not the shattered man who condemned me to die. For Henry would never order that death, only the magpie flies swarming in and around his head made him crazy at times. Spirit Possession? Perhaps it was. Kathryn was said to have hexed us. She died a most horrible death because of her own evil spirits swimming within her brain. She, too, loved Henry in her own way. Henry's spirit was much too alive and young for the likes of dear Kathryn. Theirs were worlds apart. She could only nag her displeasures in his constant ear. Henry had a tenderness very few ever knew except those of his innermost circle. How difficult to feel this tenderness while ruling lands, money and people. Henry was never cut out to be a king – a poet or prophet but never a king. It put far too much stress on him. Henry never ordered my death. I knew that – oh, his hand signed the paper but not his heart – for his tender heart cried with blood tears. He was a fine man – so fine few could see it – a smart man, too – a kindness that had to be covered with a hard shell of those who advised him. He was a kind man. That is all I will remember of him. I never did blame nor bitterness feel. He was a good man. Those who saw differently never knew my big, bold tender boy King – soft and tender was he."

What complicated webs of Karma we unconsciously weave. While they reap their sadistic sensations, it seems as though inwardly each of them, see or sense an inward success in me that they have not yet experienced, so in loosing, I have also won, although I have been unaware of the competition. One stood out as sort of a spokesman for the rest. As I saw his spiritual head bowed, I held out my hands, palms upward to offer compassion and forgiveness. There were sparks of energy that went out of my hands, like a rainbow that became a swirling vortex of energy in and around him. The regressionist attempted an exorcism of my enemies. I saw a bright light; they became silhouetted against the light. One by one they seemed to be vacuumed into the light. Only one seemed to hold back.

February 17th, 1987

Anne Boleyn speaks: "The time is nie to right the wrong – the truth at last to be. I stood in no halls nor haunted thee. Other lost souls, perhaps, but never me. Too busy am I for this. With the exception in Elizabeth's day – nay, ghost not, but a loving mother proud to be of one so clever thus amongst men. You should have seen her – how she took them on, one by one. Clever girl – some times too clever be – for sadness and loneliness was she as Queen of the realm. I am sorry, Child, I did not wish this upon thee. Nay, not a spirit haunting as though me it be, but a mother loving a child in side a woman strong and powerful beyond any man who preceded her on the throne. She needed me. She knew I stood behind her in the later years but not the time they attempted that awful exorcism of me. Truly, it stood me many lives to ward off these, especially three. Thus, now, I speak at last, the curse is broken today in full. "Speak not, never more" they pealed, thus now we broke the code. The more is one at last, power though he be. We broke the code, at last free to say things never uttered in the past. You seek to know the truth at last. Strength of two now at best."

(A friend named, Susan, was working with me. She had been Anne's closest lady in waiting and was with her in the tower before Anne's execution.) "

To be here now no longer frightens me – Trials, oh trails of woman falsely accused. History written in the times by men, rarely stated truths that smut be known. There were those women who wrote, thus destroyed by men. Ah, yes, "a man's world" is truly be at things like the writing of history. Sins destroyed by men of men. We women speak now in freedom as never before known on this earth. Speak now; speak well, we tell you now, not Anne Boleyn, alone thus written about. Public person Elizabeth had far more truths written than of me, but, too, Elizabeth's private thoughts stood time alone. She was "no spring chicken" (this life's expression) when she left her body royal but child she was when she came thus to me. We walked freely, Elizabeth and me – through time and space as though Elizabeth never was Queen of England and all Brittany. Nay, I was not a good Queen like she – nor BAD as was said! I did as best I could at times bad for the likes of me – clever though I be. Truly we *(Susan and me)* came to know each other in splendor. It was a ball that you were introduced in court. It was the Duke of Gloucester who brought you there. Eii, like me, you came thus to court fresh from France and fancy tutoring by English standards. You stood tall to me, yet petite in body. Your hair shimmered in the wind, like brown silk, through light in color. A child of grandeur, like me though pure and simple you be. I asked you assigned to me be. Henry gave me my asking. He knew I asked little for my times, thus he gave to me thee. Thirteen be your age of green. Thus linked we were - you and me. How then we know the fate to come – nay, we could not imagine a fate so grim. Truly to thee be – a kindness of heart no where found within the realm. Thus, be said for naught, it be a time of so much tragedy. "Karma" you say today – truly karma was past and found. Found subtly upon thee for low these many fields – for today the cup is passed to and fro you go, thus at last to last to be – to free – Silence still no more. Truly be me, Queen of all Brittany.... "

June 28th, 1987 CHANNELING: ANN BOLEYN

Coventry Castle (Henry VIII[6] went to Coventry, it was the Bishop of Coventry and Lichfield who married HenryVIII to Anne Boleyn.) – Henry – Anne lived in an era when women had but few choices. "Ways were hard. Instruments of men often concealed various orders of things, here to fore referred to as Annapolis heralding. Straight from home to brothels many young lass. Taking on royalty was quite an undertaking for the likes of Anne, with style quite unique, even to the French courts. Ah, yes, she had a way with both men and women, called manipulation today – cunning – remarkably sure of herself and her own countenance."

Her sisters were mild mannered, strict in their Catholic views while Anne rebelled at teachers of laws of God – "Humph," said Anne "Laws of man, they be!" I'll not have of thee" she shouted to the Priest. Her family in good stead, the Priest muttered nothing about Miss Anne's antics. She stood tall amongst bible scholars. Oft to shame she put those who professed to be of knowledge. Eii, a Captain once told me that I must always hold my own with the church. He said the church may be the rudder to the ship but where would the rudder be without a ship to steer its course? Laugh we would at his jibe dear man, he. We went to and fro upon his sea. Many a time he told us tales, none so true as the one he oft times told. Forget he did – so oft repeat -- he told us of sailors, young though they be – who for lack of better to do, did jump into the sea – "Walk on water we" – "Drunk they be" he said. Well, walk the water they did but not as Christ Jesus. Wade they did to where the rocks were few but step they did from rock to rock. Fool be those who watched with glee, for thought they did, water walkers be! Pay they did, but so did, poor souls, the sailors with their own dear lives but not that day. Later, when the sea was high, overboard washed all three. Was it a curse of God that they should scorn the tale of our dear Lord – No, God would not treat them thus, but if he did, would I know a God so vengeful? Vengeful though he be, Henry truly was a God of man. He told court with wedded plans to be with the likes of me. How did I soothe thee, savage beast – Ah, the likes of me – sooth thus to thee, sweet honor be on Henry's steed – love that animal "three of a kind" he said, no, not so, none be like thee, Sweet Ambos – a steed so rare, fit for none other than me. Have this horse I will – I will – I will – for I am Anne of Leads – Ann of all Brittany – Anne is me. Holy God, I see it now, Queen one day I will be – I will I will – I will – I will!"

"Bromley, there's a man of honest face – seems trustworthy enough to handle my mare" "chose" he said. "That one" said I. He laughed "THAT one?" said he, "is my only rare breed!" "Breed as you like" said I to he "but that one is for me!" Laugh he did and handed me the reins

– Happy day – happy day. Sweet Henry and me – I love to dance – I love to sing – happy, happy, joyous all are we!" "Thumpty dee dump – thumpty dee dump – I love to dance – I love to sing – glorious melody – sing – sing and glee.

Taking hold of one's own dear life is free of pain. As a child, thus I thought, I might die when I had to take hold and plan my day, though; surely I had the challenge to do just that. Hope to go to Leeds tomorrow – sleep now – be peaceful – rest and sleep – ah to dream, to dream of wonderful things to be -- Anne of all Brittany. I curse not the day Henry wed, for I do know one day – one way, it will be me! It will - It will – It will – It will! Oh, hold fast now, Anne, for today you see sweet Henry in the presence of this house. Still and tall he stands with such grace for such a man as he. I love his collar and his hair – a lion and his mane, did I dare tell – sinny, sinny, sin, sin, sin, sin, sin, sin," (this was a peppy song in my head).

"Since I hold no musical skills, I must be totally clever. I must know what to say at the right time – 'Oh yes, Dear, hold these" he said to me, placing his gloves upon my hand – He and me know the secret thus – we held hands, if only by his glove. Still, hold hands thus we did – Henry and me! Oh, I could go on and on about silly things we did to still curious eyes but say here now that love I did for Henry, King of all England. I had my flings, but love I did, most ardently. Take now from me this chalice, too long upon my head. This weighty chalice is the cause of my headaches in this life, these days which doctors have never cured, nor meditation or healing thus. How can one not have headaches with such head-heavy decisions? Carry my head in my hands – can it be – How awful this! To detach one's member from the other – no greater sin to can than this one to another. This be the chalice I handed to thee."

FROM THE INTERNET: ANNE'S LETTER TO HENRY FROM PRISON:

SIR, YOUR GRACE'S DISPLEASURE, and my Imprisonment are Things so strange unto me, as what to Write, or what to Excuse, I am altogether ignorant; whereas you sent unto me (willing me to confess a Truth, and so obtain your Favour) by such a one, whom you know to be my ancient and professed Enemy; I no sooner received the

Message by him, than I rightly conceived your Meaning; and if, as you say, confessing Truth indeed may procure my safety, I shall with all Willingnes, and Duty perform your Command.

But let not your Grace ever imagine that your poor Wife will ever be brought to acknowledge a Fault, where not so much as Thought thereof proceeded. And to speak a truth, never Prince had Wife more Loyal in all Duty, and in all true Affection, than you have found in Anne Boleyn, with which Name and Place could willingly have contented my self, as if God, and your Grace's Pleasure had been so pleased. Neither did I at any time so far forge my self in my Exaltation, or received Queenship, but that I always looked for such an Alteration as now I find; for the ground of my preferment being on no surer Foundation than your Grace's Fancy, the least Alteration, I knew, was fit and sufficient to draw that Fancy to some other subject.

You have chosen me, from a low Estate, to be your Queen and Companion, far beyond my Desert or Desire. If then you found me worthy of such Honour, Good your Grace, let not any light Fancy, or bad Counsel of mine Enemies, withdraw your Princely Favour from me; neither let that Stain, that unworthy Stain of a Disloyal Heart towards your good Grace, ever cast so foul a Blot on your most Dutiful Wife, and the Infant Princess your Daughter:

Try me, good King, but let me have a Lawful Trial, and let not my sworn Enemies sit as my Accusers and Judges; yes, let me receive an open Trial, for my Truth shall fear no open shame; then shall you see, either mine Innocence cleared, your Suspicion and Conscience satisfied, the Ignominy and Slander of the World stopped, or my Guilt openly declared. So that whatsoever God or you may determine of me, your Grace may be freed from an open Censure; and mine Offence being so lawfully proved, your Grace is at liberty, both before God and Man, not only to execute worthy Punishment on me as an unlawful Wife, but to follow your Affection already settled on that party, for whose sake I am now as I am, whose Name I could some good while since have pointed unto: Your Grace being not ignorant of my Suspicion therein.

But if you have already determined of me, and that not only my Death, but an Infamous Slander must bring you the enjoying of your desired Happiness; then I desire of God, that he will pardon your great Sin therein, and likewise mine Enemies, the Instruments thereof; that he will not call you to a strict Account for your unprincely and cruel usage of me, at his General Judgment-Seat, where both you and my self must shortly appear, and in whose Judgment, I doubt not, (whatsoever the World may think of me) mine Innocence shall be openly known, and sufficiently cleared.

My last and only Request shall be, That my self may only bear the Burthen of your Grace's Displeasure, and that it may not touch the Innocent Souls of those poor Gentlemen, who (as I understand) are likewise in strait Imprisonment for my sake. If ever I have found favour in your Sight; if ever the Name of Anne Boleyn hath been pleasing to your Ears, then let me obtain this Request; and I will so leave to trouble your Grace any further, with mine earnest Prayers to the Trinity to have your Grace in his good keeping, and to direct you in all your Actions.

Your most Loyal and ever Faithful Wife, Anne Boleyn

From my doleful Prison the Tower, this 6th of May

In a regression, I realized Anne practiced the execution for days before it actually happened. She worked to put herself in self hypnosis, practiced with a black hood over her head and laying her head down over an open back velvet stool, like an Egyptian throne. She was able to face her death with dignity in a hypnotic state. Her emotional body had left the physical body and darted directly to Elizabeth, where she became a guiding spirit to watch over Elizabeth as she grew into womanhood. Elizabeth was accused of practicing witchcraft but it was only Anne channeling information to her as she meditated or in dreams. Many of her decisions were influenced by Anne working through her. There is no way to prove this.

Proving my intuitive perceptions of Ann Boleyn's life that differs from the established history of her is for me to trust that my information is correct. No one knows for sure. No doubt writers have surmised and assumed many stories of her life are true but have no proof either. If she was a witch as accused, she was a "white" witch as many saints and healers were. She was totally committed and dedicated to God and purpose at all cost to her own personal martyrdom. She loved Henry dearly and realized the power she had over him. She wanted only to use it to help the people of England and other countries. Out of that union came the most powerful queen that England ever had -- Queen

Elizabeth I. Elizabeth brought forth fabulous wealth and world wide territories ruled by her.

Through the union of Anne and Henry VIII, they were responsible for the initial major break from Catholic control in Rome. Henry VIII was responsible for the Church of England. Even though she was very religious, she became the scapegoat for everything Henry's court was angry about, and then called a "whore" and all sorts of terrible names. Hatred for her grew, spawned by the men closest to Henry. No historian understood how committed to God Anne was. Her quest for power was to bring new understanding of God to mankind. Anne sensed the corruption in the Popes and Higher Archery of the Church.

It was annoying that Anne's grave is under the floor of the Tower of London while lesser royal members are laid to rest in Westminster Abby and other notable places with huge statues and tombs. The strongest memories associated with Anne Boleyn seem to have involved the time of her death. My goals in this life and many relationships seem to be heavily tied to that life. Anne Boleyn has been so totally misjudged by historians and scholars. Certain paintings are said to be Anne but I know that Henry had every likeness of Anne destroyed. Those karmic ties in Anne's life related to my life today.

As I allowed my mind to just flow where it will, Anne Boleyn's youth came into my thoughts a number of times. Anne had been riding a horse straddled which women did not do in those days. Anne fell from the horse and hurt her back. In this live, I have had back problems with scoliosis. My hips were always crocked and I assumed it had to do with carrying school books on one side before I knew of my scoliosis. For weeks I had a terrible time staying up after my daughter was born when finally a doctor suggested wearing a girdle which helped. As a fashion model, I have always had back pain when having to stand for long periods. That pain remains. Today, it takes time to get to where I can move and stand in the mornings and never without pain.

Life after life I have traveled alone in many or most of my lives. Mostly, in the body of a female striving to become compete and balanced. I believe it is only now in this life that I understand my path. I can now, though learning about reincarnation, remember many errors and so much learning to be done. Past life regressions and memories have been as helpful for me as I also see events that, if people understood their past life karma, they could resolve present life problems. It has brought into focus those events that otherwise would remain unexplained. I would just pile more and more guilt on myself.

As I asked myself the "whys" -- the father of my daughter came to mind. Newman was so very insignificant in this life, other than impregnating me in my late teens, yet he left a permanent indelible print on this life I am living. We were in the same classes in college. To me, I considered him a pest as he seemed to follow me around and would sit with me when I was having a meal. Everyone though he was such a nice guy. When there was no other guy that I wanted to date, I would accept dates with him. I did not like to kiss him. I felt no attraction for him. I was heartbroken over Roy, whom I fell madly in love with at fifteen but distance kept us apart with no way to see each other. While I was dating Newman, Roy broke up with me saying he was dating someone else. I didn't have much confidence in my choices after that so with everyone urging me to LOVE Newman, I just went along with it until I got pregnant in his car, fully dressed without insertion, which didn't happen until our wedding. I hated sex and felt no pleasure from it. What better way to even the score with me than to impregnate me, force me to marry him and have a child that would never live past age eighteen. By the time my daughter was around three and a half, I divorced him much to everyone's disagreeing, except my doctor and minister. Both advised me it was the best thing for me to do. His last name was the same as Anne's first love - coincidence?

In another vision I saw a very old witch-like woman, dirty, poor and sickly. She was watching for a certain carriage to pass her way. In a fancy carriage was Anne Boleyn's pregnant mother. I became aware that she was crunched down in an alley way. When she saw the carriage coming, she forced her tired, limp body to lung in the path of this carriage so that the wheels would finish off her near-dead body. She knew that the pregnant mother was affluent and that if she could die at that moment she could attach herself to the forming fetus and continue to live in a new body in near-royal circumstances. At the moment of death, a small girl looked under the wheels at the dying old witch. Did the two pair of eyes meet at that moment - did that attach the spirit of my daughter in this life? In one regression I had seen Debbie as Elizabeth.

I had wondered if the old witch my life just previous to the life of Anne Boleyn.

As I lay on the sofa struggling to fall asleep in the miserable sultry Texas heat, the night light lit the face of my poor, old withered once pretty mother. A dentist had left only two lower spread apart teeth and with her upper plate out, I couldn't help seeing her looking much like the stereo type old witch. How terribly afraid to die she was. She chose to be bed ridden and had rather lie helpless, having everyone wait on her. This was her effect on the cause attempt to force her spirit into that near royal birth of Anne. That old street witch was not my spirit after all but my mother's spirit attached to me for 400 years! While I am aware of many past lives, I seem always to drift back into clearing karma of the Anne Boleyn spirit.

My daughter was born on my Mother's birthday. Visits to my mother always brought back memories of my daughter, Debbie, who vanished many years before. From birth I had clearly seen her happily married with three children. Going through her old souvenirs still opened stifled grief within me. I constantly question our human ability to really "love" and yet mother-love is probably as close as we can come to unconditional love unless it becomes all encompassing possessiveness. Life after life, either I died or the child died. As far as I have gone with recalling my own past lives, Debbie was the only one that grew into her teen years. A far deeper love began within me from her birth forward and with the loss of my only child; I did not think I could live.

People's dying thoughts follow them into the future. Someone should be with then to encourage loving thoughts as we leave this present physical body.

As I say about genetic memory that may influence our past life memories, I have found ancestry connections with the families of both Anne Boleyn and Henry VIII. One ancestry line is the Montague family.

Copied from the Internet:

The ancient name of Virginia appears to have been Wingandacoa, the Indian name. It received the name of Virginia in honor of England's Virgin Queen —Elizabeth. **She died March 24, 1602-3 which was the same year that Peter Montague was born.** This **Queen was of**

Montague descent through her grandmother Elizabeth, dau. of Edward IV. On the same day and year of her death James the VI. of Scotland was proclaimed James the First, King of England. He too was of Montague descent through both his mother' Mary Queen of Scots, and his father, Henry lord Dernly.[2] It was during the reign of this King James, and under his special care and protection, that the first Colony was established in Virginia.

[2] Edmund Mortimer Earl *of* March, grandson *of* William Montague, by his dau. Philippa married Philippa, dau. *of* Lionel Duke *of* Clarence, son of King Edward III. From this marriage was descended Edward IV. King *of* England and a long line *of* royal personages. Mary Queen of Scots and her husband lord Dernly were cousins. **She was of Montague descent through her grandmother Margaret, the aunt *of* Queen Elizabeth and sister of Henry VIII.** who was married to James IV. of Scotland. He was slain at Flodden Field, and Margaret re-married Archibald Douglas Earl *of* Angus and their dau. Margaret was the mother of Henry lord Dernly by her marriage with Mathew Stewart Earl of Lennox. --[See Peerage of Scotland p. 335, and Camden's Brit. p. 918, and Chronicles of the Kings by Sir R. Baker p. 269, also Burke's Royal Families.]

"Peter Montague was a direct descendant of the House of Montague as were James I, who established the first colony in Virginia in 1607 and Anne Boleyn, wife of King Henry VIII and mother of Queen Elizabeth I."

I may also have an ancestry connection with Anne's mother, Lady Elizabeth Howard, however I can't be sure as the dates don't match. There are names in my Ancestry line like Earl John deVere, a line from Hedingham Castle; Sir William Norris, Governor Thomas DeClare, Earl Richard De Clare, Countess Maud DeLacy, Sir Robert De Ferrers, Sir Maurice Fitzgerald, Earl William De Ferrers, Earl William Fitzrobert, Earl Robert De Beaumont, and back 43 generations to Robert Lantbertis in the 600's A.D. It was reassuring for me when a cousin gave me our family history. I had always felt I was born to the wrong family that was generations of Texas farmers, continuing back to the first generation in America that were planters. Seeing many royal ancestors made me understand why I felt I had been born to the wrong family and with the next incarnation in France was more proof.

CHAPTER 9

ANNE MARIE OF FRANCE

GALLERY OLDHAM UK - Dreams-Stefani Melton Fisher

5/5/78 - regression with Diane (long time friend and professional regressionist)

In a regression, Diane took notes of what I was seeing in the regression. Here is how the notes read -- "France maybe 1700's, writing desk, looking out a window, rolling hills, pleasant, beautiful place, gardens, quite and peaceful, dogs barking, birds, feel joy, urn and stairs, a colored urn, burlwood, marble, fireplace clock. Cavalier - jovial man in red, hand on hip, large mustache, laughing (possibly a painting) - Cobble stone street - I feel void of feeling. Corset, peasant attire - Pub - gaiety - man in pub - I'm disappointed in him. He's my father and I feel heartbroken. Age 15, getting in carriage, crying, woman holding me, tells driver to go. Disappointment, heart broken, can't express myself. "I can't tell anyone how I feel." Something white lying on the carriage - riding on the street - looking at the sky, escaping. Doorway, small building, weathered door, old woman sympathetic, holding me, went to bed."

The notes go on for many pages. Obviously the traumatic experience of seeing my father killed, the funeral, etc. when I was 15 years old was the opening for this life in near royalty in France in the 1760 era. Past life recall comes in bits and pieces, much like our dreams, then we must lay them out in linear form.

I channeled additional information, so with the regressions, dreams, visions and channeling, this is the combination of all:

The vision of my room is very clear to me. The two tall windows in the room face the front of the palace overlooked the hills toward the valley's winding river and village below. There was a long half circle gravel driveway to the palace. The front of the place had no special gardening and seemed quite plain with low trees in the distance. There was a circular stairway at the entrance that had a huge urn in the middle. To the left of the window in my room was the ornate door to the hallway at the top of the interior wide stairway. On the opposite wall from the window was my bed. The walls were covered with a soft blue fabric with a woven design of roses. My fluffy bed was covered with the same fabric, only pale pink. The bed was so high that I had to have a small step to get into it. This had always been my room. Between the window and the bed, on the right side of the room was a chair and small table in front of a magnificently carved marble fireplace. On the mantle was a very ornate clock with matching candles. Above the fireplace was a beautifully carved gold leaf mirror. My writing desk of burlwood was on the left wall. It was a very comfortable, secure, happy place for me to always get away from everyone and everything.

(In my present life I have always been drawn to those antique ornate clocks with matching candle sticks as well a burlwood.) Down the major stairway and to the right was a long hallway with paintings adoring the walls, at the end was the doorway that opened for entering our carriages. Across from the driveway was an area of the palace that was some offices of servants and military personnel. There were a few prisoner cells. It was temporary holding cells until criminals could be taken to Paris. To the rear were the stables and rooms where the servants and military lived.

In early childhood, Anne Marie was groomed in all royal ways. Her father was related to the King, a brother, cousin or a Duke in the Royal Court. She had spent many nights in Versailles. (Where I visited with great gusto and felt very familiar. It was a thrilling event in my present life). Anne Marie had a very happy childhood. She was more loving than most children and everyone loved her. They knew Anne Marie was perfect for her royal future, possibly marrying a king or some royal suitor. That was a bit of a worry for her as she loved her freedom. She feared a life in royal society would be so limiting for her. Anne Marie's best times were playing with Dauphine, one of the housekeepers' daughter. Anne Marie was not supposed to play with her but she would sneak off and they would run and play in the woods. Anne Marie would get annoyed when her mother told her how her life was planned even before she was born. She feared that life would be too stiff and limiting for her.

In her teen years, Anne Marie was a vivacious, adventuresome but feminine young lady. Having been influenced by her father and tucked at his heels since early childhood, Anne Marie had been taught and met the challenges much the same as a son would have been groomed for adult life. Knowing her father had wanted a son when she was born made her more determined to do anything a boy could do. She was an excellent horsewoman and could duel with guns or sabers. She had read far more books than any other woman of her years yet she was totally feminine. Anne Marie could sit with the women at the palace painting or doing needlepoint. She did everything well. Somewhat spoiled by her doting father, she was accustomed to getting her own way. Anne Marie had tremendous energy and exhausted most pursuers before the every got acquainted. She had a perpetual curiosity. She wanted see into and around almost any and everything in life. Her father had taken her in places girls were not allow to go, which only added to her adventurous spirit.

Anne Marie's father's duty was to oversee a large farming and food supply area, including cattle, dairy, etc. They lived in a palace that owned the village; the small village was not far from the palace. Her father was quite a raconteur, telling stories to amuse his subordinates. He was also known for embellishing his feats to impress the women in the providence. He frequented taverns, brothels and mingled with the most common of the commoners. It created good will amongst the workers and townspeople. He was a robust man, jolly and a good sense of humor. To say he enjoyed life is an understatement.

Her mother paid little attention to Anne Marie, nothing compared to her father. By the time she was about 12 or 13, he would take her on his rounds of checking out the land and progress in all areas. He would always end up in the village.

When Anne Marie accompanied her father to the village, he left her with shop owners, an older couple from whom she received warmth and tender love. The man, John, was a tailor. His wife, Marie, baked tasty breads, cookies and cakes that they sold to the townspeople as well as the palace. Anne Marie loved helping them both. She became known by only "Anne." This routine of Anne and her father was accepted by everyone. Taking Anne with him, naively she never realized her father used her as a shield to hide his debaucheries from her mother. Her innocence and great love for her father would not allow her to admit to his drunken conditions as they returned to the palace. The carriage drivers and his helpers were always discreet in handling and helping her father back into his private study in the palace where no one was allowed.

It was one of those trips when Anne was enjoying her usual visit with the couple. As Anne grew into teen years, her father's behavior became a concern to her. As she was chatting with the old couple about party plans in the next few months at the palace, she became fascinated with a pantomime artist performing in the street. She stepped outside the shop and just then she heard shots ring out from the tavern down the street and heard a ruckus that boiled over into the street. She looked back at the old couple, then back toward the tavern where she saw her father burst out, staggering and falling into the street. With a gasp, Anne jumped and ran toward him screaming. There her father lay dead with blood flowing out of his chest. As she screamed and cried out, a man grabber her and pulled her away. He rushed her back to the old couple then hurried of to get help.

The couple was very protective of Anne and wouldn't let her go out to see what was happening. The old man went out to investigate. He rushed back in and told the woman to get Anne upstairs immediately. Anne was stunned. The woman wanted her to be quiet and just go to bed. After the woman thought Anne was asleep, Anne creped out of bed and looked out the window at the street below. It was dark and she saw soldiers standing outside. She wanted to go home but knew she couldn't. Anne had been taught not to express herself or show emotions or do anything that would be an embarrassment for her family. No one wanted to tell her anything. She was sure that her father was dead and was heart broken. Much later she found out that the man who shot her father discovered that her father had an affair with a man's wife or girlfriend. In the Pub where her father was a regular customer, a brawl broke out and the man pulled a gun and shot her father.

The funeral was like a surrealistic bad dream for Anne. She seemed in a dazed state since that horrible scene first burst in the street in front of her eyes. She was being taken in a carriage and aware of something white laying over it. She was crying until her head was hurting. A woman held her, comforting her while they were involved in a long line of carriages behind them. They were waiting for the King's carriage to join the procession. The long line of black carriages lined the front of the palace. There were throngs of people milling around everywhere on the first floor and in the garden.

Later, Anne took refuge upstairs in her own room. As she looked out the windows, the long line of carriages seemed to become black dots in front of her teary eyes. Many times she stood looking out at the rolling hills, dotted with sparse green trees. There were no gardens, lawns or trees in the front of the palace since cultured foliage represented a hiding place and an open invitation for criminals. Beautiful gardens were placed where the palace residence could enjoy them in the U shape area behind it. Most palaces were very plain in the front. There were no medieval moats to protect the castles or palaces. Anne spent much of her time in the beautiful rose garden in the palace's back courtyard. Anne's strong ties with her father had seemed inconceivable to even think of him dying and being without him. The thought of dealing with life without him had never occurred to her. It catapulted her from a vivacious, feverous girl into a more serious somber young woman. In time, as she resolved her grief she came out of her cocoon into a strong willed young woman. Her mother and older sister combined was no match for her determination. She seemed to be a combination of a strong man in mind and a feminine woman in all her ways.

The King could not leave the three woman and their servants without masculine overseer for the farms of the providence. While the wife and daughters had nothing to do with the death of their father, he insisted on having his most restrictive assistant move into the place and take charge. By law, the palace was owned by the three women equally but they followed the command of the king. The King's assistant, Sebastian, was devious and ambitious. His constant confrontations with Anne only intrigued his male ego. Consequently she became his number one challenge. He felt he had fallen out of favor with the King when he was ordered to move away from the excitement of social life in the Paris area to oversee the farm lands. However, as time passed he saw this as an opportunity to marry into the royal family. His frail forty year old body was no match for Anne's youthful dexterity; therefore it became a mind game. With his expertise as a chess player each opponent became Anne in the recesses of his mind. He was constantly planning moves to manipulate her, not only in the chess game.

When Anne was 18, it was time for her "coming out party" or presentation ceremony and was about to begin. She wore satin shoes with buttons. Her dress was pale blue. Anne was feeling very happy, excited, and exuberant but knew she must be in control! "It is a ball for me! I am so excited, I can hardly stand it. On one hand I feel very beautiful but also silly" were her thoughts. The trumpets were sounding off as she walked down the stairway. Some men of royalty met her half way and escorted her the rest of the way, which was very comforting as she became terrified. Two of the young men seemed very interested in her. She was almost too scared to enjoy the evening. She wanted to just sit down but her mother urged her to talk to the King, whom she hated. He hadn't even watched her as she came down the stairway. She bowed and spoke to him, he took her hand and kissed it but to her he was just so sloppy. After all the fluff and fun, everyone was enjoying the ball, no longer paying any attention to Anne. She didn't even know where her mother was as she seemed to have disappeared. She felt very alone and was feeling she had rather be out in the garden near the roses and the green grass.

After that evening, the two young men became competitive suitors now that Anne was datable age. Dating was fun for Anne. She enjoyed the company of men more than women. On one occasion while riding in a carriage with one of them, they were laughing and joking when the carriage suddenly came to an abrupt halt, jerking them both backwards. The door swung open, two men dressed in black capes dragged her suitor out, shot him. He fell face down in a pool of blood while the killers raced away on their horses. The carriage spun around to take her back to the palace without even checking the young man. Here was another man DEAD because of Anne, she thought, as she had taken on the guilt of her father death even though it had nothing to do with her. Just because she had been with him just a short time earlier, in her young mind, she put the blame on herself. She felt that if she had insisted they go back to the palace, the shooting would not have occurred.

In the restless 1700s there were those who had plenty and those who had nothing; two classes – upper and lower. Only a very small middle class existed. It was from this linage Sebastian have been born. He had inherited his philosopher father's brilliant mind but also his mother's devious, scheming ambition. It was her influence from early childhood that had driven him to attaining his high and close position with the King. Anne's family lands were the richest farmland in the kingdom. With proper management it helped fill the King's coffer.

Sebastian began to realize that he had not fallen from the King's grace but the King had laid open the way for him to become part of the royal family by marrying into Anne's family. Anne's older sister,

Katherine, held no challenge for him. It was Anne's ever present independence that sparked his ambitious nature to tame her.

One of her independent acts was her insistence in working in the rose garden. Side by side with the gardener she would dig into the soil to plant and care for the roses. This garden was more of an experimental garden to test, grow and develop new and various types of roses. This was not an act for a lady of the royal court. This was a time when Sebastian could observe Anne since in all other circumstances she avoided him every chance she could. His living and working quarters were over the grand ballroom on the back side of the Palace that overlooked the rose garden. Few words were ever exchanged between Sebastian and Anne. Those few repetitive statements by Anne were usually "But you are NOT my father!" His mocking reply was "No, Dear Lady Anne, I am not your father but I am chosen to be head of this household by your King." She knew of his commoner birth and resented his impertinent attitude.

The Palace was built in a "U" shape with the family quarters overlooking the gardens in the center of the U, however, in her youth Anne had chosen one of the guest rooms at the top of the stairs because it overlooked the drive, the expansive view of the valley and the Village far below.

Sebastian was not the only man who was constantly observing Anne in the rose garden and stables. Marc had been born in the village to the older couple who looked after Anne on her father's village visits. His father had been a Priest and his mother a nun. When she became pregnant with him, they were both excommunicated from the Catholic Church. With great compassion for them, Anne's father had provided the shop and plenty of work for them to make enough money to send Marc away to school at the age of eleven. Before that, Anne and Marc had played together. Anne's father had provided an irrevocable contract guaranteeing Marc a lifetime position as a royal palace guard when he returned to the village at age twenty. This protected him from the petty gossip regarding his birth and the rejection of the church.

While being a member of the royal family necessitated maintaining diplomatic relations with the Catholic Church, Anne's father had remained a frowned upon rebel as far as the church was concerned. This protection of an excommunicated priest and nun had not made him popular with the hierarchy of the church. Her father was a rare member of the royal family who had always made himself available to the people of his domain. With his relative, the King, he himself had always felt like an underdog or castaway since he had been assigned the farming areas of the kingdom; thus he strongly identified with the abandoned priest and nun. Anne had inherited his rebel nature as well as his thirst for knowledge. His thirst for gluttonous behavior with commoners had been his downfall, yet even his untimely death made the villagers feel that he was "one of us." This intensified their loyalty toward Anne more so than to other members of the royal family. She had always been a part of the village whereas other members rarely visited the village. Due to her father's compassion for the villagers and nearby communities who were the caretakers of the major farming lands of the kingdom, they remained very loyal and sanctified Anne more than her mother and sister.

Anne was thoroughly a royal lady in every respect but like her father, there were two sides of her personality. From her royal heredity, she had learned her lessons and training for royalty well but like her father who was the second son, she was the second daughter. Her father had taught her to be prepared for duties like management of the estate. Still too young to assume leadership, according to the King, Sebastian's "do-as-I-say attitude" spawned the rebel in Anne even more. Much of Anne's compassionate side has been developed by Marie, the ex- nun, who had more influence over her than her own mother. Her mother was usually too busy with royal activities and travel with her older daughter to give much attention to Anne's upbringing. She probably spent more time with Marie than her mother. Anne helped Marie with her baking then played as a street vendor selling baked goods. The Villagers loved buying breads and pastries from the beautifully dressed young Princess. This also helped cultivate their love and respect for Anne and her family. Marie's undaunted love and respect for God even thought the church rejected her, her husband and son, had left a lasting mark upon Anne's attitude. Anne saw the living God of love expressed through Marie and John. Anne assisted them in their visiting and caring for the sick. Taking responsibility for those less fortunate was second nature for her. Marc had received the same youthful training but from the age of eleven, the strong influence on him had been military expectations, somewhat burying his inherited compassionate nature.

It was shortly after and because of the death of Anne's father that Marc returned to assume his military duty as head of the palace guard and household staff. This title positioned his living quarters and work area directly below Sebastian's. Ironically, both men could be seen at their windows, one above the other looking out over the garden when Anne was working or sitting reading in the rose garden. The gardeners could observe both men but discretely ignored them. Other household staff members had rooms on the third floor while Sebastian's staff occupied rooms on the second floor, both facing the stables instead of the garden area.

Anne developed a game in her mind of black and white. Sebastian representing the black Knight with his black players and Marc was the white Knight with his white players; more or less a chess game in her head. Some times she would sit in the garden sketching these little game characters with no one suspecting who they represented. She looked upon Sebastian as a non-existing human being while she secretly began looking up to Marc as sort of a saint who had come to protect her from the evil Sebastian. She kept her distance from both men as neither could be proper suitors.

Pressure was being put on Anne by her Mother, Aunts and Uncles to begin courtships leading to her marriage. She accepted this expected responsibility as her obligation but in all the lands, both near and far, there was no man who combined the character traits of both her father and John, the two men Anne most admired. At every opportunity she avoided discussions or potential commitments and "putting it off until she had more time." Anne managed to stay very busy overseeing health and welfare of the villagers, plus her art, gardening and general duties allowed her no time for social visits by or to potential suitors.

When she made trips to the village, she insisted that Marc personally escort her since there were rumors of road bandits that inhibited the once freedom of travel for the nobility. In other areas of France isolation of nobility became more prevalent as the brewing rebellious nature of the common people grew louder. Anne's family realm remained untouched by those rumors because of her father's rule and her continued care of the commoners. The underlying reason for Anne's insistence for Marc to escort her outside the palace was more for companionship of a man. She missed her father's company. Since she had known Marc in childhood and his parents had been a great influence in her life, she trusted him and him alone.

Anne's relationship with her father was like no other. They had intelligent, challenging conversations filled with humor, laughter and teasing. He loved to tease her feminine innocence yet when challenged on historical events or right judgments, he could flare with tyrannical expectations. Anne worked hard to meet his challenges and expectations. Now three years had passed with virtually no stimulating conversations with any man and she longed for those challenging debates.

Knowing both her and Marc's positions, there was no intent other than the hope of recapturing their early childhood friendship and companionship of a man. Marc's thirst for knowledge could be challenging for Anne's. He could trick her on various subjects. She loved the intellectual bantering.

As the months flew by Marc's companionship went far beyond any expectations she may have had. Not only was her intelligence and humor met in kind but sensitivity and gentleness that she had not experienced since her father was killed. For Marc, it was an adventure into himself since his military schooling had limited his sensitive expression. Beyond the trips to the village, Anne would sneak Marc into the palace library so that he could access the wide range of books. They found secret ways around the palace to spend time chatting away. Much of it was in and around the stables.

Times were hard all over France, yet their realm continued to flourish in productivity, peace and harmony. Regardless of Sebastian's reports, the King was forced to overlook many seemingly discretions due to the success of the territory while other areas were experiencing so much unrest. Sebastian's reports were pushed aside as minor for the Kingdom. The King wanted Sebastian in control but he did want him to "rock the boat" either. The King tempered Sebastian's ambitions with "patience, dear Sebastian."

Without the notice of Sebastian or others, Anne and Marc opted for a small open carriage so that the driver would no longer be required. Marc now did the driving that gave them opportunities to take off the main road, visiting small lakes where they just sat and talked – and talk they did! Both were like champagne bottles, suddenly released and the bubbles burst forth in form of exciting conversational exchanges. Much of their young lives had been forced to be of a very serious nature, now with the freedom to just be, both opened areas of joy and happiness neither had ever experienced. Marc's mother supplied special goodies for them that gave them excuses to stop and enjoy their snacks. These respites became longer and longer from only a short time to hours. Anne often tucked away one of her favorite poetry books to read to Marc. Occasionally, Anne's father had laid his head in her lap while she read poems to him, so she insisted Marc do the same. This was the beginning of their intimacy. Marc loved to hear her melodious voice and felt it vibrate into his heart. This was their childhood friendship rekindled with the richness of adult intelligence they shared from different points of view. Their friendship had grown into a very powerful adult love.

All went smoothly for the entire summer until one day when they pulled into the stable area when Sebastian was in his assistance's office overlooking the stables and happened to look down toward the stable in time to see Marc gently lift Anne from the carriage without any hesitation and momentarily held both her hands between his. Blood rushed to Sebastian's head. He whirled to his assistant demanding to know what was going on down there pointing his finger toward the stable. The assistant looked out the window then nonchalantly and calmly replied that they were returning from their routine visit to the village where Anne worked with the villagers and Marc escorted and drove the carriage for her. He assured Sebastian that Anne had been doing the same routine since she was a child. He also stated that Anne and Marc had been childhood friends. "This hardly looks like child's play" Sebastian sarcastically stated. He paced back and forth then bolted out of the room in great anger knowing his intentions to eventually marry Anne so that he would then be in the royal family. The wheels began turning in his head and he cunningly made plans. Sebastian ordered Marc to appear before him. Marc reported and in an obedient military manner. After extensive questioning, Marc would not be tricked by Sebastian. He demanded to know why it was necessary for the Captain of the Royal household guards to chauffeur Anne to the village when any of the drivers whose duty it was to do just that.

He quickly added duties to Marc's schedule and ordered him to find a suitable chauffeur for Anne.

Sebastian often dined with the family. That night, along with the family and a few guest, Anne and Sebastian sat across the table from one another. He cunningly drew Anne into a conversation about her work with the villagers. While Anne usually ignored or talked very little to him, he knew how to get to her. She always grew excited and enthusiastic over her work she would forget it was Sebastian asking the questions. When he knew he had her in a vulnerable position he let go with in his placating manner so as to embarrass her so much that she would never dare ask Marc to drive for her again. He made it sound as though the whole palace and everyone in it was left in jeopardy because Anne had borrowed the Captain of the guards for a mere chauffeur's job for her convenience or entertainment. The family and guests were lulled into Sebastian's charm and sarcastic humor. Anne's eyes flashed as she realized how he had set her up to embarrassed her. Usually extremely gracious, Anne stood up, glared at Sebastian, threw her napkin down on the table and stomping out of the room retorting "Please excuse me!"

One area of the place that had always been off-limits to the family was the cells for prisoners near the palace guard's resident rooms. The prison was small and only a holding area until the prisoners could be moved to the major prison in Paris. On occasions, Anne had heard sounds coming from that area but her family knew very little about what went on there. She really did not want to know. She was furious when she found out that Sebastian had assigned Marc duty in the prison during any of the hours that they might have spent together.

Anne's father, knowing her fiery independent disposition, had foreseen her possible calamities in her adult years. In his will he had provided for her certain decision making rights if the situation required it. From girlhood to young womanhood, she never had any desire to use those rights after her father's death.

Unaware of these rights, Sebastian felt quite smug in his power over the family. He did not know it but he had openly declared war with Anne that night at the dinner table. Anne had stomped out of the dining room and went straight to her room. She paced back and forth, growing angrier as she thought about Sebastian. Many of Anne's childhood dolls still graced the corner of her room. She glared at them, walked over, picked up one and started to hurl it across the room but stopped. She gathered all of them up and piled them in a big pile by her bedroom door.

Anne Marie sat down in front of the mirror, reached into the drawer and pulled out a pair of scissors. Her scoped out neckline was filled in high neck lace. Anne took the scissors and began cutting away the lace. She unfastened the back of her dress and lifted out the lace, then arranged her breast in the dress in a more exposed manner. She took her hair and pinned it up in the back. She pinched her cheeks, powdered her face, put color on her lips and sprayed herself with perfume. She took a deep breath and stood erect to view herself in the mirror. Anne liked what she saw – as though for the first time she was seeing herself as a young woman instead of a teen age girl. She picked up a few more childhood mementoes and chunked them into the pile at the door to be stored in the attic the next day.

By now, the dining group had moved into the drawing room for after dinner drinks and conversation, which stopped suddenly when Anne appeared in the doorway with her new grownup look. Anne walked straight to the dinner guests and in her most gracious adult manner apologizes to them for her behavior at the dinner table, noticeably avoiding Sebastian's glare. Her charm and wit then monopolized the rest of the evening to the point of ostracizing Sebastian totally from the guests. After the goodbyes were said, Anne headed for the library to search for her father's will. She then went straight for a particular section, pulled out an arm load of books and returned to her room. Where her childhood mementoes had graced the feminine child's room, the shelves were now replaced with the books from the library. When Anne sat in the garden reading, no one bothered to notice that the poetry and literature books were now replaced with management and rulership books, just as she had been programmed to do by her father when the time was right.

In front of her Mother and sister, she began questioning Sebastian regarding many areas of management of the estate. While he had long sought her attention, he became quite uncomfortable at the attention she was giving him that might expose his clever manipulation of the books of the estate affecting the finances related to the King. Sebastian had never confronted a woman with Anne's cunning feminine intelligence.

He was becoming quite cautious about his answer as time went on. When Anne demanded to be shown the records and accounts, Sebastian refused. Anne ordered and set up a reading of her father's will for all those involved. Much to Sebastian's dismay, not only did it clearly state Marc's guaranteed position wit the household "until his death" but verified Anne's right to take charge of any way she deemed necessary for the welfare of the estate.

Sebastian knew that the King had the final say over what went on at the Palace and he felt he could still manipulate him but he also realized he had made an enemy of Anne and after all, she was related to the King who assumed guardianship of the family after the death of Anne's father. It seemed that the entire household became allies with Anne. A very precautions position, indeed, Sebastian had put him self in. He took the defeat with grace and charm using every bit of cleverness he could muster. For a while everything seemed to move along harmoniously.

New responsibilities in Marc's charge were occupying his every moment. Anne could see this and did not make any further issue regarding the carriage driver being sent with her on her village excursions. The new adult woman responsibilities also made her realize the impossible direction her feelings for Marc had been going. It was no longer child's play so she absorbed herself in the daily business of running the large estate. She took a room as an office as far away from Sebastian as possible. Her Mother and sister took no interest in running the estate. The more involved Anne became, the less time she had for thinking about her own personal feelings and needs. For now, it seemed that as she became more in charge of the palace business, the pressure for her to find a suitable husband became less and focused more on her older sister. She seemed to have let go of her sweet and precious times with Marc.

On the other hand, Marc, too, had been besieged with responsibilities and problems to resolve that took up his every waking hour. Regardless of their childhood friendship, as adults they each had their respective positions to fill. Each with a separate path with the total impossibility of any kind of emotional connection, they both accepted their positions without question. For awhile, anyway but soon both were longing for the exciting times they had shared.

Mid afternoon, Anne had ridden her horse into the village to get some pastries from Maria. There stood Marc in Maria's shop. Anne was unaware that it was Marc's day off. As soon as she walked into their little shop, there stood Marc out of his uniform, looking dashingly handsome. Somehow, not wearing the uniform took away his formal duties at the place and made it seem suitable for her to share time with him. Maria gave them some wine and fresh pastries she had just baked so they agreed to take it down to the river and have an exciting conversation about a book that Marc had just read. What a happy time it was for the two of them. Minutes flashed into hours. As Marc read from his book, Anne had laid her head in his lap as he had done while she read to him in the past. Afternoon grew into evening, the light began to fade. As Marc closed the book with no more light, he gently reached down to kiss Anne. Passion lit in both of them like a skyrocket going off. One thing led to another and finally they consummated this long time friendship with beautiful love making. Then and there, they knew and accepted that they were very much in love and agreed that they would not stop seeing each other regardless of anyone's attitudes toward their different status.

Anne remembered that there was a small unused cottage in the woods about a mile or so from the palace. This would be their special place to meet. They would be able to pass notes to each other as to when they could meet. Their courtship continued with great love between the two of them. Then, one day, Anne began getting sick in the mornings. Her periods stopped and she began to realize that she might be pregnant. In about two months, the herbalist woman in the village confirmed this to her.

Regardless of taboos, regardless of Anne's family and her duties, regardless especially of Sebastian's attitude, they decided they would run away and marry without anyone knowing about it. Anne never doubted for one minute that this was the right decision but she was besieged with anxiety as well. Anne and Marc met at their exclusive little cabin at the designated time and off they drove in a carriage he had arranged to use. Unfortunately, Sebastian's assistant, over heard their planning the secret marriage. After a long ride, Marc and Anne had only been inside the small chapel long enough to be married when three armed uniformed guards burst in and shot Marc, killing him immediately! Anne grabbed a knife of one of the soldiers and as she started to stab herself in the heart, she fainted. The soldiers grabbed Anne and rushed her out away from Marc's dead bleeding body! When Anne awoke the next day, she was in her own room. She thought it had all been a bad dream but she had bruises on her arms. She donned a robe and rushed down toward the complex where the soldiers lived, crying out for Marc. Just then, one of the older maids approached Anne. Her eyes asked the question. The maid said Marc was dead and all records had been burned -- she grabbed Anne as she fainted again.

For the next few weeks, food and doctors tended Anne who would not leave her room. She wouldn't even go out into her beloved garden. The baby inside her continued to grow until it was impossible for her to be seen anywhere. Anne told no one but Dauphine who was determined to help her. Finally, Anne decided to confide in Maria. Knowing this child was her grandchild; Maria was determined to help Anne regardless of the consequences. The plan was that Anne was to tell her family that she was going to visit Italy for the next few months and would take Dauphine as a companion. Maria had a sister that lived on a nice farm quite a distance from the Palace. Both Anne and Dauphine would stay there all through the pregnancy and birth. John had a brother in Italy so that Anne could write letters to her family; send them to his brother who would then send them to the Palace so that they were coming from Italy. During the time on the farm, Anne would feel that Marc was with her, communicating with her even though she could not see him except in her visions. She felt he told her how happy he was that they had a son. She knew he would be pleased with their child when it was born. When the time came and the baby boy was born, Anne vowed that there was no way anyone would take her child from her! She disregarded a holy man's warning about the child. In the village near where her son was born, she registered him under Marc's sir name, so that her real name wasn't used.

The whole thing would disgrace for her family. How could she produce a peasant's child? Once the child was born, Anne felt she could return to the Palace regardless of anyone's attitude about her child. There were meetings with Sebastian and Anne's mother with political followers of the King. The palace staff was sworn to secrecy. Anne became some what tyrannical with everyone. Again, she took the reins in running the property. There was little Sebastian could do because the King was pleased with progress she made. She adored her son and became two very different people. She was a doting, loving mother to him. No one really knew that the child was Marc's son, Anne made up a story about meeting a royal Prince in Italy that had been killed shortly after they married. Anne could not take him to the village to see his grand parents in the beginning, later with their promise of secrecy, on occasions when she went to the village; they would see him for a short while, never admitting to being the grand parents.

In my present life, I thought I was destined to have a son, even after I had my daughter and years thereafter. When I was quite young, I saw the movie "Gone With The Wind" and even as young as I was, when the little girl was killed riding her pony, it seemed to ring some thing in my head! That scene always remained prominent in my memory. In this French Anne's life, a similar accident happened to her son.

When the boy was around five years old, the King was visiting the palace. By then, the shock of Anne having given birth to this child had died down. Her son was handsome, charming and very intelligent. The King wanted to see the boy ride his pony. He wasn't feeling well and didn't want to ride but he was ordered to ride anyway. A stable boy helped prepare the pony. Anne was not there at that moment, she had gone back to the palace to get something for her son. Just as she was returning, she heard a scream and suddenly remembered the holy man's warning. Her son had taken terrible tumble and was killed instantly! Anne went berserk!! She was screaming and grabbed a whip and began swinging it at the stable boy and everyone, including the KING! Even if she was related, NO one made any attempts on the King's life! This was a death sentence! The King left in a huff! Sebastian followed after him to Paris! Anne's mother and house staff rushed Anne up to her room. Everyone was in a dither as to what to do! Anne was again in a semi-hypnotic state. Again, the one she loved so deeply was dead - and in her mind, guilt besieged her thinking it was her fault again!! First, her father's death, then her pursuer, Marc and NOW her son! If only she had been there, she could have stopped it regardless of the King's order!

While her mother and those closest to her were trying to figure out how to save Anne from sure execution by the King, news came of a young girl in the village that had died. Anne's mother quickly sent one of her staff to secretly offer the family a large sum of money to buy the body. They created a story that Anne was so grieved that her heart stopped beating and she had died. By the time, Sebastian had returned with a new replacement, as ordered by the King. A funeral for Anne Marie was in session.

Meanwhile, in the large attic of the palace, the most trusted servants had quickly created an apartment for Anne to live in and they hid her away there. They had provided all the supplies she would need. Her books and any kind of craft work she would want was provided as was food secretly brought back and forth to her.

The whole palace was involved on the planning for Anne's sister's upcoming wedding just as though Anne had never even existed. No one was allowed to talk about her or ask anything that involved Anne. She just never existed in their respect for her. Anne did have her one very trusted friend, Dauphine. Dauphine and Anne were about the same age. She was in charge of bringing food and necessities to Anne. They had not been terribly close friends even thought they played together as young children, Dauphine's accompanying Anne to the country during Anne's pregnancy, they became very close friends feeling like sisters. Dauphine had not had any schooling so Anne took it upon her self to educate her. As they became closer and closer friends, Anne finally began to smile and laugh again. Her old self seemed to come alive. Along with it, she longed to get out in the garden, in the sunshine, ride, walk, live again! There was NO way it could be done as the King believed she was dead. She had only ONE small round window in which she could look out to the front of the palace. There was very little to see in that direction. As time past she felt entombed in the attic apartment without any way to get out side.

Anne knew there was a whole big world out there and she wanted to be a part of it. Her restlessness began to grow more and more each day. While Dauphine would visit with Anne, Anne would tell her wonderful tales of other lands, other events that take place outside their small world of the palace life. Anne's quick and adventurous mind began conceiving a plan to escape the Palace and that part of France. They could escape during the night and travel to Marseilles. There they could take a ship anywhere in the world. As they talked about it, Dauphine became more and more excited at the prospects of escaping from her servitude life. By her friendship that had developed with Anne, a member of Royalty, she felt a sense of possible opportunity and freedom she had never felt before. Anne had never treated her like a servant but only as a friend.

Little by little the two young women made their plan of escape. No one was to know. Dauphine began collecting things they would need for the trip and bringing to the attic. They made plans to escape when most everyone would be out of the palace. They had condensed the clothing and food they would need as much as they could. Anne managed to take a small amount of jewelry that she planned to sell so that they had travel money and money to live on. She had spent time carefully removing the precious stones so that upon selling them, they could not be traced. They were excited but also quite concerned for their long journey to Marseille. They had to get there one way or another. Anne was a good equestrian but Dauphine had never ridden, so they had to secretly make arrangements for various carriage rides. Finally their secret night arrived when everyone was out of the place. It would take several days to make the trip. Both were filled with tension fearing they would be discovered. After their long, stressful trip, they found a cheap boarding house and got a good rest. Dauphine had never seen a city as large as Marseille and it had been several years since Anne had been to Paris, so they felt they had a reason to see the town and celebrate with their successful escape.

After awhile, in the place they were staying, they went downstairs; they had a good dinner. They asked where they might walk to see the ships, still very excited at the prospect of sailing to a foreign land. With instructions, they headed for the docks. They walked and walked until both realized they were still very tired from the long, long trip. They peeked in a bar where there were a few women. Little did they realize the women were prostitutes. The sailors began buying wine for Dauphine and Anne. The women were very friendly. There was music, dancing, gaiety and laughter. It was good medicine for both young women. The past two or more weeks for the two women had been very stressful so this night was a great sense of unwinding. When Anne was feeling the effects of the wine, she urged Dauphine that they should go back to the Inn.

Yes, it was the beginning of a new life for both young women. Very soon they found out how popular both were with the sailors and soldiers that frequented the port. Since Anne was no longer a virgin, when she felt attracted to a sailor, she felt independently encouraged to have sex with him. The money from the sale of her jewels was running low so when he offered to give her money, she accepted. This went on each time she saw him. When she told Dauphine what was happening, she decided to do the same. The two women realized that it was easy and quick money to have sex with the men. It was far easier and more pleasant than the work as servants that they had been doing, which brought them very little money. For Anne it gave her a sense of revenge and all very new to Dauphine. This was a way to save enough money to sail off to anywhere in the world, except that it came too easy and before long, they were in business together. Since Anne was the smart one and having contributed to the management of the palace and the properties, it was easy for her to set up a business. When they had enough money saved, they didn't sail off to a foreign land but set up a very successful House of Women of the night. Anne was very generous with her girls and ended her servicing men to run the business. As business grew, Anne was always fair to Dauphine as her partner. She was eternally grateful to her as Anne would never have been able to escape had it not been for Dauphine. They were more like sisters than Anne had every been with her real sister.

A few years later, one evening while the two women were sitting in the front garden, just out of sight of their front gate, who but Sebastian was on his way into the house alone! At first, both were terrified and rushed into the house via the back door. Anne grabbed the strongest and most devious and cunning girl she had. She quickly told her what to do. This was Anne's chance once and for all to rid the world of this vicious, mean, hate filled man! The deed was done. Late at night, they dragged the dead Sebastian, with a weight tied around him and slung him in the waters at the nearby dock. They felt a great sense of relief and totally justified in their feat.

Anne and Dauphine would take trips now and then to Italy, Spain, Minorca, Malta and Oran. They were business and pleasure trips as they explored the various seaports and businesses for "the ladies." They were so well established in Marseille that they just never got around to taking that long trip to America or any far away places. The years passed and all their fears went away. By her forties, Anne was very tired of the business. It was around that time that the King arrived in Marseille. He had heard of the Madam of Marseille and he wanted to meet her in person. When Anne saw him standing downstairs, she panicked and sent her servant down to tell him she was not well. He declared that he would return each day until he could see her. For the next ten days he waited but finally brought soldiers that barged into the house, breaking down Anne's bedroom door. Even with age, Anne never lost her beauty. When the King saw her, he was astounded. Anne fell at his feet begging forgiveness and radiated a beauty that bedazzled him. He listened to how Anne had risen from being a servant to becoming one of the most respected Mistresses in France. Knowing her royal upbringing, he was so amazed and sad for her. He told Anne that her mother was near death and needed her more than ever and that her sister's family had moved to America. With his full pardon of her, she agreed to return to the palace.

Through legal channels in Marseille, she signed over all ownerships of properties they had gathered through the years to Dauphine but also offered her a permanent home in the Palace if Dauphine chose to return with her but she declined. She was content with her established home in Marseille.

When Anne arrived and saw her once strong, proud mother withering away and so near death, she knelt beside her bed. When she saw Anne, she said that she could go now, no more pain, she had always known Anne was not dead but could do nothing to find her. Within a few hours of Anne's arrival, her mother left her physical body.

Anne lived out the rest of her life in the palace, no one dared to ask any questions. She maintained just enough staff to look after the home and garden. By now, the farms and surrounding properties have been divided up among the people. Anne could once again tend her garden, sit and read there as well as reminisce over her one true love. Often she would go to the river to sit and read and think about Marc. She could hear him speaking to her and how much they loved each other and that one day they would be together again.

As she lived these past memories, as well as her ventures with Dauphine, she wrote them in her diaries until she had written a book "J'amour le hommes" -- "I loved the men" was the book ever published or was it lost in time?

CHAPTER 10

MARY ANNE - THE NUN

Since early childhood in this present life, I had a somewhat hostile attitude, as well as some fascination for major art supported by the Catholic Church and the beauty of the construction of the many cathedrals. Had I once been a good Catholic or was I always rebelling against any kind of orthodoxy in a male oriented and dominated institution.

I knew that in one life I had been married to the Church. Mary Anne was born in Southern France, probably around Aix-en-Provence or could have been Marseilles. She had an especially close playmate her own age, a boy she loved very much. One day, while they were playing near the water, she saw him drown and could not save him. Within moments as she prayed, she has a vision. With that experience she knew she would never be parted from the soul of her dear departed friend. She was also shown she was to be a nun so that she could heal the sick and save the lives of others.

From that time on in her early childhood she has a strange talent for making people well and showed miraculous powers of healing at an early age. Through the years, she talked with this young boy, especially in her dreams. For a long time her mother hid this ability for fear Mary Anne would be accused of witchcraft, which was common in those days. When she was only about twelve years of age, she and her mother had to move into a convent where her mother could work and felt that Mary Ann would be safe from accusations regarding her rare ability to heal.

The monks and nuns saw this ability in Mary Ann as a gift from God and encouraged her to use it. As she grew into her teen years, it was natural for her to follow the traditions of the Church and became a Novice, dedicated to becoming a nun, even thought inwardly, she has reservations. She felt it was her duty with no other choice. No one ever asked her what she wanted to do or to become. It was assumed that God had sent her to do healing work. She didn't understand because she felt like any normal female. The Nun's life was definitely not Mary Anne's deepest desire. From early youth she had always enjoyed the company of boys. Actually, she preferred playing with boys instead of girls. She seemed to have more in common with them. She loved exploring as well as attempting daring pursuits. Before she lived in the convent, she had been very outgoing. Since living in the convent, she could do little about her personal desires but hold them inside and share with no one. She had become very quiet and withdrawn. By the time her mother died, she knew no one but the nuns and monks.

She worked as a teacher for the children that helped her survive her cloistered life, especially when she would take them on educational trips. In my present life, as younger women came into my life, I began feeling I had been a teacher to them in a previous life. In a specific vision or dream, I saw them with me in Paris exploring the Cathedral of Notre Dame and the arts and crafts along the Scine River. This memory kept occurring as these younger women kept coming into this life. My daughter, niece and others felt it was true and felt the same familiarity.

While Mary Ann's healing ability was not admitted outside the convent, it was known and she was assigned to help Father John Mark, who attended the sick with his medical knowledge and considered a doctor in that era. He was a young monk, very serious in his work and when called upon to go out into the village or countryside, he took Mary Anne along to help him, more or less like a nurse, although he was aware of her unusual healing ability. Once out and away from the others, both John Mark and Mary Anne tended to be more outgoing and had more fun. They shared their inner feelings more than they could in the convent or monastery. He was the only person she had ever told about her doubts regarding becoming a nun.

For the next few years, their working together with the sick became known for their powerful healing abilities. It was mostly Mary Anne's healing touch, which she never understood or felt that it was any special ability. As her powers became known, gossip preceded her to the Pope in Rome. Was this from God or witchcraft? He ordered her to Rome to be examined. She was terrified that she would be named as a witch. The trip seemed to take forever for Mary Anne. She was sent to prove guilt or innocence of witchcraft. She was the youngest nun to appear in Rome. When she finally stood before the Pope, she was trembling so much, she could hardly talk. He ordered her to perform her healing on a sick man they brought to her. She declared that God's power was not to be tested. The Pope apologized and talked her down from her anger. She said "Forgive me your Holiness but God has directed me to say these things. You sit here in all your splendor and have far greater powers of healing than me, your humble servant." He asked her if she knew anything about witchcraft. She said she did not. Advisors to the Pope insisted that she be tested, so she was tested in many ways and examined for any kind of witchcraft markings on her body, which was very humiliating! It required her disrobing in front of men, which she had never done before.

She waited for his verdict in great anxiety fearing she had spoken much too strongly to the Pope. Unexpected healings occurred among the examiners without her obviously doing anything. Finally, great compliments and tributes were heaped upon her. The Pope declared

"Child of God, I humble myself before you. You will do God's work for men more than many others. Your life is blessed by a far greater soul than me. Goodbye, leave on your way and return to do God's bidding." She vowed silence for a certain length of time. When the Pope released her to return home, she could give him no answer. He understood her vow of silence. She was carried as an honorary during a sacred holiday parade. Children rode on their father's shoulders to see her. This, too, was so embarrassing and humiliating she couldn't wait to return home. Seeing Rome was a miracle to her. She saw miracles of inventions but she also saw into the hearts of many that surrounded the Pope and was disturbed by what she felt. People gathered along the way to see this mysterious num of great mystical powers.

Far from towns and villages on the return, she had a vision that perhaps was far beyond her comprehension. It was the world in the future generations, mankind in an almost godless state, many future inventions as well as sight of her own next two lives. She vowed to be a servant of God no matter what life held for her.

When she returned home, she was greeted with great honor but she wanted no part of it. She refused to see anyone. With tears in her eyes, alone in her small cell she prayed "Oh God, forgive me for speaking to your Holiness in this manner. I see now my voice often speaks out in anger which is me, not God. I vow to be still when those in authority, as the Pope, speaks to me. I vow to be a servant of God forever." She locked herself in her room for days and nights with no food, only water. When her body was tired, she saw many visions of her life in this world. She vowed to be strong and conquer all that was given. She fasted and continued having visions of future generations unintentionally developing her psychic awareness.

As her body grew weaker and weaker, she finally came out of her room. She wanted to see Father John Mark only so that they could continue their good works together in healing the sick. She told only him of the visions she has seen. While she did not understand love between a man and a woman, she felt her love for and from Father John Mark was of God. After a time, she returned to her work with Father John Mark. They again began working together. They would take long walks and talk of many things, time passed, maybe years.

On one of their trips out in the country side they were to tend a farmer's sick son. When it was time to leave, storm clouds were gathering. They had not gone far when a terrible rain storm hit with flashes of lightening and heavy thunder. There was no way to return to their homes. There was no place for them to take shelter but a small barn that was stacked with hay. They were tired and hungry. What an awkward situation. They were both very tired and collapsed on the hay and fell fast asleep. The cold air caused Mary Anne roll over and moved closer to him in her sleep. In his sleep, he rolled over toward her. When they awoke to see into each others so close, he put his arm around her and held her close. With a natural instinct, they could not resist kissing. She had wonderful feelings flow through her body that she had never felt before. As luck would have it, both were very passionate people, neither had participated in any kind of sexual activities, but nature took over within both of them. Their natural instincts kicked in. Their hearts were racing in tune to each other. Both felt unbelievable bliss that neither even understood. She had never felt such bliss and joy. Mary Anne was happier than she had ever been in her life. It was as though God had brought them together to experiences this feeling of bliss. They laughed and cried until they fell fast asleep. In the early morning hours she awoke when she rolled over onto a cutting tool buried in the hay and cut a deep gash in her back. John Mark dressed the wound and knew he must rush her back to the convent where the wound could be better treated.

The sun came up on such a beautiful day. The fields were wet and green with the sunlight dancing all around them. At first, both were embarrassed, but as they finally talked about what had happened between them. Both felt it was a gift from God but others around them might never see it that way. They agreed that it would never happen again and it was to be their deepest secret. Neither would tell anyone. That seemed to be their plan; however, within the next six weeks to two months, Mary Anne was constantly sick. When she was well enough after the cut on her back, she was called in to see the Mother Superior, who asked how she could have a hole in her skin and not in her robe. Tearfully she confessed. She was forced to wear a mark of this experience. She did not understand her continued sickness and was feeling very alone not being able to see or talk to Father John Mark. When she did began feeling better, the other nuns noticed that she seemed to be gaining weight in her stomach area. It kept growing until their vowed secret was very observable! If she had ever been cloistered before, it was nothing like it was now. The nuns refused to allow Father John Mark to contact or see her. He was confused and could not understand until finally through the small hole in the wall of the Convent, he saw Mary Anne at a distance and knew immediate why he was not allowed to talk to her or see her. He was dismissed since he had broken his vows of celibacy and asked to leave the province.

Father John Mark planned to leave as directed but was confused and distraught for he genuinely loved Mary Anne. He had a fight going on within himself as his commitment to God and to what he had done to Mary Anne. After the battle raged within him, he finally came to a decision. He returned to the hole in the wall day after day until one day Mary Ann was walking within calling distance to her. He called to her to please listen to him. She walked over to the wall. He begged her to leave the Convent as he must leave the Monastery. They could be married and raise their child together. They could find a way to live in the outside world. Just as Mary Anne was listening and considering it, the Mother Superior of the Convent saw her standing at the wall and ordered her to return inside immediately. From then on, if she wanted to walk outside, she was accompanied by another nun.

Weeks past until it was time for her to deliver the baby. What pain she felt and who could help her. She never felt so alone in her life. The nuns delivered the baby and rushed it off without Mary Anne even seeing it to know if it was a boy or girl. From that time on she was kept in a small room much like a prisoner. She was ordered to never ask about the baby or mention anything about it. If she was withdrawn in her early years, she was completely withdrawn from everyone now. The nuns were ordered to deny any knowledge of her unusual healing powers. The code of silence took hold of the convent.

With this disastrous experience plus her visions of future lives. As time passed she became more and more disheartened, more and more bitter. She refused to use her amazing healing powers that seemed to slip away. The Mother Superior ordered her to only wear a red robe with a mark on it; therefore, she did not want to be seen at all. There were times when she walked for hours in the nearby woods. She became too sad to even cry. She read and read but nothings satisfied her. Her hatred for Mother Superior had grown. As the Mother Superior grew near death, she asked the "branded nun" to forgive her but Mary Ann refused. She expressed no love for anyone or anything.

After years passed, John Mark returned to see her. Once again she felt the same longing to be with him. Love began blossoming in her heart and he asked her again to leave with him and help him in his medical work. Feeling she had lost her powers, she felt she would serve no purpose for him, plus she was filled with guilt over him being defrocked, excommunicated and forced to leave the Monastery. Again, she refused to go with him. When he left, she knew she would never see him again. She cried and cried until her heart felt empty. When she went for a walk in the woods, an elf like creature followed her. When she turned to see it, it seemed to melt in a puddle of water. A bird landed on her hand and fell and died. This confirmed to her that she was no long in God's sight but filled with evil forces. She stood so alone in the woods with the light of God gone from her more so than ever before since she first felt it when her friend drowned in youth. No matter how much she prayed and worked but nothing brought back this warm glow she had always felt. She now believed she no longer could live among men and should live among those condemned to die.

Guilt ruled her life so much so that she contacted the Pope and asked that he send her to a leprosy colony. He agreed so that it was an opportunity to leave the Convent and to serve God in a far away island allocate to leprosy. While she knew almost nothing about leprosy, she thought anything would be better than her imprisonment within the Convent! For the rest of her life, she tended the sick until she finally contacted leprosy, too. She prayed to God to let her take all the pain from the people there so that when she died, she was taking it with her. She had lived many years tending the sick until her death. On her last day of life, she was reliving that one happy moment with Father John Mark when they both felt love, joy and happiness. She died reliving her one sexual ecstasy.

That is all I ever received about Mary Ann's life. I don't know exactly where she went. I feel she never returned and that Father John Mark did leave and tended the sick just as a good doctor would. I feel that each continued to hold a special place in their hearts for the other for the rest of their lives. It seems that there was a war at the time and he volunteered to serve as a doctor, where he was killed.

I made a visit to Europe in the early 1970's. At the time, my daughter had graduated from High School and was living at the LaLanne home with her best friend, Janet. She got a job and seemed content with her life. I felt a new sense of freedom after long years of a feeling of "entrapment" from early pregnancy and the responsibility of raising a child alone. I was hoping to make a new life for myself somewhere in Europe. I worked to make it possible for me to return to Europe once again.

While in Europe, from Geneva, after visiting Lausanne, I planned to go to Marseilles but decided to go to Nice, France instead. I just didn't want to go to Marseilles for a reason I did not understand. With the revelation of a life lived in France, ending up as a madam in Marseilles, I understood why I didn't want to go there in this life. I ended up renting an apartment in Monte Carlo where I found out that the martyred patron Saint Devota's body was brought from Corsica in a boat guided by a dove. She became the patron Saint of both Monte Carlo and Corsica. Miracles were attributed to her there afterwards. That seemed intriguing considering I had mysterious visit by doves for several years. It began on a Sunday when three Sundays in a row, a dove flew into a large picture window of the house I lived in and killed itself on a street named Sierra Bonita - beautiful mountain. Never had I seen a more beautiful mountain than the one behind Monte Carlo. The word for mountain in French is Montague. Years later I discovered that I had ancestors named Montague. Another ancestral name related to the Montagues was Latane. Reverend Lewis Latane, born in Jovan, Guyenne, France was a French Huguenot minister that escaped France for England, later to Virginia where he was a minister for many years.

I, too, became an ordained minister.

In an apartment in Los Angeles before going to Europe, three days before Easter I was awakened by a loud scream in my opened window. I jumped up scaring two doves off my ledge. During that time, I kept getting things about Malta but found no meaning or connection. The first man I dated when I arrived in Monte Carlo was born in Oran, Algeria, another was a young film producer who had just finished shooting a film in Malta. I drew a triangle between Malta, Oran and Monte Carlo and had a very strong feeling that it was very important for me or some kind of major connection. Strangely, long before I had any plans to go to Europe, I had drawn a triangle from Lake Geneva to Malta and equal distance was Oran with Monte Carlo at the top. I stayed in Monte Carlo for seven months.

In Aix-en-Provence there was a church of St. Jean de Malta dating from the 13th century. When my daughter was in her pre teens, if I had the money, I wanted to send her to a school in Europe and had selected one in Aix-en-Provence, known as a University town with many cultural opportunities. The events became too numerous to be coincidental. I have a never ending quest to visit and discover more about past life connection in various European countries. Slowly the missing pieces of my Soul's puzzle are revealed to me.

$\mathcal{CHAPTER}$ 11

LEANNE OF BELGIUM

July 31, 1968 (Regression)

"Go to the birth of this life now, Ann." "I hear a baby crying -- crying. The father is upset and pacing the floor -- "it's a girl, not a son." He is so upset. He was so sure it would be a boy. The mother, in her pain, feels his disappointment and feels she is a failure to him. The child feels it too and cries all the more. "NO, I don't want to live here, let me go back." "No, Ann work this life now."

Then I connected with a vision I had earlier of a life in Belgium when I was the daughter of a ship builder that by the time Leanne was in her teens he had become one of the wealthiest families in the community. Her mother died and her father married a beautiful statuesque youthful wife. Her step-mother had never been terribly fond of her "ugly duckling" step daughter. Her interest was her social life and social standing. My name was Leanne and unfortunately my genes followed my father's ancestors - short, dumpy, large breast and average looks.

Now I see a little girl playing by a dock area. It is sort of a nice bay area. People are selling fish. The little girls move in and out of the areas, teasing and mischievously bothering the adults. A carriage goes by with a beautiful lady and a handsome young boy a few years older than the girls. The girls stop and watch. I know that I love this little boy -- he seems so elegant. While my father is wealthy, he is not elegant like this lad. Many days I see him and he sees me but tries not to look at me.

Now I am in school with a private tutor. There are five of us, he is one of us. My, how handsome and elegant he is. I am the daughter of a simple boat builder. Poor dear boy, his beautiful mother is dead and he must work to support himself. My father pays for his schooling. It is a strange twist of fate for us. I laugh at him, he is so very proud. Oh, but my, he is so beautiful. God never created a young man so beautiful of face as this. I do have problems with him. He is so proud and embarrassed now that he depends on my father's training him for our business. He knows I remember when he rode by in the elegant carriage of his elegant mother - a princess without a country. Ho, ho, what funny ways life has. I will play up to my father. He will see that he marries me if that is what I want. Yes, he is what I want and he is what I shall have.

Jonathan had an elegance way beyond all others there and even as a little girl, Leanne loved him and set her mind that she would marry him when they grew up. In the beginning, he just ignored Leanne and would hardly look at her or talk to her. He was obligated to work for her father even as a child. Leanne's father's shipyard provided most of the villagers a livelihood one way or another.

The hills were green and fertile as we walked in the shade of a tree lined road. Suddenly we heard a wagon thundering down the road behind us. We stepped aside to let it pass when all of a sudden one of the drivers yelled "Run for your life - run -- run now!" We fled into the forest without knowing why. Just as we were a safe distance away we heard the thundering of horses. There were many soldiers on horseback and were the prestigious King's guards. We considered them as normally quite peaceful. This was unusual so we just stood there in disbelief. I thought about the poor man who shouted his warning to us. What would happen to him? So many soldiers for just one old man - what could he have done? We waited until the thundering hoofs were no longer heard. There was something amiss -- an ere feeling lay across the meadow. We stood in the opening for a moment and then heard the distant thundering of hooves returning. Again we dashed back in to the woods out of sight. Why were they riding with such gusto? In our peaceful land we had never seen anything like this. Perhaps, it was related to the King's visit.

Only a fortnight ago we stood at the harbor watching the King sail off into the distance on his peace mission to our out lying empires. We were a people who understood our own nature. We knew that warring nature only destroyed. That is why we had maintained peace for six generations. There were crops to be harvested and boats to sail. The mornings were filled with everyone scurrying around doing his or her job to fulfill the needs of all. The ship decks were polished before passengers boarded. The harbor was a busy place from day break until well past noon. Our ships sailed on the morning tide. There were hundreds of workers in my father's shipping business. He built them, sailed them, sold them - anything that could be done he did. He owned surrounding farm lands that fed our people. He was a quiet man at home but oh so loud when aroused.

As Leanne grew into adulthood, she was a short brunette with large breasts that gave her a heavier appearance. As far back as Leanne could remember, the servants seemed more her family. As an only child, she had few playmates in her own social standing but played with the children of the docks near her father's ship building business. When the servants did their shopping on the docks, she was free to play with the other children. Her father had little time and paid little attention to her. When he did, he was teaching her things fathers taught to their sons. Since he had but one child, no doubt he was disappointed he had a daughter instead of a son. She was a bright little girl. Her father's teachings gave her an interesting perspective both from a male point of view as well as a woman's. Since she spends much of her formative years playing alone, she created games that involved watching people, sometimes mimicking them. She loved observing the many different types of personalities around her from royalty, politicians, and socialites to the fish wives, dock worker and beggars. In her games, she manipulated these different personalities like puppets. She was exceedingly successful manipulating her father as well as other men and women. The female household staff members could generally see through her childish manipulations but even they got caught in her web occasionally.

Leanne looked upon her step-mother as a queen who rarely passed her way. Her father not only built ships but owned a ship line from passenger ships to a fleet of fishing ships and freighters. She enjoyed the fish market and dock people more than her society friends and relatives. This did not set well with Kathryn. Leanne learned rapidly from her private tutors but she also learned from the dock people. She could switch dialects as needed. At an early age, she set her ambitions on marrying Jonathan, her primary obsession. His background and ambitions were the opposite of Leanne's. He watched longingly the rich and socially prominent and longed to be accepted in those circles. Jonathan's mother was accepted when she was alive but with a questionable background. His handsome smile set ladies' hearts afire from all walks of life and all ages.

Jonathan's limited education did not limit him as he was quite intelligent. What he lacked in formal intellectual studies, he made up for in charm and personality. He had an inborn lust to be socially accepted. Because of Leanne's social position and hoping to learn as much as possible about society, he would tolerate her following him about and constantly talking to him, even as he worked. Aggravated thought he might be, since Leanne was the daughter of the owner, he could do nothing about her hanging around him at work. Little did he realize that from a very young age, Leanne has set her mind that she would marry him when she was grown. Little did he know that she memorized almost every word he uttered. As soon as she got home, she kept a log on Jonathan. She knew everything about him, his favorite foods, activities, even the qualities in women that gleaned his attention. She recorded his every desire. She knew how he longed to go out to sea. He daydreamed of ventures in foreign lands. Since she had traveled to foreign ports with her family, she could entice him with stories about her travels.

As Leanne reached her teen years, her beauty had not improved. She knew that the one thing that she did have was her family's social connections, money and ships, which Jonathan had no way of getting on his own. She knew she could outsmart any woman to whom he might be attracted. With all his good looks and charm, no socialite woman could ever been seen with him, much less marry him. He had to achieve success so that he could have the things he thought would make him happy. Leanne always knew she would have to carefully learn how to manipulate him with her intelligence. Each time he mentioned anything of interest to him that she was unfamiliar with, she would pour through books until she could tell him tales about every where in the world he longed to go. She taunted him with her tales, romanticizing every detail.

She knew his favorite spot was sitting on the rocks far out on the jetty near the lighthouse where he could watch the ships come and go, dreaming all the while. She would sit with him and talk about the ships her father build and owned. Often she pointed them out to him as they sailed by describing many details. She spent years, carefully, methodically spinning her web by wetting his appetite for everything he desired. She romanticized each detail of a perfect ship that she wanted her father to someday build for her, including everything she knew he wanted. She filled his head with the glamorous social events she attended and those that were held in her home.

She knew her plan was almost perfect. Knowing how Jonathan loved beautiful women, she tried to capitalize on her step-mother's beauty. How could she know it would be her undoing! She would describe in details her mother's clothing, jewels, beauty habits and secrets, the aromas around her mother, which she often used on herself. In her youthful mind, she thought by selling him on her mother's charm and beauty he would associate it with HER. She hoped to blind him to her own shortcomings. Leanne had a hypnotic affect on him. Unbeknownst to Leanne, eventually with her romanticizing her mother's beauty he secretly fell in love with Kathryn. He knew he could never be in this gracious lady's presence, except through Leanne. Jonathan was also unscrupulous regarding his own self-centered goals. His self-love and self-admiration left little love for anyone else.

Leanne would borrow ship blueprints from her father's office convincing Jonathan her father wanted his opinion. She gleefully watched the gleam in his eyes and felt confident her long range plan was working. While she had his attention on the ship plans and designs, she filled his head with stories of riches that could be brought back from foreign lands. With the right ship, any man could become vastly wealthy and acceptable in any society. She would tell him of her father's plans to build this ship for her and her future husband. With this ship and her knowledge of lands where riches lay on the ground for the picking, a man could reach any goal regardless of his background. Wealth and power -- without it, how could any man born in a fisherman's village ever end up being anything but a common street beggar.

He knew he could have any woman in his part of the town but none could bring him wealth and power that Leanne promised. For several years Leanne filled his head with Kathryn's beauty and glamour, the marvels of social life and position, excitement of wealth and freedom of the sea. How could any man resist Leanne's determined plan.

Slow to comprehend it, Jonathan finally realized Leanne's husband-to-be was him! He realized that this little girl who followed him around had grown into young womanhood and possibly is only passage out of life-long poverty and loading cargo aboard ships that would always leave him behind. Even so, he could never seriously consider marriage to her. She was still filling his head with day dreams day after day, month after month, year after year. When he would close his eyes as he listened to her tales, she would impersonate her mother's voice, which was so seductive it caused him visualize Kathryn instead of Leanne.

One sure way to make him marry her was if she could seduce him and hopefully become pregnant. This would make her father force him to marry her. She began making her plan, listing everything she wanted to do when the opportunity was right. She patiently planned and waited. The seduction had to happen in her home. How could she ever arrange that? Finally plans were made for her family to attend two weeks of royal functions in London, England. Leanne enthusiastically made plans for the trip, carefully planning a wardrobe, having new outfits made even though secretly she never planned to go. The day of departure arrived. Leanne waited until all the luggage was aboard her father's most luxurious ship. Just before it was to depart, while her parents were settled in their cabin, she called on her most dramatic talents to fake a fall and cried out in fake pain, with a twisted ankle. She told them she would never be able to walk in London at the various events and insisted that they go without her. She said she knew how Kathryn was looking forward to all the social events and her father needed the trip to promote his business. With all the help at home and she was now old enough to look out for herself, she bayed them goodbye, "Have a wonderful trip!" With phony tears Kathryn bid her to take care of herself while inwardly happy that she didn't have to have people look upon her as having a grown daughter, especially one that wasn't very attractive.

Leanne was so happy she almost forgot to limp away as the driver helped her into the carriage. The carriage drove away before the ship left the dock. As it headed out to sea, not yet out of sight, she ordered the driver to stop the carriage. The driver was stunned as she bounced out of the carriage heading for the market without any sign of pain. She was dressed in her finest travel outfit. It didn't take her long to buy all of Jonathan's favorite foods as she raced back with the full basket. She told the driver to return in about an hour. He drove away shaking his head. She took a deep breathe, awaiting the lunch hour horn to blow and strolled toward the dock where Jonathan worked. She quickly unbuttoned her jacket and blouse exposing her well defined cleavage. As he walked out, she invited him to share her lunch on the jetty as she wanted to watch the ship sail away. As they walked toward the jetty, her heart swelled with satisfaction knowing that the first step of her plan had manifested.

She failed to mention that her parents were both on the ship sailing to London, instead she made up a story that her father was taking the ship out to test some new equipment and that from a worker's stand point and he would still like to have her get Jonathan's opinion on the designs as soon as possible. She asked him to come to her home that evening to check out the plans. He agreed as the lunch horn was blowing for him to return to work. His thoughts were on Kathryn, that this might be an opportunity to see her. Leanne rushed to her father's office plowing through plans to find a new one to show him, then rushed off to the waiting carriage.

As soon as she arrived home, she grabbed the menu she had planned months before and gave it to the cook. She set a most elaborate table using her parent's finest wares. She went over her lists very carefully that she had made out through out the previous months of planning this event. Everything had to be perfectly in place, including the timing. She had to get Jonathan intoxicated for it to work. In each room of the house, which was more like a palace, she carefully placed a decanter of her father's finest liquor. The coup de gra'ce was her mother's bedroom.

Not only with her father's finest liquor but fresh flowers and incenses she purchased that promised lust and love.

Leanne raced through Kathryn's wardrobe hoping she had not taken the blue satin dress that she wore in her portrait that hung above the fireplace. Getting it to fit was quite a challenge. Kathryn's willowy statuesque body did not allow for her shorter bosomy body but her plan was to scoop up the skirt with silk roses so it would not drag the floor. She wanted to expose as much of her breast as possible, the tight dress made that possible and her nipples barely hidden. She did not want to involve any of the maids or cooks. After the dinner was properly prepared, she gave all the servants the night off.

If it was possible for her to appear beautiful she was going to do everything she could to create the illusion of Kathryn. She tried to make herself look as much like Kathryn's portrait as possible - the dress, the hairstyle, makeup, et al. She select a long necklace of Kathryn's to draw attention to her breast. It was the one attribute that she knew would attract Jonathan's eyes. She took a beautiful lace scarf to cover her breast so that when she answered the door, it would not be so obvious. So far, everything was perfectly in place when the doorbell rang.

Her heart jumped and was racing as she opened the door. She dropped the scarf just a little so that when she extender her hand for him to kiss, his head would be near her breast. She had to make good use of this one asset that she had. She invited him into the parlor. She took a seat directly under Kathryn's portrait after she poured Jonathan his first drink. He asked about the plans. Mimicking Kathryn's sexy voice, she urged him to have a drink. She had his favorite foods prepared that he must try first. There was plenty of time to look at the ship plans. As she stood filling his glass again with her father's most potent liquor, she dropped the lace scarf on the floor and leaned her buxom breast toward his face. The luxuries that surrounded him, the drinks, the atmosphere began taking the effect she had planned. She would point out the most expensive artifacts around the room knowing he had never seen such elegance. Leanne had laid out the ship plans on a table but never invited him to look at them. Jonathan was totally unaware that her parents were not there as they sat down to the elegant dinner, just set for two.

He was overwhelmed with all his favorite foods laid out before him, such a feast he might only dream of. She continually filled his glass, laughing and making gestures that Kathryn often did. When his eyes focused on the necklace she was wearing, he complimented it. Leanne jumped out of her chair and leaned over for him to look closely and touch it as she also jiggled her breast; her heavy breathing was moving it in his face. His head was swirling as he was becoming intoxicated, not only by drinks but the elegance, the great food but also Leanne and Kathryn's portrait seemed to merge into the one.

Suddenly, she grabbed his hand, jerking him out of his chair like the exuberant child he had always known, she rattled on about showing him something wonderful and exciting. She yanked him up the stairs and into her mother's fragrant bedroom where she had incenses and candles burning. She sat him on the bed as she began filling a brandy glass and urged him to try her father's very best brandy. She then took one of Kathryn's jewel boxes and dumped them on the bed. She told him to wait; she has something special to show him. Quickly in the next room she dropped everything she was wearing and slipped on an emerald green fur collared robe. When she returned, she picked up a beautiful emerald necklace and asked him to fasten it on her. As he put his arms around her, she slowly dropped the robe off her shoulders until her breast was completely exposed. She pressed toward him as he took her breast in his hands. He could no longer resist the temptation to take her sexually as she dropped the robe exposing her nude body as she pressed him back across the bed. Her plan was a total success! Her night of ecstasy would remain her secret. All the years of planning were finally a success! If he thought he had made love to Kathryn, Leanne didn't want him to awake in bed and see her instead of Kathryn. As he began to sober up a bit, she helped him dress and escorted him to the door very quietly so the servants would not know he was there. He had to find his way home as best he could. Before dawn, Leanne had meticulously replaced everything so there would be no trace of her night of love when her parents returned from their trip. She was ecstatically happy with her state of bliss and accomplishment.

After that night of Leanne's bliss, everything turned back to normal. She and Jonathan acted as though nothing happened as though neither remembered it. They would meet or walk out on the jetty and discuss her tales as always. After about six to eight weeks, Leanne's venture was a complete success when her physician confirmed that she was pregnant.

Again Leanne prepared a basket filled with Jonathan's favorite foods and sweets. They met on his lunch break. This time she carefully selected her most innocent demure dress. Actress that she was, soft tears rolled down her face as she recalled the evening he came for dinner. She confessed she had never had a drink of alcohol before and not responsible for her actions. She was a virgin as he well knew and now she was confessing she was a mother-to-be. Her tears of concern were for Jonathan's welfare since her father had such a horrible temper as well as strong political connections. Jonathan realized he was entrapped. Whatever she wanted, he had to resign himself to do. He cared for her but not as a woman and lover. She told him that her parents would never allow a marriage to take place and their only hope was to run away and marry in a nearby province. She said she could have their carriage drive them there. What joy of winning she now felt!

After the deed was done, her parents put forth superficial objection to the marriage but in truth, each was so busy going their own way, Leanne's activities had never been a high priority for either of them. Her father was now obligated to give Jonathan a job in his company. He arranged for him to be an apprentice in the shipping offices. Jonathan desperately wanted this kind of job so the deal wasn't so bad for him after all.

While Leanne's parents were not happy that she was marrying beneath their social status, it was an opportunity for her Mother to have a big party, so a large beautiful wedding was planned with all the socialites from the surrounding areas invited. It was the perfect wedding except for one thing -- a despondent, sad bridegroom! Leanne was so angry that he embarrassed her on her special day when she actually felt pretty. Jonathan spent the reception with everyone but Leanne. "Oh, how could he do this to me? How could he embarrass me and my family who he owes everything to us -- a despondent bridegroom? And me, the most worthy lady in town! I will make him pay for this. "I shall never forget this day as long as I live." She said to herself.

Leanne's long awaited joy of being Jonathan's wife was almost overshadowed by her consistent illness that went along with pregnancy.

It was Jonathan she wanted, not a baby. The baby developing inside her womb limited her newly found enjoyment of marital bliss.

CHANNELED:

"You would not lay with him on your wedding night, nor days afterwards, you were so cold to him. The marriage was very negative. When he did lay with you, he felt no love for you. He asked if you wanted to die. You asked "Why would you ask me that?" He told you that long ago he loved you but now he hated you and the baby you carried. A war was going on so he went to war. You had your baby without your husband with you. When your baby was one and a half, he returned from the war. By then, you were longing for him and thought he would have forgotten your harsh vows but he lay with you no more. He was known to lay with any woman in town. His vow was to stay with you. He wanted love but not from you. Your father wanted him to leave the land, you begged him to give him another change. He agreed but with the vow that if he ever shamed his household, off to American with other refugees he would go. You forced the baby on him, thinking this would bring a bond between you but the baby acted in reverses. It drove him farther away."

Leann's father owned several houses so she selected the one nearest the docks. It was certainly a step down from her usual life style but she didn't care, she had Jonathan now all to herself. It was certainly a step up to where he had lived all of his life. Leanne's father hardly approved of Jonathan but he could not have Leanne's husband working on the docks. Knowing well what he wanted, Leanne continued to prod him with future plans for his career unbeknownst to her father.

When Jonathan returned from the war, he wasn't all that interested in making love to her. He was blissful but not because of the marriage, it was working at a job he loved, plus he saw Kathryn at the office now and then and at the weekly family dinners. He could hardly keep his eyes off of her. Quite often, Leanne had to lie down after dinner. Her father's age required his early retiring to bed which left Kathryn alone with Jonathan. He acted in the most gentleman fashion, as the cool Kathryn gradually warmed to his continual charm. How could any woman not succumb to his handsome charm? After all, he had done the honorable thing by marrying Leanne. After the long years of admiring Kathryn from a distance, now he had an opportunity to be near her and get to know her. He had made no agreement with Leanne to give up his tavern wenches and the likes. It was his nature to use his flirtatious charm on all women. Kathryn was no exception.

With Jonathan's irritable charm and Leanne's constant chattering about him since childhood, plus her father's aging habits made Kathryn realize she had missed out on a very important aspect of life. She found it more and more difficult to resist his charm as the next few years passed.

When their son was born, Leanne had no role model for parenting, except her own childhood. So as her parents had done with her, she turned him over to a Nanny. As he grew, they would take him on picnics out on the jetty. Both were proud of the son they produced that held them together, plus with Jonathan's elevated social position, he became even more enthralled by his own good looks and charm. He wanted so desperately to be a part of the social structure that he learned social expectations quickly by observation. He had always been a diamond in the rough. He and Leanne attended many social gatherings. Hardly a woman, young or old, was not seduced by his charm and handsome looks. Leanne accepted his flirtations in painful martyrdom. She was desperately afraid of loosing him so she would do or say anything to constantly appease him which only added to his self centered vanity.

By the time their son was almost four years old, none of Leanne's promises to Jonathan regarding what her father would do for him had come to pass. Leanne had created her own monster for now he was obsessed with wanting his own ship that she had promised - the ship her father was building for her that would be THEIR ship. Arguments grew into explosive excuses for him to retreat to the Tavern for the evening where he had boasted about having his own ship for the past few years. It had become a joke to all. The Tavern's patrons' laughter, along with the alcoholic exploding in Jonathan's head made him more determined to get his own ship from his father-in-law. Where Leanne had failed, he knew Kathryn could succeed.

The years had brought Kathryn and Jonathan so close that once he decided to turn on the charm to get her in bed, she could no longer resist. He knew Kathryn was there for his asking. He seductively taunted her until he decided the time was right. Their rendezvous was a small Inn at the edge of town, an area never traveled by Leanne's father.

Jonathan would wait downstairs in the Tavern and at the appointed time the cloaked unrecognizable Kathryn would enter through a back door and up the stairs to their special love nest. This went on for some time before anyone discovered the pair and their tryst.

Leanne's blind love did allow her to see what was going on between her husband and step-mother even though there were little subtle flirtations at their family dinners. She made an effort to try and believe any tale or excuse he gave her. She could never believe any tale of her step-mother actually cause Jonathan to fall in love with her. Even less could she imagine her step-mother willing to betray her father. Each year Leanne had become more desperate and afraid of loosing him.

These rumors and gossip began reaching the ear of Leanne's father, who still did not like his son-in-law and merely tolerated him for Leanne's sake. Leanne's father was a very prideful man. These dirty rumors were an affront to everything he stood for. He would put an end to the gossip. In his anger, he struck a pistol in his belt before he headed for the Inn at the edge of town. He had his wife followed to this Inn. Could the gossip possible true that this dock worker scum had cuckold both his daughter and now his wife?

He was so angry he was ready to explode. He quickly climbed the stairs of the Inn and threw open the door of the appointed room and there, much to his shock and disbelief was Jonathan making love to his wife, Kathryn. Jonathan and Kathryn were frozen in shock as they caught sigh of him standing the doorway with a pistol pointing toward them. Just as the shot rang out, Jonathan lunged across the bed. The bullet found its mark, only Jonathan had moved out of its path. It hit Kathryn directly in the heart and she was killed instantly. When Leanne's father realized what he had done, he let out a fierce scream "I have killed my own wife" as people gathered outside the room attracted by the gun shot. Jonathan had quickly scrambled into his clothing and departed out the window. Leanne's father lunged toward Kathryn's limp nude body. Just as he did, he grabbed his chest, let out a gasp and slid to the floor. It was only a matter of hours before he, too, had departed life with a severe sudden heart attack.

Long before the news reached Leanne, Jonathan had rushed home to her. He passionately kissed her, telling her she was his very life since she was a young girl -- he lived only to make her happy -- she was the only thing in his life that had any meaning -- on and on he went filling her head with his distorted tales that only Leanne could accept and believe. He begged her for forgiveness for everything he had ever done that could have made her unhappy. He had been an innocent victim of her step mother's aggressive quest and her father's vindictiveness. She was stunned as she had no idea what had caused this outbreak and confession even though it did not include the fact her father and step mother were now dead!

It was after Jonathan had made love to Leanne as he had never made love to her before when there was a knock on the door. The police came to arrest Jonathan. Leanne was convinced of his innocence. Even though she was grieving over her father's death, she believed Jonathan had nothing to do with the death because it was natural causes. After all it was her father that had murdered her step-mother. She believed her step-mother had seduced Jonathan with promises of giving him the things he wanted -- like a ship of his own! Whatever the truth was, it mattered not to Leanne. All she cared about was keeping her husband safe.

Within a day or two, she was off to Paris to obtain the best attorney available. She had just inherited everything her parents owned so money was no object.

There were plenty of witnesses to prove that Jonathan had killed no one but unfortunately his reputation for seducing women was also well known. The judge was determined to get this raucous Lothario away from the women of the town. His options were tenuous at best. He decreed that Jonathan was to be abolished from the Continent of Europe or England. With the next sailing of a ship of criminals to American, he was to be shipped out with them.

Leanne was working with her attorney to get the decree rescinded when her attorney suddenly had an emergency and had to return to Paris. She was devastated. With her father's fortune now her own, she threw money around attempting to buy Jonathan's freedom. She was sure she could accomplish her goal. During the few weeks of imprisonment, there was an unbelievable gentleness and sensitivity that came over him. If Leanne had loved him before, it could not compare with her love for him now. Even Jonathan seemed to feel that he had always loved her without realizing it. His loving words to her now seemed very sincere. She kept a constant vigil at his cell and brought him ever possible comfort and food. Neither doubted that he would be freed. She needed him more now than ever since all her father's businesses had suddenly fallen on her shoulders. Jonathan could run them all. What a dream come true for him. The world was his oyster, together they had it all! He could now build any ship design he desired. They could sail the world together. Even though there were jail bars between them, they were happier than they had ever been together. There were times she could pay the jailer to allow her into Jonathan's cell. Her sensual appetite was filled beyond her wildest dreams. Their day dreams together were reminiscent of their days of her childhood out on the jetty. The adventures and fairytales she had filled him with through the years were, at last, coming true.

Leanne was in the park playing with her young son when a young boy came running to her to tell her he has seen Jonathan on a prison ship at the docks. For a moment she was frozen not knowing what to do first. Could they do that? How could she stop a ship! She grabber her son and dashed off frantically, running with the young boy and carrying her son toward the docks. The boy led her to the ship. Without warning there was a ship leaving for American that morning. During the night Jonathan was hustled aboard. Leanne searched the deck from the dock, finally she saw Jonathan in shackles. She was trembling as she sat her son down and screamed at Jonathan. As he stood up to find her voice, the ship began moving away from the dock. She ran to try to jump on the ship, totally frantic and sobbing. As she leaped, the distance was too far to reach and she fell into the water. She was a capable swimmer but her petticoats and skirt weighted her down. She finally managed to unfasten them and swim out of most of her clothing which floated back toward the dock. She crazily swam toward the ship. There was no one on the dock but the little boy holding the hand of your young son. The two boys stood there not knowing what to do but watch Leanne struggle toward the departing ship. There was no change of her catching the ship. Jonathan kept screaming at her to return to the dock but she kept swimming further and further away from it. The ship seemed to have caught the tide and was moving rapidly out to sea. Jonathan could barely see the dot between the waves as Leanne continued swimming. She could no long hear his screams to go back. Guards were laughing at her effort. Jonathan dropped to his knees with tears streaming down his face and prayed to God as he had never prayed before. First, asking Leanne to leave the body as he saw the shark and she disappeared under the water. "God be merciful, don't let her feel pain." He promised his life would be dedicated to God's work if God would only spare her life for their son's sake... "Just take her back to shore, never to leave it." In his heart, he knew it was too late.

Leanne had moved with super human strength until she pushed her body beyond its endurance. When she looked back at the shoreline and realized how far out she had swam, she cried "Oh, God, if you let me get back to shore, I will never leave it." (July 31, 1968 - vision clearly opened and I heard these words) "please don't go -- please -- please -- growing so tired -- must keep going -- where am I going -- I can't go back, Jonathan don't leave us -- must keep going -- oh is that a shark -- the boat is almost out of sight -- I can't go on -- I can't go back -- Oh, God -- Dear God, I didn't mean to die -- I didn't mean to die -- its closer - its closer' (choking) Just at that moment Leanne felt an excruciating pain. 'Oh, it's salty -- death? I come now -- swirls of blue, swirls, shocking pain -- red -- blue -- foggy -- foggy - there's someone coming for me -- oh thank God -- I am not alone after all. It is an older man - I don't remember ever seeing him -- As she looked up, an old man in a biblical looking grey robe with a very long grey beard reached his hand down toward her. Leanne struggled to reach for his hand, then felt herself being lifted upwards.......how can he walk, I am in the water, no, I am standing -- I am not in water -- I feel strangely light" —"Yes, Leanne, you are now in the land of the soul world" "Am I dead?" "What you may call dead is life here, come with me." "Yes, Leanne, you are now in the land of the soul world."

In that meditation, before I knew about this life, I saw a horrible scene of a deteriorated body that lay on a remote beach half covered with sand; dried skin scantly covered the skeleton. I seem to know that it was somewhere in France or Belgium. I realized that a long silvery blue cord ran from this deteriorating body up to what seemed to be -- me! I felt that I was trying to detach from this grossly mangled, rotting body, as I was drowning, the words came to me "Let me see land again, I will never leave it." It seems my spirit was tied to this body until I reviewed the negative things I had done in that life.

That was my first memory of Leanne's life that began during a past life death experience. It was the vision of the sea adventure of the old man pulling ME out of the physical plain, which was long before any of the sequences of Leanne's life had fallen into place. Perhaps in the in between plains of existence, Leanne's soul was not allowed to see what happened to Jonathan or her son. While I did not know the details or location, I seemed to know that Jonathan has kept his commitment to God and became a priest in the new world spending the rest of his life serving and teaching others the perils of sin. I was told "As he watched you struggle in the water and knew you could not make it back to shore, he called out to God to be merciful to you and not let you feel pain. He vowed to enter life of God at that moment. "If you will not let her feel pain, God, I will work for you all the days of my life and eternally work for God." You felt only the first pain, not the tearing of your limbs off. When he saw blood, he knew you were dead and watched the shark swim away. On the long trip to America he saw only that sight of your death. He was lead around like a bind man. He was out of his body for the voyage. The day land was sighted he came back. He was first to see after not seeing, he proclaimed "Land!" He lived a life of service to God. He lived with the men of God in a priest's robe. He went on to be very high in the church. He became a priest, then a bishop."

Somehow I felt that Richard, in my present life was Jonathan in that life. What a twist of fate. Richard had such a hang up on women's with absolutely huge breast, not pretty ones just huge! His preoccupation was a bit "sick" even though I tried to figure out why he had this obsession. It wasn't necessarily pretty large breast but huge ones that were in the magazines he collected. He would flip through the magazines and watch videos with women with huge breast while jacking off. How we set our own hell on earth in past lives. Cause and effect! In five years of a friendship relationship, we made love only a few times and spent the night a few times without making love. I loved him so much, yet, the real passionate feeling I felt in other relationships never happened. He never wanted a relationship with me that would lead to marriage. So here in my present life, we came together once again, with a great fondness for each other unable to break away until he found a woman he wanted to marry, leaving me "on the shore" again!

In this present life I was a good swimmer and swam with a water ballet group but hated swimming in lakes, oceans or any waters where I could not see what was in or around me. Was it because a shark struck Leanne and caused her untimely death? I always hated the sickening smell of fish, the sight of shrimp crawling or fish stacked, yet I loved the air out on a pier of jetty and enjoyed climbing and exploring the shoreline rocks.

What happened to my young son? Did my unthinking jump in that water that created my deserting him create this life time of loosing my only daughter in her teen years so that she deserted me leaving me without her life and my future grandchildren? Was she my son in that life?

CHAPTER 12

LONG LOST LOVE

A long time friend and I decided we would take photos of each other. We both needed current ones and both had been fashion/commercial models. As former models, we understood angles and soft lighting. As an amateur photographer, Cheryl had good camera equipment. After our photo session, she asked me to stay for dinner. While she was preparing dinner, I sat next to at least a foot high stack of magazines. I picked up one called "Playgirl" which I had never seen before. I leafed through a couple more of the magazines.

After dinner we were discussing the kind of man we would each like. I recalled one guy in the first magazine, so I got it, went to the stack of magazines and showed her his photos. She took one look and said "I wouldn't like HIM; he's too stuck on himself!" I wondered why people make such quick judgments of a person because of their looks. I knew that both of us had been misjudged many times because of our looks. She shunned the magazines and said her daughter must have left them. She told me to take the magazine as she didn't want any of them. I laughed and said I hardly needed a magazine centerfold when I had dated famous actors, singers, professional athletes and other glamorous men. However, as I read the article, I was intrigued as I read about this one guy. He had lived with the Monks - now a college instructor and had the guts to pose in the nude - some kind of nut, even nuttier than me! I tore out the photos and article and took them home with me.

As an artist, Cheryl had recently seen an article about an artist in a magazine that intrigued her. She had written him. Now they were dating. That was probably my inspiration as the next day, I scribbled off a quick letter to this captivating centerfold, never expecting any reply. I had said what I wanted to say; which was a way I release the thoughts that I keep mulling over. I certainly never expect to hear back from him as I didn't even know if he would receive my letter as I just sent it to the University where he worked. About two weeks later, late one morning I answered the phone and did not recognize the man's name. Once it registered that it was my centerfold guy, I must have risen three feet off my chair! The teenager in me was alive and well! I was thrilled!

A few days later I wrote in my diary -- "4/14/81 10:40 P.M. Today was quite spectacular day. Columbia space craft returned to earth 10:17 AM in perfection.

I go to L.A. tomorrow morning -- will I see Richard? Could he be gay? I have myself together so I am not counting on anything -- ANY thing would be a bonus! The fantasy I have lived since Richard called has been such a welcomed up lifting feeling. If it has no finish or completion, I can handle it. (What a strange statement to make at that time) I just get so tired of TEST - I would really like to feel fulfillment!" No matter how much knowledge I have regarding metaphysics, still, I seemed surprised at what we call "coincident."

The friend I was to visit in Los Angeles lived only two blocks from Richard. At their house, I carefully applied makeup, combed my hair and dressed. The magic time arrived when I was to go up and ring Richard's gate bell. My heart was in my throat. When he buzzed me past the gate, my heart was thumping so hard I could not believe my reaction at my mature age. He opened the door - there he stood in living three dimension colors -- an Adonis come to life! With all the good looking hunks I dated, he was magnificent to me. In his skimpy black bathing suit, he was every thing I thought he would be after falling in love with the magazine photos. He apologized for the bathing suit explaining he had little time for sunning on his lunch hour - (I'll bet -- he just wanted to show off his perfectly sculptured body!) We never got around to having lunch. The conversation was fast and furious for two hours when he announced he had to get back to work. My Gemini Adonis was sweet, interesting, intelligent, uptight and inhibited. When

I returned to my friend's apartment, I felt I had to take a nap. I felt as though I had been in another dimension - a far faster dimension and had to return to normal vibratory rate by sleeping. I knew Adonis lived once again to fulfill my Venus - Taurus nature.

That was on May 15th, 1981, two days before my birthday and one month later after agonizingly awaiting for his phone call that never came; I called only to be told that right after we met, he ran into an old flame and had rekindled their romance. Since he worked two jobs, he had little time for socializing. I knew it was a brush off and even though he knew nothing about reincarnation, I calmly said "Well, obviously you have some karma to work out with this woman, so call me when it's over… I'll still be here." What a birthday gift! I let go but in my heart, I still believed we had unfinished business together. Life went on and

I begin dating a darling musician in Newport Beach where I was living.

I could never stay away from Los Angeles for very long and felt I would have better chances to make a living there. I put my house up for sale and seemed to take forever to get it sold, finally by mid October in 1982 it sold. I decided it would be better to find a place to live and work in the same place. I found an apartment upstairs in a commercial building that was perfect for my living and work. Ironically, it was on Westwood Blvd. just about four blocks from Richard's office, although by that time, I had let go of the incident the year before.

I sent out a notice of opening my office to everyone on my mailing list. Apparently he was on the list. On January 10th, 1983, about 11 PM I was almost asleep when the phone rang. When he gave his name, it didn't ring a bell.

I scanned over names of my clients -- "Don't you know who I am?" he asked. "I'm sorry, I just can't place you." He then slowly stated his first - middle and last name. I sat up in bed with my heart pounding again -- another teenage thrill! We talked for a long time and made a date for Sunday night.

That began four of the maybe the hardest learning years of my life -- painful, degrading, the epitome of rejection. Subconsciously, I seem to be seeking the impossible. I rationalized everything would come out OK. One kind word from him and I would be lapping at his heels -

ENSLAVED! For some reason, my unusual spiritual growth comes in weird ways!

Our first date was fun but awkward. At the time, Before AIDS, it was still in the free sex era that seemed to flourish after the 1960's and the advent of "THE PILL." After waiting two years, I was much too willing to go along with his every desire. As we sat on the sofa, he awkwardly put his arm around me while we discussed our individual needs from the opposite sex -- a rather adult approach intermingled with my teenage crush and feelings. As up tight as he was, eventually I suggest a back rub. He removed his shirt and lay on the floor -- gorgeous -- but so tight and tense. As gorgeous as he was, there was no sensual feeling. While I felt "madly in love" I was not turned on. Considering his involvement with academe and my acting training to let go of inhibitions, I excused his uptightness compassionately. As we stood in his kitchen, he continued to explain his need for establishing friendship first and foremost, not meaningless sex acts. I said "Well, if you're really serious about friendship and it's not because you are not attracted to me, I am willing to go along with it."

From then on, our time together consisted of me going to his office and waiting for him. He taught me to use one of the computers. We would go by his apartment for a short time, maybe a quick dinner and back to work. Eventually he gradually introduced me to a form of sexual interaction that was totally foreign to me. Strange as it was, there was a great deal of realization about him in it as well as a lot of compassion on my part. Much of what he did, I thought was testing me and my reactions. I had never known a man obsessed with women's HUGE BREAST or who enjoyed masturbating more than intercourse. There was no participation for me; yet, I wanted to be with him and to try to understand him psychologically. At that time I was doing more psychic counseling and regression work than working in TV or film, which only came now and then. Trying to understand his lust seemed a natural thing for me to do.

I felt a lot of compassion, especially after he told me about a male neighbor that had emotionally raped him as a young boy. Maybe he was fearful of a close relationship with a woman and developed his sexual satisfaction via watching sex videos and looking at sex magazines with women who had -- not pretty large breast but HUGE breast! Richard has such a perfect body, I wasn't confident with mine. I had lost thirty pounds but gradually began regaining it back as his activities were affecting my self esteem. Naturally, I had to think his obsession was "sick" and though I tried to remove myself from him with other lovers, still there was a sweetness, almost naiveté as well as light hearted fun. I enjoyed him and often thought a part of him was better than all of another man. He showed his friendship in many ways. When I needed someone to help me, he was there. If I had car problems he was there. One time I went with a friend to a strange kind of meditation that was so long, I got very bored and didn't feel good with the surroundings. I felt like I was being set up for almost a forced membership. I called and he came immediately to pick me up.

The mere mention of his name to friends brought on a hostile attitude and negative remarks from friends. I couldn't blame them. They didn't know him and the friendship we shared. When we finally did make love in the mid 1980's, it was tremendously satisfying for me. Maybe it was because I had waited so long. Finally, I thought we were set in our relationship with love making included. Quite the opposite, he ran. His excuse was that he wasn't interested in a committed relationship that would be necessary for me.

I would leave him alone for weeks at a time hoping he would pursue me but it was just the reverse. I would find some excuse to go by his office or call him.

He would not reject me totally so I would continue to go back, perhaps taking him his favorite cookies. I took a birthday dinner to his office. If sex was so good those few times, I knew it would be again. Unfortunately as the relationship developed, he felt that if he made love to me, it would seem to him that we had a committed relationship and he wasn't willing to commit to me. I was a few years older and with a hysterectomy could no longer have children. He wanted to have children although I was convinced he was too self-involved to ever care for children.

I truly liked him and felt so much goodness in spite of his self centeredness. While I felt I was in love with him, I never had the fiery desire or passion I had felt for other men. I worked very hard at attempting to make myself indispensable to him. He and his partner worked at getting their new business going, night and day, seven days a week. I became an excellent maid servant in cleaning and reorganizing their office while allowing my own to become a cluttered mess. Every penny he made went back into the business so he spent almost none on me. I paid for food, loaned him money, while making very little myself but it was a choice I made and was totally responsible for my choice. I knew he would pay me back and he always did. I made my apartment as comfortable as possible for him to do "his thing" -- the porno videos and magazines -- seeing his pleasure from women I though were cheap and unattractive, probably not too bright either, really pushed my self esteem further down the drain with mounting sexual frustration. I did not enjoy sex with other men. I was sure that such a ridiculous relationship could only be because of past lives! At that time I did not realize how TRUE that thought was!! If I had rejected the relationship, I would never have worked off all that karma. Because of that experience I had a far better understanding of soul mating. My soul mating experience with Richard and other men has been my greatest growth tools. Even though I had lectured on soul mating, these experiences showed me that we have far more than just one "soul" mate. My journey was a far cry from any thing I could have imagined and a life path that others cannot understand.

It is difficult to know when and how the awareness of past lives filtered into consciousness -- was it a dream -- a book, movie or a meditation that brings back a memory. I had been active in serious psychic development and past life research since the mid 1960's. My friends that weren't into any of that could not understand the relationship. I saw what I wanted to see in him. He had several degrees -- an excellent academic education, he was very sweet and funny. He was a better friend to me than any guy had been. He was THERE when I needed help. He never lied to me. He knew what was necessary for his life and his work. He had a perfect body because he worked out daily. As perfect as it was, when in contact with his body, it did not have any cuddly warmth. It was too much of a hard body.

With all my mature wisdom and experience sexually in relationships I maintained a lot of compassion, patience and understanding. He had chosen the priesthood in his younger years for a few years. With his Catholicism he couldn't open up to the thought of reincarnation, yet, I knew that he, too, felt we have been together before. He once commented "Maybe we have been together before, but now it seems unlikely, maybe in our next life..." I interrupted with "Sorry, I am going to do all that I can to clear up all these karmic connections this time around. I don't plan to return." With his unusual sexual satisfaction and more of a frustrating one for me, I realized we were doing sort of a tantric dance. I felt it was a bit of a soul mating of body - mind and spirit on a higher plane. At the time I had not made the past life connections that came in later years, which all made total sense. So often what we see as reality is really illusion and illusion is reality as it has no ending.

With his love of skiing, he met a woman that was an airline stewardess, meaning free travel all over the world. In addition her parents owned time shares that they could use. She was still young enough to have children. His work was picking up enough to buy a new car and take off to go places. Her timing was perfect. In his mind, I don't think it was ever a romance although after he began serious dating with her, he did say to me that he wished he could combine the two of us and have a perfect mate.

It was 1986 and time for changes. I "86'd" two other men that had been in and out of my life for over twenty years. Tom was in a position to help me with my career but never lifted a finger to help me. He was married and I didn't want him to divorce his wife. He lived in NYC and our long relationship had been almost a love/hate one. On the other hand, Burt had been the most intense relationship of my life. Both men lasted longer than any husband ever had.

Burt had found a potential wife - his doctor's nurse. As he was aging, I figured he might need a nurse to take care of him and it all made me very disgusted with him, too. I had never had the manipulative skills of other women to entice men to help them. I made years of mistakes of "hanging in there" with several men that I thought would eventually be a marriage or something with more meaning. Yes, it was time for a major shift in my life. And shift I did!

April 12, 1986 I wrote:

"It seemed appropriate that I say "goodbye" to Richard at 10 AM, almost to the day he first called me those years before. The "goodbye" was my emotional tie to him when I took him to the airport for him to fly away to his Kathy, his airline stewardess from Denver. How ironic that my ex,

Bob, married a beauty contestant in Denver, too. I awoke this morning having a dream about him and in reality, I awoke to several realities -- In this life, Richard is in his "harem consciousness" - and I am in my "nomad consciousness", traveling through this life, attached to nothing and no one while he is attached to so many women. Richard loves me in a way but he doesn't really see or appreciate me. Perhaps in that long past life when I ran away from him is part of why he runs away from me in this life. It was April 1985 that I last spend a night with Richard. I think it was then that he began his romance with her. Richard helped me grow in many ways. We had a valuable friendship for five years. He knew that I was a woman for a relationship with just one man and knew that he needed the attention of many women, still in that Harem consciousness! I think I understand and accept what is!" When I think of it, in past lives and now in this life, problems with women with names like Katherines, Kathleens, Kathy, et al.

On that April day, I did my best to release myself from feeling so much love for him; however, I began remembering other times. I relived that one weekend we spent together. That weekend when my friend loaned me the key to her cabin in Big Bear. Knowing how much Richard loved to ski, I invited him to accompany me for the weekend. Snow was on the ground in the mountains. Richard was delighted at the prospect of skiing. He brought a large light that would plug into the cigarette lighter and he knew how to put the chains on the tires. As we headed up the mountain, it began to snow and felt it was time and the need to put the chains on the tires. I pulled off in a parking area. I held the light for him and left the engine running so not to run the battery down. Suddenly the engine stopped and would not start again. My driver's side electric window was down and no away to get it up. I had to hold an umbrella to keep the snow out. He could not get the chains on, especially with no light. No chains on the tires, no battery, no going anywhere when finally the Highway Patrol stopped and offered to call the Auto Club. He slipped on several sweaters he brought. We cuddled in the back seat with his arm around me -- precious moments of loving his arm around me while freezing and wanting to get on our way. It was more than an hour before the Auto Club finally arrived and got the chains on. More frustration followed when we arrived at the cabin as we couldn't get the heat to come on. We were tired and decided to go to bed. When he told me to sleep in the other bed, I wad shocked as we had slept together several times in the past. There we were both cold and a perfect night for two people to cuddle and keep each other warm. His excuse was that at home we had slept in his king size bed and these beds were too small for two people. I felt like a puppy that had just been kicked. Now I think how uncanny that it was so similar in those same mountains in Hanna's life with her monk friend who was Richard in that life.

Another past event came to my mind. It was the holiday season and I was going to my best friend's elaborate party. "Absolutely, positively, NO!" Richard's words hit me like a hot poker. I thought he would go with me but he said he had work to do. I knew he had a heavy work load but my intuitive feeling was the he was retreating again since we had just spent 48 hours together in the mountains. As I hung up the phone, I wondered why we couldn't have a more normal dating situation. We had been seeing each other fairly consistently for the past two years, plus knowing each other for nearly five years. How strange and confusing -- for years I had wanted someone to love and care for me for something besides sex, now I had all those things, almost everything I thought I wanted in a relationship -- except sex. I kept asking myself why we couldn't have normal sexual communication. We had made love and spent the night together many times. That same morning he had held me tenderly and lovingly in his arms. The battle raged within me wondering if I had pushed him too hard with my aggressiveness, then I rationalize and make excuses for him. In my counseling I was perfectly capable of helping others with my intuitive counseling but when it came to my own life, I drew a blank. Since Richard was younger than me -- was that why he pulls away I wondered. The past few years' experience with younger men had force me to deal with the fact that most men I felt compatibility with were younger. With my reincarnation research, I realized a few years one way or the other was minor in the grand scheme of life. If we have karmic circumstances to work out, regardless of the many circumstances in life, we will come together again to work them out. Age has nothing to do with it.

Feeling lost and alone, as I held the phone, I felt the need to talk to someone but who? Generally I handle my problems alone but occasionally I felt the need to find a compassionate ear. "I've got to get

out of here, if I sit at home, I will just be sad and feel sorry for myself"...
so off I went to a movie. As frequently happened, destiny again too hold
as the movie I selected was filled with beautiful aesthetic presentations.
It soothed my emotional upset so that I reminded myself that it was my
responsibility to get back in charge of my emotions. Later, he called and
decided he would to go to the party with me. We made an extremely
handsome couple -- in my opinion and probably the best looking couple
at the party.

In recalling past events with Richard, in the mid 1980's I knew
the relationship with Richard was hopeless so I gave up my office in
Westwood, stored my furniture and moved back to Texas to try to help
my mother, however, I got tired of receiving only negative responses
from both my brother and sister, I gave up after a few months and
returned to Los Angeles.

I found an apartment in Palms, not far from Westwood and
Richard's office. I got my furniture out of storage and attempted to re
establish my psychic counseling and past life regressions and to merge
both with crystals and color therapy in my counseling. I taught classes
through the Learning Annex, did lectures on crystals and color. After
appearing on a national TV show I developed an audio tape "Rainbow
Regressions." I received over 500 phone calls with people wanting to
experience past lives. I created the tape with the intention that it would
help them research and discover their own past lives. All went well
for a couple of years then less and less income no matter what I tried
during my experimenting in my Multi Level Marking era. It was in this
apartment that I lived during the on and off romance with Richard.

When my rent was increasing, I rented out a bedroom and bath to a
young man. That didn't work at all. My next door neighbors, next to my
bed's wall, had recreation activities every night in the wee hours. With
continued loosing sleep, I was feeling very stressed out. The ending of
my friendship with Richard made me want to just get out of California,
at least out of Los Angeles. This was in the Shirley MacLaine area of
popular books. She was also presenting expensive seminars. I began
making plans to buy a travel trailer and head out of California to do
less expensive similar seminars in smaller area less accessible for her
large seminars. I would do weekend seminars, teach some classes and
do counseling. Yes, that was my plan!

My recall of the life of an Egyptian woman, who was kidnapped and sent to the Sultan's harem, did not come to me while in the relationship with Richard. As time passed, the pieces of the puzzle began falling in place. His Harem attitude of having many women and my dying statement "If I can get back to him, I will never leave him" made perfect sense and I knew that Richard was the Sultan in that life and several others. I seemed to identify more past lives with him than any other man. Putting past lives in linear time was the proof that I needed in my present life association with Richard in order to release myself from all those past lives connections.

CHAPTER 13

THE CABIN

It was in the mountains at Lake Arrowhead, CA that I had my first psychic experience with a non physical soul mate that came to me through automatic writing. He had been the one that sent me into this physical incarnation. In a vivid and lasting memory I had seen him in a powerful meditation. When we were walking in the woods in another dimension, he insisted we lie down but I didn't want to as I suspected something was wrong. Sure enough, when we lay down on the fallen leaves, I seemed to go into a trance and couldn't move as he covered me with the leaves and some how I knew I was being forced back into physical incarnation. These communications went on for several years. I could never "see" him but his name was Mark Troy. I felt his presence. He became so real to me that on one occasion a good friend could see him and described him to me, the same as I had imagined. On another occasion, again at Big Bear, while I sat in my car waiting for my daughter to finish her skiing, I was conversing with him as I often did to tolerate boredom. When my daughter got in the car she said "who was that guy in the car with you, Mom? Humorously I replied "Mark Troy, who else? - There was no one in the car." "Mom! I SAW a guy in this car! He had on a turtle neck sweater!" We both sat silently that our joking around with a non reality suddenly seemed mysteriously real!

After my 86ing any thought of successful romance with Richard, Burt or Tom I felt I had successfully gotten rid of my obsessions related to these men. In early summer of 1987 I planned to present workshops throughout the southwest. I was determined to get moved out of an apartment, stored furniture as I had bought a 22' travel trailer and felt content to live in it and travel. About 11 PM a friend came over to help me finish up and clean the apartment. I slept until 5 A.M. - hitched up the trailer and off I went to a three day Past Life Conference in Uplands, CA. It had been a great plan to become a poor man's Shirley MacLaine and give enlightening seminars in smaller areas. My goal was to do weekend seminars and write during the week. It all seemed completely feasible. However, almost from the moment I pulled away from my apartment, it was one thing after another with either car or the trailer problems.

After the conference, I began my journey. The car broke down just before heading up the Cajon Pass. Finally, a mechanic drove me to a RV park, left the trailer, took the car to be repaired. After the repairs, the next day I drove up the very long Cajon Pass so stressed out, I didn't know if I could make it. I finally arrived to visit a friend out of Victorville. After a relaxing visit, a dip in the pool and a restful couple of night, with a bit of anxiety, I started out on my new journey across the desert, heading toward Sedona, AZ, however, before I could get out of her community gate, a bar holding the trailer leveler snapped and the hitch dropped on the street. I didn't even get out of California before that trailer broke down. At that point, after the several days of problems with car or trailer, I felt it was an omen that I had to give up the idea of traveling. In only a few days, I had spent over $400. on repairs! With the car unhitched, I drove up the mountains to see if I could find a place to park the trailer, live there and do my writing. The next day, I managed to haul the trailer up the San Bernardino Mountains and found a place to park it in Crestline. Sitting still seemed to be the answer. My beautiful plan had burst but being adaptable, I figured I could do my writing and start some classes, maybe even bring people to the beautiful mountains for seminars. When we become in some kind of harmony with our karmic responsibilities and balancing them, it doesn't matter what plans we make, the Universe directs our course. I have learned to be pliable and make immediate adjustments to my plans.

Some twenty years before a friend and I moved a few miles out of Crestline near an old boy scout camp that could make a prefect Spiritual Retreat. Acting on faith, we believed we could raise a million dollars to buy that camp. That was our goal. My daughter was to enter her last year of High School and when the fall came, the fog also came! When I realized she would have to be driving in that fog, I decided to move down the mountain to Palm Springs. That was the end of my part in the Spiritual Retreat and soon my friend also gave up. It was an interesting experience as I began getting little memories of my life as Hanna in those same mountains.

It wasn't long before I had established weekly classes in Lake Arrowhead with some interesting results. It was summer and the mountain area was beautiful. I felt happy and content. Even though I was content in my travel trailer parked by a small stream, for what ever reason I decided to just drive around familiarizing myself with the mountains. While driving near Lake Arrowhead, I came upon this old, lonely, desolate cabin that was for sale. Why was I drawn to it? When I looked inside through a broke window - I said to myself "NO WAY!" It was a disaster! I don't know why but I found myself driving by it time and again.

The first time I saw the cabin; it looked as though someone had just gotten up and walked away from it in the 1930's and never returned. The cabin was in terrible shape. It had been five years since anyone had used it. Squirrels and mice had taken over. Anyone would think I was crazy to buy it. When I first saw it, it seemed to call to me and I saw "charm" in it knowing I could fix it up the way I wanted. There was no way I was about to tackle the necessary renovation to make it livable! "Never say Never" -- something about it kept calling me back. On the spur of the moment, I called the owner, made him an offer, he accepted, next thing I knew I was the buyer of this monstrosity! Clean - clean and clean - I hired Mexican laborers, clean, clean and more clean, hired mountain handymen who never completed anything - every thing was half finished -- plumbing done three times. I spent until I had nothing to spend and without a working heating system. Without heat, I had to abandon it and stay at a friend's apartment in Palm Springs until May when I thought the weather would warm. I have always had this "thing" about taking something ugly and making it beautiful - turning the ugly duckling into a beautiful swan! There had to be a karmic connection with this cabin or one very similar. At the time, it was the largest project I had taken on for myself as it was totally unlivable and had to have a lot done to it before I could think of living in it. Inside it was about 18' high vaulted ceilings. There was only one small bedroom. It was divided down the middle with a bedroom, bath, kitchen, utility room on one side; the other was a large living room with a homemade rock fireplace. On one of the panels about 8' up in the bedroom was a large somewhat crude painting of a baby. I did not like it and intended to replace it. Weeks later while looking at that painting, I thought, "that's my nose" then I recalled my own baby photos -- "My God! That baby could be me!" I wondered who painted it. There was no record of the painting.

When I bought the over fifty year old cabin with enormous work needed, my students had offered to help. Of course, when the work began, they all disappeared. I kept wondering what possessed me to buy it. With the psychic attachment, I had to wonder if I had lived in that area in a former life. Did the man who built it know me in a past life? Did he love me or feel some sort of guilt that put vibes in that cabin that drew me to it? Did he do the painting and did he have a psychic impression of what I looked like at as baby in Texas? Was my karmic debt to bring life, love and beauty to the cabin some where in the vicinity where I had taken my own life? In my present life I had learned to use a rifle with three of my college semesters consisting of taking marksmanship. I was a good shot but could I have actually pointed a gun at my own head and fired it? One thing in this life that I have not had is any suicidal intentions. Years before I had an inkling that I would someday live in Lake Arrowhead, however, under far, far different circumstances - like having luxurious circumstances!! This cabin was the reverse of any luxurious circumstances!

I have realized that "endings" can be achieved with love. When two people have karmic ties, one can release from the other by loving that person and learn to loving let go and be some what indifferent but wishing them well on their life journey. We don't have to like them but love their total soul, then release them. It is the same with locations or circumstances.

It didn't take long to consider selling the cabin. With a couple of 'maybe I would like to live there' trips to Sedona, Arizona proved not to be the right place for me. Searching throughout North San Diego County for the right place felt fruitless as well. Gradually, I was drawn back to Los Angeles, realizing that my friends there were my "family".

On one of my many trips to visit my Mother in Texas, a voice in my head said "Go to Arkansas and get some quartz crystals." I replied "NO! I am involved with enough with metaphysical pot-pourri, I don't need crystals!" Again and again it repeated: "Go to Arkansas and get some quartz crystals." Alas -- I went -- and bought crystals. I met a young man that had a pickup with crystals. He said he would like to go to California to sell crystals. I gave him my number and told him that if he ever goes to the Los Angles area, I would try and help him find the places where he might sell his crystals. I have read that there maybe major crystal clusters within Earth that regulate the North and South poles, that we resonate so perfectly with quarts crystals and the we can program them and use them to focus energy we may not even understand. I find it interesting that with the use of oil and coal to run our vehicles and many other things, crystals are made of the same elements. Perhaps crystals can help us travel in our physical vehicle toward shifting collective consciousness from fear and separation to unity and love - the transformation of Planet Earth energy, at least which seemed to be a theory tossed around in the Metaphysical community. Many people do not realize that as this nation has transitioned from the Industrial age to this electronic age that it has been greatly influenced by quartz crystals. Now becoming more known are the electro magnetic grids throughout the world, areas like Sedona, the Great Smoky Mountains and areas all over the world where energy is the highest. Ancients seem aware of these energy vortexes as they built their spiritual structures on them.

In my psychic counseling work, any client coming to me needed healing whether it was emotional, physical or needing past life connections. I gradually incorporated my knowledge of crystals, color and past life karmic connections that needed resolve. Many years before, a psychic had told me I was destined to be a film star. While I didn't consider it, I did move from Texas to Los Angeles after my divorce. I felt California was a more desirable place to raise my daughter than New York City, the only two places to continue my fashion modeling career. I had daydreamed of becoming successful enough to produce my own films or television that lifts the consciousness of the masses rather than the trend toward any and all sorts of crime and violence that inundated TV for the better part of 40 years. Obviously if one has a criminal mind and desires to be a criminal, methods are laid out on TV every night. How could I even consider that by studying acting would make me go deeper inside myself and meditation would bring up my own psychic ability. In the mid 1960's, I began reading metaphysical type books, I found more things that made sense to me than any of the different religions I had been searching through most of my life.

Eventually, it made sense to me that all life is a huge stage and we are each playing out a character. It is not up to me to judge these characterizations that others are cast in but to do the best in my own character, no matter how far it is from the character I thought I wanted -- a housewife and mother of three children married to a successful husband. If I meet a totally despicable character (and I have many times) I can simply bless them and know that they are playing their character to the best of their ability and know that I never have to play that character since they are playing it so well. That makes it easier to tolerate the multitude of lower states of consciousness human beings. Perhaps it is like a rainbow of colors with many different shades and hues -- it takes all of our colorful personalities to evolve the planet. We humans can get very annoyed with weather or other things we confront, yet, even though we may tire of continuous rain, Mother Earth needs it. I feel our thought vibrations affect our weather and the chaotic conditions around the world.

Through my years of individualized searching, I seemed to subtly pass over a psychic bridge or it all comes together like an electric magnet. Our greatest growth seems to come very subtly, where things seem to be the opposite from what they appear to be as though I am looking from the other side of a mirror, as said in Corinthians 13:12: " For now we see through a mirror, darkly; but then face to face. Now I know in part; but then shall I know even as also I am known." Observing others from the other side of the mirror has continued to separate me from them, realizing that my destiny was set to be a solo journey into soul evolution. I see those who profess to be the most devoted to their own religions can be the most judgmental of all toward those that are not of their particular religion. Regardless of one's religion, since my basic has been Christianity, Jesus' and others' great teachings are so simple and all teach that the thing one needs is - love, love, love, compassion, nonjudgmental, respect, understanding and tolerance. Jesus was the Way Shower and his last name was not "Christ" - it is a title reverberating from him - he showed us that he reached the Christ Consciousness, which we can also attain. While what we call Devil or Evil is the Gate Keeper of Fear. (**F**alse **E**vidence **A**ppearing **R**eal) As long as we fear, the Devil holds us behind the gate of physicality and we are caught on the wheel of reincarnation, learning our lessons one by one. When we are ready to move to the center of that wheel, where all power lies, into the Oneness of all, we are then released from the outer manifestations of life after life. Another essential quality, in my opinion, is having a sense of humor. We get so caught up in the emotional immediacy of our situations, which we should rise above it to look at it from a God-like perspective. "If I was God, how would I view this situation?" We need to acknowledge that we see only a pinhole perspective and cannot see the whole picture. As God you would see both sides of any issue and would love both equally regardless of which appears to be good or bad.

Our dreams should prove that we work on more than one level of consciousness and more than just the physical. The physical level is the least level of our evolution. Many years ago, I saw with my mind's eye a whirlpool of humanity and in the center was me. I heard the words: "There is no I, there is no me, we are all one." Just add an "l" to alone and you get all one. Intellectually, I understood but it took many years to "feel" that oneness.

The evening breeze brought cooling air across my skin. I cherished the wonderful silence of my mountain cabin while sitting on the long L shaped deck I had built. The remoteness had also made me a bit frightened. That was before a two story grey monster was build across the road with loud rock music blaring and kids screaming, which also blocked my view of the valley below. Many times I considered selling my own albatross cabin, which I had a love-hate relationship with. Eclectic was hardly the word to describe it. It was crudely but solidly built of solid wood slats about 3" thick and 12" wide that was both the inside and outside walls with no insulation. It was over 4' off the ground at the front that allowed cold air to briskly blow around under the floor. Almost everyone that looked at it found its faults and never saw its charm. It had a hold on me like no place I had ever lived. It seemed to have some sort of karmic debt that had to be paid.

"Nothing tomorrow" was the reply that came back over the telephone from the "General Hospital" casting office. I had mixed feeling of not having to drive into Los Angles to work and anger since it had been almost a month since I had worked. I had worked as an actress nurse on the show for quite a number of years and depended on it for income. It felt degrading to have to call in for work when I had first been cast by a different Casting Director, the office called me when I was to work, not me having to call in with constant busy signals with others calling during the allotted time period. There was no thrill in working as a background actress with the occasional few lines. Yet, I knew that there were unlimited people all over the world that would PAY to have the same opportunity and but for the union, would work for free! If it had not been for the Insurance, I wouldn't have bothered to work the show.

It was well into June and I was still freezing in this damned mountain cabin. I thought winter had passed! I watched the smoke curl out of a neighbor's chimney. The trees were green - the air seemed fresh and alive. The distant mountains were clear and serene. I was layered in warm clothing unable to get any heat because of a handyman's failure to complete the job, as all handymen seemed to do. The cabin owned me, I did not own it. For years I had visualized perhaps living in these mountains or some on the Eastern USA; however my vision was living in far more affluent circumstances. The cabin was meant to be a retirement home but with the long winter's cold, I had listed it with a Real Estate Agent just a year after I bought it. It became a monster to me with the over powering needed work and reconstruction. I longed to have a place where I could feel settled in one place, yet I felt so lost, alone and unsettled after having moved away from Los Angeles.

There had always been something very haunting about the cabin but it was not "haunted" -- deja vue - seemingly very familiar to me. Generally, I tried not to fear anything but being alone in this cabin; I did begin having an inner fear almost a terror of bears. When I would have to come home at night, I would rush the door, key in hand to enter as quickly as possible. I just knew a bear would come around the corner and attack me! There were far more "whys" to my lonely cabin experience than answers, yet it was an awakening time related to a past life.

My thoughts went to Hanna's life -- was this cabin or one similar associated with her? When life in it was so hard for me, could she have survived in even worse circumstances as I was feeling had happened to her? Did she travel from Northern California to Southern California? What really happened to Hanna? Or was there no connection at all?

CHAPTER 14

HANNA - CIVIL WAR AND BEYOND

Collection GALLERY OLDHAM – UK – Tying her shoe,
Sir Walter Russell

Having developed my psychic ability in this present life, I can ask for those memory banks to open to my conscious mind. I cannot be detached from the painful suffering of my soul evolution nor can I be emotionally detached from others' painful experiences in the present or past. The further back in time, the lesser the attachment. The year 1842 came to mind, was that the year I was born as Hanna? Some times I refer in the first person, sometimes as an observer in the second person.

My sister in this life was my older sister in that life, too, and she married the same man in this life. Before the Civil war they moved to Texas. I am aware that their oldest son in this life was her husband's son in that life. They set up farming in the same general area where they lived in this life. My sister was older and we were never very close. It was the same in my present life, only after we were both mothers, our bond seemed to grow, for some years anyway, then it all ended with her never speaking to me after our father died.

Life on the plantation grew very hard. It was difficult to plow the fields - plant the seeds - toil and labor as never before. How could we keep plowing - planting without any harvest? It seemed no matter how hard we prayed God had deserted us. The war was getting under way, taking so many of our young and middle aged men. (In my present life I married a man who was my third and last husband in this life.)

Hanna was born to a wealthy plantation owner before the Civil War. The stately plantation set amount beautiful trees with swaying Spanish moss. Probably my first hint of a past life in this life was when my Mother and I took the train trip to Houston, Texas when I was about ten years old. On the way, I was fascinated with the Spanish moss hanging from trees that had a strange familiarity to me even though I had never seen it before.

In a past life regression I recalled Hanna's christening day. As a baby Hanna was aware of being in a ruffled crib with flowered wallpaper in a feminine, frilly room. She was aware of a fat black "Mammy" huddling over her dressing her. In the crib Hanna was aware of hearing the arrival of a carriage as she could hear it approaching on the gravel rock driveway. Hanna was picked up by her father along with her mother, carried her down a circular stairway. Hanna was wearing a long white embroidered dress and was the center of attention. It was her christening. Even though she was only a few months old, Hanna was aware of a five year old boy she seemed to know.

Other than having a carefree, worry free childhood, memories of Hanna's life skipped to a time during the Civil War in the regression. This boy she was aware of as a baby was also the young man she was to marry. It was known from early childhood as their families had planned it. By joining forces for more land -- more power and then the War had taken both parents - the plantation -- the land.

Hanna's older sister had married a man with a son from his previous marriage. Our parents did not approve of him, so they moved to Texas before the war. Kathryn was more serious than Hanna and seemed jealous of their father's attention toward Hanna as well as Hanna's fun loving, passionate nature.

Plantation life had been a true blessing prior to the drought and approaching war. The family cared for the slaves as individuals and all shared good times. On each plantation there was their own social system and combined work with play when they could. It was more likely that they shared secrets with a dark companion than white ones as secrets were met with more compassion and without gossip. People today cannot know those feelings shared between black and white. It was not always the horrors presented in films. Conquering the South went very deep in the spirit of those who experienced the real and true South. There had never been a social structure as had evolved in many areas of the Southern states. The war never ended for those killed spiritually by the pain and suffering. Some people today are still paying emotionally without realizing it is from their genetic ancestral memory.

Perhaps one can be raised too safe -- too happy - in childhood -- too unprepared to face life's realities. Hanna had a charmed, happy childhood, filled with many beautiful frilly, feminine, fluffy dresses and petticoats that had been so important to her. Her father sheltered her from ugliness of any kind in that life outside of their domain and she was ill prepared to be face to face with the outside world of reality. The bedrooms were upstairs - Hanna was putting on a beautiful white dress, white petticoats - white corset being tightened as she heard carriages arriving outside on the circular gravel road. The bedroom was the same one she had since birth, then her thoughts drifted back to a long white christening dress and as a baby, she knew she was to be the star of the event. Hanna's childhood flashed before her. One of the servant's daughter was her best playmate and was the same age. They played in the front yard where there was a fountain - Hanna was wearing a ruffled dress and was playing in the fountain with a boy. Her mother yelled at her for being in the fountain in one of her best dresses. She was embarrassed in front of the boy. From then on, as she grew up, she always felt embarrassed when she saw him. Hanna never wanted to grow up and never wanted to leave the beautiful, happy plantation home. Hanna was only day dreaming about another white dress and white petticoats that would be her happy wedding day.

It was September 11th, 1861 when they came. There were only four of them but more savage than any twenty uncultured natives of any land. The war had not really touched us on a personal level at that time. We were sleeping when the ruckus began. Our Negro foreman was ordering these men off the property when their horses encircled him and they began shouting "Dance, Nigger!" and shooting at his feet. As I looked out the window in a half sleep state - a bullet riddled his back, then they just kept shooting as Martha, George's wife stood by helplessly. I can still hear her shrieks, ungodly death screams. One rider grabbed Martha by the hair and drug her round and round the circle, then slung her on top of George's body like a sack of garbage. The inhuman laughter was followed by shots rang through my head. There had hardly even been a day in my life on the plantation without Martha and George. Two dear loving spirits were not to be found any where. At that moment a hate and bitterness began that would stay with me the rest of that life.

What followed was too harrowing for me to even remember now. It had been a hot, sultry evening. We had our evening meal on the veranda. My father must have sensed some sort of unrest although it was not expressed in that manner but in nostalgia, memories of things I had done as a child, which was boring for me. He spoke of our honor of family -- all of which I had heard many times before so that inwardly I was impatient and angry at his reminiscing. How little patience we sometimes have in our younger years. My mother would just tune him out at times like that. I would live to regret my attitude that last night of our peaceful, sweet life together. My father seemed to talk forever and as was our custom, no one left his presence until he decided the evening was ended. There were some ten or twelve Negros of all ages gathered listening to him. These talks were also very educational opportunities for all who wanted to listen. One evening of listening to my father spouting moral character gave a person more than a year of listening to a preacher. Honor - truth - respect - love of country and fellowman with emphasis on all men, regardless of race, creed or color. He could quote the bible better than most preachers without looking up passages. Unlike them, he was well read in other philosophies and history. Since he was my father and all I knew - I never really appreciated the truly special man that he was until after he breathed life no more. Considering we began life at dawn, to stay up until well after 10 PM was a very late evening. With his arm around my shoulder, I grew impatient and sleepy with his reminding me of family traditions and his "Remember, I will always love you with all my heart." "Really, Papa, I know that, I want to go to bed." "Sweet dreams, little Princess." Why couldn't I sense his hanging on - why was I so irritable and impatient - why couldn't I have sense the impending night of disaster but if I had, what could I have done. At my age, no one listened to a woman's thoughts or wisdom. There are memories with Martha from when I was a baby that flashed through my mind that were profound. How could I remember as a babe - I never thought we remembered younger than about 3 years old.

One rider burst through our veranda doors that have been left open for air circulation due to the heat. The doors were on the back of the house facing the servants quarters which we thought were protected. Perhaps the screen doors were locked, I don't know. I did not see him enter but heard his horse's hoofs in our foyer. My father ran to the top of the circular stairway - I did not see this but heard the shot ring out - a loud blast - then another and my mother fell behind my father. As I ran to the top ledge, the horsemen were in the dining parlor and did not see me. When I saw my parents sprawled dead at the front of the stairs, I fainted, escaping the rest of the massacre.

That beautiful gentle home was so much more than a house and became a tomb for my beloved parents and nearly for me had it not been for one of our Negro slaves who risk his own life to save mine. One of the servants, who was sleeping downstairs in the house hearing the ruckus, entered the foyer carrying an oil lamp. Two of the horsemen reentered the foyer, shots rang out, one hit the lamp, scattering flaming oil in all directions. The flames quickly spread. The robbers had ransacked the dining parlor for silver, then forced to evacuate from flames. They were on a drunken rampage and found the burning mansion thrilling excitement "Burn!" "Burn!" they laughed and shouted. Their swearing and shouting had held the servants at bay. One of the teenage boys managed to hide away, entering the flaming house, running up the stairs as the stairway began to crumble. He dragged me across a room out of view of the robbers, out on the roof of the veranda and pushed me onto bushes below to break my fall. I was unconscious and came to as he dragged me under the arms safely away from the burning house. We were on the far side of the goings on at the house. With the noise of the crackling, burning, timbers falling, we could hear only muffled screams, not knowing what was happening to the others. Was my aunt rescued from the flames? I wanted to believe what I had seen of my parents' death was a bad dream. I passed out again.

I awoke to the blinding sun and the horrible stench of the fire still smoldering. About seven or eight of our slaves were standing over me. The women were sobbing. The doctor wearing his black coat was standing over me. "She's coming out of it" -- I heard "Oh, God, what's this poor chile to do!" This is a dream - I am still asleep - this is all a very bad nightmare! "Mama - Papa" I began to shout out as I sat up. Oh, God - NO! - There it was - a heap of smoking embers -- My hands grasp my cheeks - I am not asleep, this is no dream, this can't be real! I jumped to my feet and started for the house still shouting "Mama - Papa" when someone grabbed me from behind, holding my upper arms. "No - no - the embers are too hot to go looking for them." "Chile - they're gone -- They're in heaven now with your Aunt Helen" -- "NO, not my aunt, too!" I sank to the ground sobbing, feeling more dead than alive.

In a half- crazed daze, the weeks that followed, even now, seem only a vague impression. An air of desperation began taking hold of me. I now had no family - no dowry - everything was gone. My father had a terrible experience with banks in his youth and did not trust them, plus with the approaching war, he kept everything in cash, certificates and deeds in a safe in the house. Perhaps the robbers knew about it and were after the safe. The flames were so hot, it and everything in it was melted.

In present day, people cannot understand how devastating it was for people of the South, especially a cultured young lady to no longer have a dowry. No well bred young man could possibly marry a young woman without a dowry. It wasn't as materialistic as it may sound but a deeply engrained custom of women prepared to serve as a housewife and mother for in those days, we considered husband and family, serving God and country each the highest most important thing we could do. Having servants who served our needs -- only meant that we were able to serve them with their needs. We looked upon all, as servants to a benevolent God. With the fairy princess life that was suddenly jolted away in a half night's events into a hideous world of reality, I was totally unprepared. The "benevolent God seemed a part of the fairy tale world now gone. While I didn't know the word "atheist", that was what my silent self became. I had to think. I had to be clever. I had to have a way to survive. In the months that followed, all plantations were hard hit as were the people in all walks of life. There was almost no food or necessities which became a way of life. I feel sure this is why many people today that lived a previous life in that era so easily identify with Scarlet O'Hara in "Gone With The Wind." Even as a young child in this present life I identified with the experiences of Scarlet - her youth, the young men around her, scrounging the earth for a potato "I will never go hungry again" and her daughter's death. Those scenes connected so strongly inside of me. I don't know why the war was called "Civil War" there was nothing "civil" about it. White men against white me - very uncivilized. We had "red" men to fight against. All over the world wars had occurred with race against race, not countrymen against countrymen. Our forefathers had escaped Europe's repression to create such a strong class culture, how could we be a part of anything so totally uncivilized!

I was living with friends of my parents but they could hardly feed their own household without me leaching off of them. I was trained to be a woman cared for - I was also taught to be responsible and not leach off the good fortunes of others. In this case, they no longer had good fortune! I had to do something to take care of myself. My older sister was living in Texas with her husband. We were never close and lived very different lives. When I was quite young, she had fallen in love with a man that was not in our social standing and my father disapproved.

They decided to head West and ended up in the middle of Texas where he established life as a farmer. I didn't feel that I knew her at all. As the younger sister, I had a lot of attention and would be called "spoiled" and raised more like an only child. After my parents' death and destruction of everything, she urged me to move to Texas and live with them. They had plenty of room and food as the War had not affected their lives as much as in the Southern states. To me, it seemed like an unexplored, wild foreign land. At first, it was just unthinkable, yet staying was reliving so much pain and fears. Those four men were never caught and punished. I prayed that life would punish them for their dastardly deeds! What to do? Where to go? My uncle had died several years before and formerly had a business partner that moved to California. Perhaps he could help me if I ever got that far out of the South, which seemed more unthinkable than Texas. With my fairy tale life gone, I didn't want to keep imposing on our friends. My emotions grew very cold and I began growing more and more calculating as to how I would manage life as an adult. I could not stand feeling so temporary - little could I imagine how that state of mind would follow me through future lives and past ones that I didn't know about. I did not want to stay and I did not want to go. With a socializing life in the past, I didn't realize how tightly knitted we were on our plantation. My parents, my aunt and our servants had our own social communal structure. With everything gone, everything and every one seemed so distant to me. I felt like a tree and I was a limb, yet the tree was destroyed and I was the limb floating in life. I had to find a tree to be attached to again.

John (my husband "Jack" in this life) was a quiet pharmacist who had more than a passing fancy toward me since I was a little girl. He had always been a grown man ever since I became aware of him. All the younger men were off in the war, plus the problem of no dowry. He was a good man, not rich or from any particular significant family. Actually he was from the North but had lived here for a long as I could remember. He, too, had no one. This seemed to bring us together, as two rudderless ships which found some directional course together.

He was a nice man, gentle and kind. He was educated and intelligent. That held some fascination for me. He was unlike any of the boys I had thought I would fall in love with. Since they had all been away for so long, my memories had faded or shut down. Any thoughts of the past seemed like childhood fantasies as I tried to adapt to this new unpleasant way of life. I was building a fondness for John that I thought was becoming a more mature "love." (In other words, I talked myself into being "in love" with him, just as I did with him and my first husband in my present life!) I didn't think he had any interest or the courage to ever ask me to marry him. Many of the men his age had sons in the war. Marriage and family never seemed to be his goal. One day, sitting under a tree, I coolly said "John, do you want to marry me, leave here and go to Texas to live with my sister and her family -- maybe later to even travel to California?" Just as coolly he said "yes I do." There were no bells ringing - no sudden emotions, no passion, not even a hung and kiss - it was simply a subtle business like agreement. Thus began my married life in the Civil War era. From early childhood I had envisioned a huge wedding at the plantation - the social event of the season. I had designed dozens of wedding gowns - huge, bouffant satin and silks - a long train, with at least 5 to 10 bridesmaids. I would float down our circular stairway on my father's arm with everyone gasping at the beauty of the fairy tale bride and the handsome young man waiting for me in our largest parlor that had been added and called the ballroom or in our garden. The mansion has several parlors befitting the season of the year and size of any gathering. Calling it a ballroom seemed pretentious so we called it our gathering parlor. Papa said it was for parties, his political meetings but I knew it was built with my wedding in mind. Gone -- all gone now - my wedding day was nothing more than two people standing before a judge taking vows. How sadly lacking was this world of reality for me.

When Katherine married William, our father objected but consented to have the wedding at the plantation as it was the thing to do and mainly an excuse for a social event to invite everyone to our plantation. It was sweet and charming but insignificant compared to the social event mine would have been. Her marrying a widowed man with a son and not of our social standing was usually not well accepted; however, since our father was a strong in politics, all who were invited came. In my childhood, she had helped take care of me and I looked up to her. She was like a Nanny in many ways. She seemed like a very compassionate person, especially with her writing letters to me insisting I come to live with them.

The journey to Texas was long and tiring. We went part of the way by boat to New Orleans, the rest through Louisiana and Texas by carriage, stopping many times along the way. It was hot and miserable. Long layers of skirts were not cool apparel. Unloading and loading trunks became an almost impossible task even for a man. John had never been very physical in work or pleasure. His sport was croquet and parlor games. As for sex, as a virgin, I avoided it as much as possible. It must have been so insignificant that it is difficult to conger up memories of any strong emotion between us. He seemed patient and adapted well to my youthful joie de vivre.

Kathrine had two children, her husband's son who was about 17 and they had a daughter around 8 years old. When we arrived, all seemed happy to see us and begged us to stay. They had an extra small house where we could live. It was fixed up but had been for darkies. After the long wagon trip anything with a roof was to be thankful for. Katherine, William, her husband, and John got along well as they were closer to the same age than I was. Her step-son, Lester, William's son was closer to my age. That had been one of my father's objections to her marrying William. To me, Lester was such a wimpy boy. There was something about him I really disliked - a sneaky, untrustworthy, dishonest nature. (He is my sister's son in the present life). He seemed to have an abnormal attachment to Katherine. Years later I was to find out that he had a sexual affair with her which seemed second nature after him viewing his father's disgusting actions.

On a hot, sweltering Texas late afternoon, John had driven the wagon taking Katherine into the town to shop. I didn't go because of the heat and I was involved in making art craft items which we sold in town. I needed seeds for my work and went to the barn to get some. I was unaware of William entering the barn, besides it was natural to see him there. I realized he had been drinking when he called out sarcastically, "Hey, Sister what are ya doing out here all alone?" I replied "Just getting these seeds for my work." As I turned, he said "here, let me help you" with that he pushed me into the batch of seeds and hay. Suddenly he was on top of me penning me down so that I couldn't struggle free. He threw his hand over my mouth and told me if I screamed he would kill me just like the pig they butchered the day before. He knew how that had upset me after all the human blood I had seen. He said I had been leading him on ever since we arrived. He assumed I had been raped by soldiers, so one more wouldn't matter. He raped me holding his hand over my mouth. I could feel the grit forced into my mouth from his dirty hand. Later, I found out his son has peeped through a hole and witnessed the whole thing and threatened to tell so he had me beholding to him. I hated him from that day forward but couldn't say anything for fear someone would know. Because of the heat I was wearing a simple tie string dress with nothing on underneath it. It never occurred to me that one quick pull of the string left me nude! A loose fitting sack dress with a draw string would not seem "sexy" even then. William was so drunk that his painful thrust caused him to have an immediate organism - just enough to enter my body. In pain and humiliation in tears was all I felt as he flopped over seemingly passed out. I struggled to slip back into my dress and rushed to the house to wash away this horrible, disgusting rape! I was horrified and didn't know what to do. I felt so alone. All I could do was wash myself over and over, feeling I could not get the filthy experience off of me. I could not tell either my sister or my husband. I couldn't chance upsetting her marriage and we were soon to leave for California in the spring. I kept it to myself hardly able to be courtesy to the monster who raped me! I couldn't wait for spring to arrive so we could get away from there. I felt so miserable and uncomfortable around either of them.

In this life, William and Lester were father and son once again. They carry some terrible guilt for both hated me for no reason in this present life. They used me for a scapegoat for any flaws in any woman. I know my husband then was my third husband in this life. My sister was the same. A few years ago when in Texas I asked my higher mind why my sister and brother-in-law hated me so when I had done nothing toward them to have so much hate thrown back at me from these church going people -- it came to me about his fathering my son and in that past life, they were still angry at me for just being. The next day, I drove to the local cemetery to visit my beloved father's grave in my present life. I searched among the headstones of the old cemetery's section to see if I could find one for a child in the mid 1800's. There were pre and post Civil War headstones but none struck me as the one I looked for. There were many unmarked graves in the old section. In those days, probably many graves were on the farm property, not in public cemeteries. That night I sat in meditation and asked why was I sent on a "wild goose chase" since I had not discovered a grave to prove this sensing of my son's death? At that moment, on the movie screen of my mind, the picture of my father's grave stone popped up! That made sense! I knew my father in this life had been my son in that life. I had been his favorite child and my daughter had been his favorite grandchild that created jealousy with my siblings' families. I just knew that this area of Texas was where my sister and her family lived in that life and the present. My father always wanted to move back to that area while we lived in the western part of Texas where I was born in my present life.

My parents had lived in that East Texas town when my sister was a baby. My Dad succeeded in moving back when I was in High School that really ruined my last two years of High School. I hated that town and to this day, I still can't stand that town filled with so much mean-spiritedness narrow mindedness and hatred. Before my parents even moved to that town, I never liked it and rebelled when he decided to move there. I did not know why I disliked it so much --- until I began getting this past life of Hanna. I realized my child who died at 4 or 5 years old was buried in the local cemetery. Suddenly I understood so many things. My father and brother-in-law never liked each other. My father hated California and always wanted me to move back to Texas. Through the years hurtful people always greeted me in that town. My father did everything he could to try to "hog tie" me there. When he was in the hospital the day before he died, he said he wanted to talk to me alone but my sister would not leave me alone with him. In that life, as my little son in that life, he had choked to death and in this life at age 80, again his death was because of choking.

Years before he had throat surgery for cancer, since that time he could not sleep on his back. He warned all of us not to let him sleep on his back while in the hospital. After his death all hell broke loose as he was the bonding force within my family. My sister's husband was now determined to destroy every thing related to my father and me. Little by little it all fell apart until there was nothing left, even all communications with my sister's children ceased even though I had loved them almost as much as my own daughter. Inwardly, I know that this man will return in his next incarnation as a woman and have all the crap thrown at him that he has done to women in this life.

William was curt and said thing to me that were too sensitive. He made accusations that were totally unfounded. I was empty of love for anyone. The best I could muster was what I though was respect but even that was most difficult after his hideous abuse of me. Kathryn had not seen any of the war in Texas. William had not served in the army so they had little knowledge of the suffering we experienced. I was much too sensitive and could still see all that blood of my mama and papa when they were shot and killed, then burned along with the mansion. No one understood what was behind my eyes, then having to deal with my own sister's husband raping me forced me to secrecy that was devastating for me. She was so snippy toward me. I couldn't seem to please anyone. The three of them, being close to the same age, seemed to talk down to me like I was a dumb child when in truth I was smarter than them all. Now that I can look back at that life I know any sickly feeling I had was just plain fear of my husband's actions toward me. He had been so kind and gentle with me before we came to Texas. One wouldn't know him to be the same man.

My older sister in this life was in a similar situation having been Kathryn in that life. In both cases, she was accustomed to telling me what to do and bossing me around. I resented it in my present life as well as that one, too. Now that I had assumed adulthood, having her tell me what to do all the time got very tiring plus having to live in their domain. The money John has saved was almost gone. We were at their mercy. We didn't have the money to continue on to California and after the rape, it was imperative for us to get out of this situation. To help pay for us being there, John tutored Lester and their daughter. Neither John nor I knew anything about hard farm labor. At our Southern home, as females we were taught to cook, sew and do household duties as well as rearing children. As a pharmacist John often acted as a doctor for family and friends that gave him a small bit of money, which we saved every penny. He always seemed to know what to do or have the right answer for health or accident problems. He was better educated than William so he was able to help him with books, finances, etc., but we seemed indebted for our existence. Texas began to be affected by the War, not like the South, but there wasn't much actual money around. Mostly, people bartered for services, however, it wasn't possible to barter our way across the country.

Their home was not fancy but it was a large farm house. Each year, as we moved toward the winter months, it was too late to try to make the trip to California. Fear came over me when I realized I was pregnant. Unfortunately, it soon became obvious that I was pregnant. I did not know any joys of sexuality. I hated it and avoided it, now I would bear my sister's husband's child. I was overwhelmed with grief and defeat. I had to pretend it was John's child. I was taught never to lie; now I must live a lie! (I had to live the same lie with my pregnancy in this life.)

From that day of the rape, William acted as though nothing had happened. Was he too drunk to even remember? His son sometimes had a disgusting knowing grin. Since I had never seen William drunk like that before or since, I wondered if his scheming son might have gotten him drunk. He was not a man to drink. Who could I confide in -- certainly not Kathryn. Knowing that her husband did not drink, she would never believe me. I couldn't tell John as it would be so hurtful for him. Deceiving him over the unborn child was an unthinkable choice but a choice I had to make. Intimate acts were just not discussed with anyone, even one's closest friends, in those days. There were far more acts of incest than anyone care to admit, then and now!

Within weeks the signs of pregnancy were obvious. I had to give in to having sex with John even though I found anything involved with it quite disgusting, even more so with the rape. "Rape" was not a word a well brought up Southern girl would even know or ever use.

Almost nine months to the day of the rape, miserably I gave birth to a baby boy. The event intensified me knowing the truth but having to live a major lie. It weighed so heavily upon me; I had to choke back tears when I should be happy about our "blessed" event. My excuse for sadness was the absence of my beloved my parents and that I was not feeling well. I asked to be left alone so I could sleep. Poor John thought he could no longer foster a child and was delighted. Only I knew that probably he could not.

Regardless of who fathered a child, a mother's love for her baby is no less intense. My secret and my losses seemed to wrap my life totally in my son's well being. Perhaps I was too attentive or did my inner self want to savor as much mother/child love as I possibly could? Carrying the burden of this terrible secret was the main reason I wanted to leave for California but there was the matter of money to make the trip, so we stayed and saved all that we could. William's son could not know for sure who fathered the baby. If he suspected, he never revealed it. I just never liked to have any conversation with him and as little contact as possible.

Most of Hanna's life was revealed to me in several meditations while visiting my Mother in Texas. I knew that my sister in this life was Kathryn and that her husband now was William. I feel fairly sure that William's son was their oldest son in this life. Interestingly, my sister's husband in the present life never carried the name "William" but "Billy" and my father's first name was "William." My sister in this life is Kathleen and Kathryn in that life. In this life, they lived on farm land twice but never really farmed, instead raised cattle.

Howard was a man of thirty in the Civil War. He was from Bolorei, MS and fought against General Grant in the siege at Vicksburg. Bolo Rei was the name of a sweet bread Portuguese Christmas Cake. Manuel Gayoso, Portuguese born, built a fortress to defend the Mississippi river from Indians. It was a very small community, no longer there. Union soldiers had shot Howard in the eyes, the last sight he saw was Hanna, whom he had known and had adored her. His last dying thought was of Hanna. It was this connection that brought him in as Hanna's son and was not enough time for him to reincarnate, thus he could not remain in the physical body more than five years. He died of consumption and choking. Still wanting to hold on to Hanna to obtain her lasting love, he was able to draw her into this present life as his youngest daughter, even though his wife had desperately not wanted this child. My father in this life's name was Howard.

In present life's circumstances, my sister and her husband did not meet in that town but did move back there when they married. He never got along with my father and they seemed to hate each other. I was also on her husband's hate list. Without ever spending five minutes to get to know me, he so harshly judged me that he made my life miserable for many years and did succeed in beating me out of any of our parents' inheritance even though it was stated in their will that I was to receive one third. In this life, I adored my sister and all her children, just not her husband! For years he had used me as a scapegoat for everything he didn't like in any woman. Was his unexplained hatred toward me his own guilt for past life shame? I am sure that if I could check back far enough, I would find that I had done something to him in a past life that created his hatred in this life, besides the rape. It took me a half century to understand that my sister and brother had always resented me. She and her husband turned their children against me. When I put the pieces together of the past life and present life, it all makes far more sense as to why attitudes were formed through possibly eons of time!

Sometimes, I feel that past relationships of desired control over another may reincarnate as our children that do seem to have an unidentifiable control over our lives for many years. Was the soul incarnated as my child in that life to express control but through illness died as a young child, then incarnated to be my father in my present life? I adored my father and what ever moral structures I may have was put there by his devotion to Masonic morality. He was the most moral person I have ever known. In this life, again, I had an unwanted teen pregnancy and in a forced marriage even though I wore an engagement ring from the father. If it had not been for the pregnancy, I don't think I would have ever gone through with a marriage to him. Again I had a marriage without passion that should have remained only as a good friendship.

Even though four fifths of the world believes in reincarnation, fundamental religions rebel against it. Unfortunately, it stifles their real spiritual growth not knowing where this life experiences originate. They sell their congregations on "sin" and forgiveness comes only through their churches that must be supported with their members and guests money. Frankly, understanding past lives experiences make forgiveness far easier and completions are made so that we don't have to keep repeating them! Karma is about "balancing the books" -- the sooner we accept that we do create our own reality only it may not be in our present lives but brought over from a past one so that we can resolve and end the repetitious process and experiences. These revelations make forgiveness, completions, letting go so much easier. Even if I cannot prove that my life at that time existed as it has been presented to me and as in any past life, if it resolves issues in this life, what difference does it make if I have no proof? Again, I say that one of my most important revelations in this life is to love oneself and be able to forgive ourselves for what we think of as mistakes, etc. Never succumb to other's option of you!

CHAPTER 15

WESTARD HO, THE WAGONS

John and I had saved and saved for the past four years as well as read everything we could about how to travel westward. Since we had felt settled in Texas, it was not an easy decision to make to leave the sheltered house and family to strike out on a long wagon train journey with possible Indians, weather, mountains and all sorts of potential problems. Those problems we heard of were small in number compared to those who died along the trial, killed by Indian attacks or just couldn't make it all the way to the Gold Rush of California and often just settled along the way. Some even had to turn back. Today we know of the perilous journeys of those who choose the Wagon trains -- the weather, the mountains, lack of supplies no matter how well prepared people thought they were. There were breakdowns with wagons, Indian attacks, wild animals, etc. For a cultured Southern belle it was an especially hard decision to make. Each trauma we face, we think it is the most difficult until we meet with another, another and another and so it goes. This was guaranteed on wagon trains. Each train group felt since others had made the trip before them, theirs would be easier -- or perhaps the promoters of the wagon trains sold them on the idea. In our RV lives today, I have often wondered if RV lovers were wagon train travelers in a past life. In either wagon trains or cross country RV travel, no one really wants to know the hardships they might face. RVs break down, too.

John kept me reminded that we had made it this far to Texas so California was just a little bit further. To me, it seemed a whole lot further! Even though we knew there was gold in Georgia, John never considered trying to go for it but with the enthusiasm we heard about the Gold Rush in California, it seemed a viable choice. John's calm nature became almost excitable as we took weeks preparing our wagon. With our different backgrounds, John was able to get along with the Texans so that the men often helped him with ideas for our travels westward.

To escape our confinement in Texas, we read stories to each other regarding traveling west. During the four years, we scraped to save, collecting things we needed. When we had a chance, we had bought two stout, young healthy horses, named Dan and Charlie. (Once living on a farm in this life at age six, we had two horses by the same names.) If instructions called for two of anything, we took three or four, if seven, we took ten. We wanted to be as well prepared as we could. Knowing Dan and Charlie would have a heavy load to pull; if light weight materials were available we used them. The idea of a new beginning with the possibility of more truth in my life, not having to hide the major secret, grew excitement for me, too. While I dreaded the trip, I also wanted to get started. I had left my southern home because of all the death and destruction, now leaving family and home behind because of the death of an unwanted, but loved son. My secret was now buried with my son. I vowed I would no longer carry it with me on our new journey.

In recalling past life experiences, scenarios do not fall in place in linear time or fall in place in time sequences. These memories came together over a very long period of time. As I write these memories and put them in linear time, more memories flow. Our memories flow into our conscious mind when we are ready for them. I state "ready" - millions of people are never ready to open to those past experiences, even though they help in their present life. They may have past life memories but they assume that it is just from a movie they've seen, a book they've read or in dreams. To me, repetitious dreams are past life memories trying to bleed through to the conscious mind. As we resolve these past life events, we leave space for new experiences. The more emotionally attached we are to people, things, places, etc. the longer we have to keep on the wheel of reincarnation. We can love people, things, places, etc. without allowing them to control us emotionally. Earth life is a spiritual school for us whether we want it or not.

My memories are scant about the travel from Texas to California. I don't know exactly when we left or how we hooked up with the Westward Wagon Train.

I know that it was far more difficult than I could imagine. I gained strength that I never knew I had. I have never been shown exactly the time my son died - I just know he never made it to age five. We were regular church goers during the Plantation life. To me it was more socializing than any kind of religious experience. My father had freely quoted the bible. It was a part of our way of life for him to read to us from it. After the horrible deaths there, then the rape and then death of my little son, I didn't have much faith in "a loving God". Like so many people today, I blamed God for my miserable experiences of taking away everything meaningful in my life. Now I understand Karma that I set in motion in another time and now have the opportunity "to balance the books." I kept my feelings to myself. In that life, as well as this present one, even with people I always felt alone and never understand why or what I could do about it.

Little could I imagine how much more I would face before that life of "Hanna" ended! I would need every ounce of courage and strength I could muster. During the travels to California, John became friendly with a religious group. They ate together, prayed together, dressed alike, read the bible together and similar in mannerisms. They were sweet, caring people but I wasn't interested in their religion. John seemed to get swallow up in their group. It was OK with me as it meant I could spend less time with him. I preferred to be alone with my thoughts - imagination - day dreams or reading a book in our quiet time.

I preferred talking to the men about horses or how to raise food. I had always preferred conversations with men rather than women. I learned as much as I could about prospecting for gold in California, the potential farming and anything I could read or learn about California.

John was a good traveler and fit in with the men and the women. The women in the group he joined seemed fascinated by him. Since it was the first time I saw women paying attention to him, perhaps it created a small amount of jealousy. Maybe I began to look at him in a different way. We always seemed good friends and companions, but never passionate love. It had never been an issue since I had never been with another man willingly, so I really didn't know that I was missing anything. In that era couples were more reserved about expressing any kind of affection in public. John had lightened up after the stress of living with my family in Texas. He began to laugh more and showed a side of him I hadn't known before. We grew closer than at any time during our marriage.

We had just headed for California and decided to see which direction we wanted to go after we got there. We had been in contact with an ex-business partner of my uncle's that was in Northern California. He would help us get settled there if we chose to go in that direction. John had read so much about all areas; we had no definite direction as to where to go. He was so influenced by the religious group and they wanted us to follow them to Southern California. Our decision would not make any difference since John would never make it out of the Southern California desert.

John and I had grown so much closer. With the past few years of tragedies and hardships had forced me to grow up and see things very differently. After we had entered into California and almost across the desert, we stopped near a mountain that had a stream trickling through it. There were very large boulders on each side of the creek. We had walked there, a short distance from where the wagon train was camped. We dipped our hands in the cool stream and cooled off our bodies. We found a rock formation and sat down to rest. John put his head in my lap. I leaned back on the rock. We both closed our eyes and day dreamed about our future now that we had finally reached California. As I heard a whizzing sound, John grimaced. I looked up at the blinding sun to see a silhouette of an Indian holding a bow high above us. The Indian stood there as if he was frozen and for me time also seemed frozen. Suddenly I was jolted into the reality that John lay there with his head in my lap dead with arrow in his heart! Again, I looked up at the Indian and at the moment a ferocious hate welled up in my heart. That hatred would remain etched in my heart for the rest of that life and into my present life when unknowingly, that Indian entered my life again. John was buried at the foot of that mountain and the wagon trained moved on. (John was my husband in this life and we met in the

Palm Springs desert and married there, a continuation of that past life. He couldn't wait to leave California to move to Florida. I had no desire to live in Florida as I had spent most of my adult years in California.)

John and I were just about to finally begin our new life together in a new land when my whole life fell apart again. Now I was totally alone, not like at home where everyone knew my family and we knew every one. There were no major decisions that I ever had to make until now. What to do? Where to go? I knew only of the one man, Mr. Huntington, who had been my uncle's partner in Northern California. The minute he got word of my husband's death, he sent an escort to bring me to his place in the Napa Valley area of Northern California. He owned a general merchandising company and other investments. Obviously, he had no financial problems. He also owned houses. He provided me with a small four room house that had fairly large rooms built in the old fashioned style with no hallways.

Hanna never told Mr. Huntington about William's rape; of course he knew of John's death and had been so caring for Hanna. He was providing everything for her. She had become cold as steel. The thought of any form of sex was far beyond any consideration on her part. She wanted sex with NO man! Mr. Huntington patiently waited for Hanna's morning for her husband to end. Perhaps, because he was providing everything for her, totally supporting her, even though she felt she earned her keep by working in his store, he apparently felt he might have sexual pleasures with her and eventually began making romantic overtures toward her. This was a role she was not willing to play! Hanna cleverly got around Mr. Huntington's ambitions toward her. She hired a prostitute to be around and available to seduce him and take care of his sexual needs.

In my present life, this same man was in my life for many years. He was a powerful executive in the TV industry and at any moment, he could secure my acting or production career! Did he? NEVER! Interestingly, in this life he was born a Southerner and maintained a heavy southern accent. What he DID do was gently give me money, which I refused, however, he would give it to me as a birthday gift or he told me he wanted to help me by giving me tips on stock market investments and I was to invest the money there. He never gave me the tips, more and more degrading to me, feeling I was taking money like a prostitute! What better way to get back at me from rejecting him in Hanna's life! Who was the prostitute in Hanna's life -- none other than my daughter in this life so that I could guide her and teach her good morals. She loved and often visited that same Northern California area. That same man was in my life as Anne Boleyn. Anne was responsible for his death.

There was a young, handsome Indian who worked in Mr. Huntington's store also. His constant gaze at Hanna made her very uncomfortable. After John's horrible death, she hated all Indians with the depths of her being. The young man sat on the porch of the store on a large bucket turned upside down and acquired the nickname "Pan". He was intelligent and very well built. He watched Hanna come and go for the first year but if their eyes met, she looked at him with disdain and looked away. Even though both worked for Mr. Huntington, Hanna would have nothing to do with Pan. He had a caring nature and wanted everyone to like him. He had charm that eventually won over everyone's attitude toward him -- except Hanna. People lost sight that he was an Indian, except Hanna. Mr. Huntington would be gone for months on business ventures so Hanna ran the store for him. For all the fun loving nature she had in youth, she was now cold, withdrawn, strictly stayed to her self and made friends with no one. All family ties had been broken. She refused to "darken the doors" of any church after John's death.

If Hanna was not at the store working, she sat in a chair reading with three oil lamps providing ample light for her lust for living with her books. Night after night, while she sat reading, Pan crept near her window, silently climbed into a nearby tree, sat for hours fascinated by her focus on reading. He was falling deeply in love with her but had no way of expressing his feelings with her continual ignoring him. When he did try to talk to her with limited use of the English language, she would only glare at him with her hatred for Indians and shout orders for him that only added to his frustration.

Hanna always loved to be out in nature. Since her arrival in California a few years before she had done little but work and read, plus she had no close friends. She was friendly to the customers but never allowed any of them to get close to her. As a child she had been an avid horse back rider and spent much time out of doors. She felt her best when she was away from people and in nature. Hanna had a terrible longing to visit the ocean where she had been only once when Mr. Harrington had arranged an overnight camping trip for his employees with tents and needed supplies. He had taken her there by horse and buggy.

When she expressed her desire to Mr. Huntington, he ordered Pan to ready the horses very early one Saturday morning. He ordered him to go with her and look out for her. Pan dared not to ask questions and did as he was told. If this was her only way to visit the ocean, so be it. She prepared blankest and baskets to carry across the horses. She had been taught to use a gun and generally carried a small rifle. Even with her sharp mind, she had underestimated the time it would take to get there and back home. Since they were riding horses, she thought the trip could be made in one day. It was into the afternoon before they arrived. Pan knew the way as he had made it many times before. He selected a high cliff that was an open flat area with one huge wide spreading oak tree. (This same wide spread tree overlooking the Pacific Ocean appeared in repetitious dreams in this life.) It became obvious that being able to spend any time there to enjoy the fresh ocean breeze, it would be necessary to also spend the night, yet not as prepared as the previous trip. She ordered Pan to secure the horses and gather wood for a fire so that they could stay warm during the night. Hanna walked down to the beach and took a long stroll while Pan sat atop the cliff watching her ever move. She ran and played like a little girl. He had never seen her like this and seemed to fall more in love with her in spite of the fact she would not have any conversation with him. This day seemed to soften her attitude toward him.

As the day turned into evening, Hanna took out the food from the basket and served Pan and herself, still without conversation. The huge oak tree offered a protective solid covering. She gave Pan the blankets and ordered him to sleep on the opposite side of the fire. With the way Hanna had always treated him, he could have easily deserted her but he stayed. As she fell asleep, he lay there just staring at her. She seemed to have no fears. Pan had never seen a white woman as brave and as self-contained. He did not understand this nature.

As the morning sun awakened Hanna from a deep restful sleep, it was as though she was back again in childhood with an overnight camping out with her father and cousins. A joyous feeling came over her that she had not felt in many years! She flung back the blankets, leaping up and racing toward the cliff taking deep breaths of the ocean air. He leaped up and followed her toward the cliff. She was smiling and he had never seen her like this. He was confused. He did not know whether to tackle her fearing she would fall off the cliff or let her do what she pleased. Confused and fascinated, he was totally in awe of this personality change. She climbed down the steep slope with ease and grace, with Pan following behind her. Being a practical person, she was one of the few women who dared to wear men's pants. Her father had taught her that it was OK for a girl to wear pants if the situation called for it. Since his death, he had become a saint to her. If he thought it was OK, it didn't matter what anyone else thought.

Hanna ran along the beach with her head thrown back laughing. All the years of pain, hostility, fear, resentment she had held inside burst forth now into joy and laughter. It had been so many years since she felt this exhilaration. Pan made no attempt to do anything but gradually merge with her swing in mood and began laughing with her. She was a totally different person than he had ever known. She ran until she fell exhausted on the sand. Laughingly, he picked her up and cared her to rest against a large bolder. As he laid her against the rock, they both looked at each other with a total communication for the first time. At the moment, Hanna was a beautiful youth filled girl and Pan was a handsome well-built young man. At that moment, there was no hatred on that beautiful Sunday morning of new birth. Even thought she refused to got to church on Sundays, it was always a special day of new birth, new beginnings and regeneration. This was the first time Hanna had felt alive in a very long time. She was happy!

Hanna was the one who insisted that she and John come to the new land in the West. Once she had to face total aloneness, she had retreated within her own cocoon. This day was like no other. It was as though it was the first day of her life in this new land. Pan and Hanna were in a time warp; nothing and no one existed except that moment of feeling wonderful. Pan gently kissed her forehead. As Hanna looked at a very close range at his lightly tanned body with his shirt opened to the waist, her heart was pounding from her run, now her body exploded with millions of electrical charges going off simultaneously as she ran her hand across his bare chest. There on that beach with the morning sun beating down upon them, Pan and Hanna made love as neither had ever experienced before!

After they had redressed themselves and walked peacefully arm and arm back toward their campsite with Hanna's head resting on Pan's broad shoulder, she was a totally transformed person. For the first time, they were talking. For the first time Hanna was laughing and gay. The youthful girl was OUT alive and well within her. It was a day of days. Pan's head rested in her lap as she read aloud to him, under the giant oak tree. Even thought Hanna had been married to John and raped by William, she had never known the joys of a good sexual experience. That day was truly a day like no other in her life!

By early afternoon, she knew they must start back home. In the beginning of the return trip, Hanna maintained her youthful, fun loving attitude but as the miles passed and each on a separate horse, her mood began to change. She grew silent as Pan observed the change come over her. He tried to talk to her, reminding her of their joy at the cliff and the beach. She only grew more silent. It was nightfall by the time they reached home. Hanna was totally back into her previous silent, withdrawn personality. Even though Pan felt like a strong man, he could do nothing about this change that came over her. Again, he crept outside her house, climbing in the tree, with his strong emotions, tears fell down his face.

In the weeks that followed, everything was back as it had been. Hanna was cold and rude to Pan. Born an Indian, close to nature, he did not know how to deal with his awakened feeling that had been opened then so drastically shut down just as suddenly. Hanna seemed to totally cut the memory of that Sunday as though it never existed. For Pan the memory grew so strong that it became an obsession. He hardly thought of anything else.

A few months passed. Word came that Mr. Huntington would be returning in another month or two. Now Hanna carried the secret burden that she was pregnant by Pan. What a predicament to be in. Mr. Huntington, a friend of her father and uncle, had taken her in when she knew no one, had no where to go and no money. He had set her up securely for the rest of her life with no money worries and a home registered in her name. He had been good to her and through the years continually made sexual overtures toward her until she had hired the prostitute to service his needs. This was a humbling experience for a highly successful, powerful man.

Hanna had made may excuses for her disinterest in any kind of sexual activity but NOW it was obvious that she had sex with someone. Any time Hanna knew that Mr. Huntington would come around, she always had Deidre, the prostitute with her in the house so she could offer him Deidre. It was like a game she played with light heartedness and he was too proud do anything about it but now she was showing her pregnancy!

One night as Pan took his usual place outside Hanna's window, he grew very upset seeing her pace back and forth, wringing her hands, not taking her usual place, sitting and reading a book. He had no way of knowing of her pregnancy and wanted to be near her to comfort her. As she went into the other room, reacting to his own emotions and concerns, he silently raised the window and crawled into the bedroom. She heard nothing as she was so preoccupied with her own worries of how to handle her unwanted pregnancy and had necessary planning to do. When Pan appeared in the doorway, totally shocked and frightened, so lost in thought, she did not recognize it was Pan and grabbed the gun off the mantle and fired. Being an excellent shot, the bullet hit its mark, Pan slumped dead on her floor! Horrified at what she had done, she could not stand the sight of Pan's dead body that she had so enjoyed in their sexual encounter! She grabbed a sheet and dropped it over him. She went screaming out of the house "Rape - HELP - Rape!" She told the Sheriff that Pan had raped her.

Hanna would have to stand trial. Simeon was Mr. Huntington's attorney and was called in to represent Hanna. Simeon had been a kindly man toward Hanna in the past and felt she could trust him. She would relate the story of the trip to the ocean and say that Pan had raped her there and when she saw him in her house, she was so shocked fearing he would rape her again, she didn't mean to kill him. She tearfully told her deepest dark secrets to Simeon regarding the previous rape and heartaches at the Plantation. She felt that if Simeon would use this information in privacy to the Judge, she might be freed of the murder charge. The trial was simple and almost totally secretly processed. Simeon had carried out the deed with perfection. Hanna had little or no remorse and had a strange feeling of justification. She believed her own lies regarding Pan, that, in truth, she secretly loved him, if only she could have allowed herself to be free of the hatred she felt for Indians after John's murder by the one on the cliff.

Hanna knew that she had to go away for the rest of her pregnancy. What to do with the baby she would think of later. To cover up her pregnancy, she talked Mr. Huntington into adding a section to the store featuring European fashions for both men and women. She would go to Europe and shop for the merchandise. She worked out the story so well that Mr. Huntington had no idea of her deception. She felt confident of her plan. She felt confident that Simeon would help her carry out her deception.

Hanna was totally naive to Simeon's devious nature. Now Simeon had Hanna exactly where he wanted her! This gentle, intelligent man became a lustful, greedy, sadistic old man. As Hanna stood before him sitting at his large hand carved desk, Simeon explained in vivid, gory detail exactly the sexual plans he and made for her and him. She could not believe what she was hearing. He was a totally opposite of what she had thought he was. This was total blackmail for the rest of her life. He was leaving her no options. As Simeon reached across the desk and hurtfully grabbed hold of Hanna's wrist while expressing dirty vulgarities, Hanna spotted an antique dueling pistol and hoped it was loaded. Again terrified, trembling and heart pounding she had no thought of the consequences as she grabbed the gun, fired it, a direct hit right between Simeon's eyes! The horrified expression on his face would remain with her for years to come as he slumped in a heap in his big chair.

There was NO way Hanna could get out of this one. She could not believe she had taken the lives of two men in a matter of weeks. Who would understand? Who could help her now? Think Hanna! Think! Think rationally! Get away -- disappear - vanish - just go! Hanna knew that the small hand carved wooden chest was locked in Simone's desk that held a large amount of cash. He had shown it to her trying to impress her. His keys had fallen out of his pocket when he slumped down in his chair. She grabbed them, fumbled to find the right key to the desk. She grabbed the little chest and ran out as fast as she could. She knew she had to get as many miles between her and Simeon's dead body as soon as she could. At the house she grabbed a few clothes, food took the money from the chest and all the cash that she had saved, saddled her horse and off she rode as fast as possible before anyone could find Simeon.

Where would she go? She was heading south not knowing where she would end up and beating the horse to go faster and faster. Finally, she was brought back to her senses hearing the poor horse gasping. She had always been so gentle and caring for horses, now she had almost killed one without thinking.

Her concern was far greater for her horse than the man she had just killed. She and her horse rested by a stream where they both partook of the water.

She petted him and apologized for her inconsideration. "I will find you a new home with people who treat you well..." After the rest, she continued to ride for several hours, stopping to rest now that she was further away from her home. When she came to a small community, she found a blacksmith shop. Hanna figured that the law might be looking for her horse when they found she and the horse gone, leaving without any arrangements about her small house. She asked the blacksmith if he would be willing to trade horses with her. "Your horse looks half dead, Lady." She said "He'll be alright tomorrow. I was being chased by some bandits and had to outrun them." He took off his hat and scratched his head - "We haven't heard of any bandits around these parts for years." Flushed with fear, she quickly began asking him about a piece of iron work - "Did you do this?" "Yes, Mam" he replied, so she quickly changed the subject with flattery for his work. "Please sir, will you trade horses with me, my father is ill in Oregon and I must be on my way." In case her horse was discovered here, she didn't want the authorities to know she headed south. He said "Lady, you just rode in from the North." "Yes, I had to stop to see some friends just north of here. They told me about you and how kind and generous you are." Even though her horse was a better one than the one he offered, she offered a bit of cash to seal the deal. This horse would be her lifeline to God only knows where! She slowly headed north until she got out of sight of the Blacksmith's shop, then headed around the community, sped up and continued south.

In that one day, money, security and all the nice things she had in her life had no meaning, just saving her own life was her only goal.

Fortunately, Hanna's training with her father's overnight camping and her trek across the country in a wagon train had taught her survival skills. When she found a community with a store, she picked up needed travel items and food. When she bought a pair of man's pants, the shopkeeper seemed a bit shocked. She could carry very little on the horse. Between the cash that was in Simeon's little chest and the cash she had at home, she felt she could get by for several months even if she had to loose everything she had worked for back in Northern California in the area that is near Napa Valley.

She followed the coastline as much as possible because she didn't know the terrain and feared having to travel through mountains. Hanna had no idea if the Indians were still dangerous or if the event with John was an exception. She could still see the face of the Indian that shot him with his arrow. Her survival determination took over her fears. She loved being in nature - little could she know how much of it she would face the rest of her life. She had to stop at dusk and prepare to sleep somewhere as she needed the sun to know which direction she was going. Hanna had never ridden cross country on horseback but if men could do it, she could also. This was the first night she had ever been totally alone out in nature. At first, she was so committed to being totally self-sufficient, building a good lasting fire, preparing something to eat and spreading her blankets for sleep. Her rifle lay next to her hand as she lay there starring at the fire. How did she get there? Was this all a bad dream? Before she could think about the day's events, she fell fast asleep totally exhausted. She was awakened by dew dripping on her face from the tree, she grabbed her rifle, swing around but there was nothing or no one there. "Oh! God! Is it real -- did I really kill Simeon - did it really happen?" Hanna began sobbing hysterically - she cried and cried and cried until there were no tears left. Her eyes were red and swollen. As she stood up, pulling her shoulders up trying to fill her lungs with the fresh morning air. "Hanna, get hold of yourself! You can do this! You can make it! You CAN survive!" It seemed her father was putting those words in her head.

There was that ocean she had longed to see, now, she was getting a bit tired of it. When she had to sleep near it, the sand was damp and hard. The nights were cold - the wind would blow out her fire. It was a struggle to keep it going. Hanna had nightmares about getting turned around and ending up in Simeon's office again. Her nightmares include a mean looking old judge shaking his finger in her face screaming, "You die by the gallows for killing two innocent men... You Vixen!" She lost track of time or what day it was as she restlessly rode on from sun up until sun down. She pushed herself beyond human endurance. During the whole horrendous experience, she had forgotten about her major problem of unwanted pregnancy -- until one morning she was awaken with excruciating pain. Hanna doubled over in pain. Was this it? Was she going to die alone on the beach... finally the gross pain aborted the fetus. There it was a heaping bloody blob lying on the beach beside her - she began sobbing with another death that had passed through her body. In a frantic release of joy and pain, she grabbed the mass and ran out into the ocean and threw it into the water. She watched the tide sweep it out to sea as she cried and laughed at the same time, with tears streaming down her face, she screamed "Now, Pan take your bloody Indian baby with you -- it is yours -- take it with you." Her body weak and exhausted, she limbed back out of the water and dropped lifelessly on the sand.

She was awakened by her skin feeling parched and a man's hands under her arms pulling her out of the surf. The tide had come in and was nearly pulling right along with Pan's would be child - out to sea - to Never - Never land. He was a bearded young Mexican man that had wandered by while he was fishing. After he bundled Hanna's belongings on to her horse, he laid her limp half-conscious body across the horse. He led her inland but she was not conscious to know where he was going. She vaguely saw the small shack with the smell of fire going, dogs yapping, numerous small Mexican children jabbering in a language she could not understand. She passed out.

When Hanna awoke a few days had passed. A gentle looking Mexican woman in her late thirties was leaning over her jabbering excitedly when Hanna opened her eyes. The young man and children came rushing in -- all jabbering at the same time. Hanna was confused and disoriented. She put her hands to her ears to block out the sudden noise. The woman shushed the children and sent them scurrying out of the room. They could be heard excitedly outside, with a small boy climbing to look into the window. Even tired, sick and limp, Hanna saw a rare beauty in these children she had never seen before.

Hanna struggled to get up but fell back in her weakness. "I've got to get out of here -- who are these people - are they Indians or what - if they are Indians and if find out I killed one of their braves and his child-to-be they will kill me -- I must get my horse and leave..." Hanna smiled weakly at the woman, took a deep breath and with every ounce of strength she could muster, forced herself to get up. At first, she sat on the edge of the bed. She looked at the cotton night gown and looked up at the woman. The woman understood, smiled and went into the other room to bring back Hanna's clean clothing and laid them beside her. Hanna thanked the woman who exited the room giving her privacy. Hanna looked at the child peering in the window - he quickly dropped out of sight. Hanna struggled to remove the gown and replace it with her own freshly washed blouse and pants. When she stood, she dropped back on the bed several times before she could get her balance. Her boots were a real struggle. Finally she stood fully clothed and held onto the wall as she edged her way toward the adjoining room. There was strange food she had never seen before. Never mind, she thought "they eat it and they look healthy enough -- I need my strength -- I gotta keep moving on." Had they found the aborted fetus -- did they know - could they know that she was a murderer -- a murderer -- Hanna could not believe her thoughts - a woman brought up in such genteel refinement. As she observed the children around her, she recalled her own affluent childhood. All those children would never have the toys and childhood joys she alone had experienced. Her heart went out to them and their simplistic life, but they seemed happy and that seemed all that mattered now. As she struggled to adapt to the strange food, sadly humorously thoughts of the past few years how she has struggled to save money, build up securities, what good was it now when forced to leave behind. Even if she wanted to buy toys and things for these children, she had to save every penny she brought with her not knowing what she had to face or where she could live without being caught by the Northern California authorities.

She struggled to get on her feet and motioned to the young man, gesturing riding a horse. He quickly jumped to his feet and motioned her toward the outside. There in a nearby stall stood her horse. She slowly walked out and reached for her saddle. The young man grabbed it and rattled in his own native tongue, began saddling her horse --

"Thank you - thank you" as she reentered the simple shack. The woman motioned to Hanna's supplies neatly stacked on the floor. She took the woman's hand and thanked her. She reached in the saddle bags to place some money in the woman's hand. The woman tried not to accept it but Hanna insisted wishing she could give her more for her kindness.

The young man entered the cabin and picked up Hanna's supplies, then loaded them onto her saddled horse. He had also saddled a horse to ride with her for a little way. He apparently was asking her where she was going but since she did not know, how could she answer him? She looked toward the sun to find directions then pointed south. Other than that, she was totally disoriented and did not know how far they were from the ocean. He rode along with her for awhile but since they had no means of communication, Hanna thanked him and motioned for him to return home. As she rode off he exclaimed "No - No - NO Senoia!" She continued on having no idea why he kept calling out "No - no - no!"

After a couple of hours, still very weak, she had been riding in an almost unconscious state. She then understood why he said "No - No - NO!" The sun was sweltering hot. The horse was sweating. Hanna removed her jacket and neck scarf to wipe her brow. Her clothing was soppy wet. The trees and every living thing had disappeared. "My God, I have ridden into a desert -- which way is out?" She didn't know which way was back to where she started. She kept riding trying to head south. Finally the sun began to drop in the West.

The air began to cool down with a slight breeze. She found some large rock formations to make camp for the night.

The next day was even worse - was she riding in a circle - would she find her way out of this blazing desert? The third day was worse than the previous two. About mid day Hanna's horse reared up dropping her to the ground. In an almost trance like state Hanna raised her self up on her elbows only to be staring at a rattle snake within inches of her face. "This is it..," she closed her eyes awaiting the strike of poison venom when a cracking sound made by her horse startled the snake, which slithered off in the opposite direction. Hanna's heart was pounding so hard, her head was throbbing that she wasn't sure if the snake's venom might have been a quicker death that what it seemed she was experiencing. Was this all God's punishment for what she had done! She struggled to a large boulder, grabbing hold of it trying to pull herself up to a standing position. As she starred directly at the bright sinking sun, she was momentarily blinded. She had a vision of walking in a beautiful forest. The air was fresh and cool. There was a nearby brook - small animals played at her feet -- birds dipped and sang near her. As she walked through this beautiful forest, there was a brilliant light ahead of her which she walked toward. Peace and contentment that she had never experienced. Suddenly she was distracted from this beautiful vision with water being poured over her face. Her blurred vision seemed to reveal a silhouetted gowned figure standing over her. Had she died and gone to heaven. Would they be pouring water on her? "With God's help, you will be saved, My Lady." As the sun had burned her flesh, she then wondered if she was dead and had gone to hell instead. Was the figure standing over her the Devil? Why wouldn't her eyes clear up - everything was still a blur - then it all went black.

A hot wind bowing on Hanna's face awoke her out of a deep sleep. She was wearing a white robe. Was she in Heaven or Hell - whatever it was -- it was quite warm! This definitely was not the beautiful cool wooded area she had seen in her vision. The walls were white adobe. She lay on a simple bed with a straw mattress, atop leather strapping. There was one open window and an open door that allowed the suction for the warm air to flow through the room. She lay there starring at the ceiling -- "Am I dead or alive?" Just then a little fat bald brown robed man appeared in the doorway with a big smile. Hanna saw a huge cross hanging from his robe "It must not be hell or there wouldn't be a cross." "Ahh - how wonderful to see those eyes opened at last" he said with a funny accent. Hanna tried to raise up on her elbow but fell back too weak to sit up. "No, now no need to rush yourself; I have brought you some nice porridge that will help give you strength. I will help you with it."

Hanna asked where she was. Brother Timothy explained that Brother Paul was transferred from the mission in Santa Barbara to their small mission near the foothills of the San Bernardino Mountains. While crossing the desert area, Brother Paul came across Hanna who was near death. Brother Paul had brought her there where she and been for several days recuperating. "Many prayers have been said in your behalf for you to live." Here she was, among men of the cloth -- God's servants and she had no longer believed in God, the church or any other religiousness. She looked the blank wall, except for a crucifix affixed in front of her. She closed her eyes to avoid looking at it and asked "My horse?" Before Brother Timothy's answer could register in her semi state of consciousness Hanna again drifted back to sleep.

Early in the morning Hanna was awakened by the hustling about in the hallway. Again she tried to sit up. She finally managed to get herself in a semi sitting position. As she looked around to see what to prop herself against, she saw Brother Paul silently standing in the doorway. He was so big that he blocked the whole doorway. Hanna glanced at him - now her eyes were in focus. There stood about the most handsome man she had ever seen dressed in the clothing of a monk - a man dedicated to God. "Well, Dear Lady, I am happy to see that my efforts were not in vain." Hanna replied "You are the one who saved me..?" He replied "Let us say with God's help you are here with us today." He began talking freely to her in a melodic voice that vibrated rapturously that put her in a state she had never heard before. She did not hear what he was saying but heard him as she had never heard a man before. His eyes penetrated into her very soul!

The days turned into weeks. Brother Paul talked and walked with Hanna. Soon her strength was back. Little by little she began to help at the little mission. There was nursing to be done which seemed to come easy for her. She had never professed to be able to cook but she helped in the kitchen as was permissible. As the few patients came in and out, soon she was the only one left. It became awkward for her to be there. She felt she had overstayed her welcome but where would she go. Brother Paul strongly urged her to join the order of Sisters but Hanna felt totally unworthy of God's consideration in any way after her lurid past. How could she tell anyone of her past experiences? Who would ever understand what she had been through? What had driven her to react in the way she did - even God would not understand. After all God was a man. What man could ever understand her inner feelings or experiences? Brother Paul was a man, yet he had a gentle soothing warmth that warmed Hanna through and through. At times she was so ashamed of her thoughts about him; she felt she had to get away from this totally hopeless situation. How could she have those sinful lustful thoughts about a monk committed to God!

Hanna would venture out with Brother Paul as he went visiting the sick. He was to go up into the mountains to help a family that needed a strong man's help since a tree had fallen on Mr. Parker and he was unable to care of his family. Since Hanna had been such a help to Brother Paul and could ride a horse, he asked her to go along and help him. She was delighted to accompany him any time, any where!

The mountains had fascinated her from the first day she had seen them. It had been a very long time since she had been so high on a mountain. The pine trees seemed to beacon her. The smells in the air were the best she had ever experienced. It felt good to be riding her horse again as it gave her a sense of freedom.

When they arrived at the home of the Parkers, it was late afternoon. The family greeted them with great appreciation. A warm friendly meal was shared. The small house was bursting at the seams with the family members. Both Hanna and Paul helped with the chores until it was almost dark. It was dangerous to ride the horses down the mountain at night. Hanna and Brother Paul decided they would find a place to sleep in the barn. Even though they found separated places to sleep, when the rain began to pour outside, a strange deja vue came over both Hanna and Brother Paul. As Hanna lay there with her body aching to go to Brother Paul -- how could she be so disrespectful and sacrilegious!

(Just as I was channeling this past life recall and writing it down, Richard called, who was the *same* man I called Brother Paul in that life and the Priest in a French life. In the Belgium life, Jonathan became a priest when he was sent to America. In this life Richard had studied to be a priest. Talk about synchronicity!)

Brother Paul was in the loft above and could still see Hanna below. He had very little to do with women and this woman was the most beautiful women he had ever seen. His entire body pulsated with feelings he had never before experience. A crash of thunder startled Hanna out of a dream - or a day dream - "How could I have this dream" -- she seemed to have a dream about Paul as a priest in another time making love to her as a nun in a barn much like this one. Guilt consumed Hanna as she recalled this dream over and over. She turned away from Paul - even though she could not see him, she buried her head under her arms in shame. From Paul's perspective, he faintly saw her movements in the light from the flashing lightening - "she must fear the thunder" Paul thought as a part of him wanted to reach out and go to Hanna and hold her to protected her from the elements. How could he, a monk, have such feelings! Both Hanna and Brother Paul lay awake most of the night with the lightening and pouring rain. Both struggling with a magnetic pull toward each other, nether knew how to handle their feelings.

As morning came Brother Paul was up chopping wood, hustling about getting man's chores organized and done that Mr. Parker could not do with his injury. Even though he was a large muscular man, he seemed to have super human strength. Hanna was busily nursing and nurturing the family. Since there was so much that needed doing, she assumed that they would stay on for several days. The evening meal was prepared well before the sun sank in the west. Brother Paul announced he had to return to the Mission. Everyone knew it would be well into the dark before he reached the bottom of the mountain but he insisted he knew the way and had Divine protection. It was settled that Hanna would spend the night. She wondered if Brother Paul had felt the same magnetic draw that she had felt for him but also knew that it had to be stopped and ignored. He assured them he would return as soon as possible and continue Mr. Parker's chores.

Mr. Parker told Hanna that he knew of a deserted cabin that had been used by foresters if she needed a place to live, she could take it over. He said it was only a couple of miles from there. "Thank you -- that would be nice as I really need a place to stay as I have no home." She began to feel a small measure of joy and relaxation move over her. "Yes, this might be the perfect place to hide away. Perhaps they would never find me here." she thought. Her body ached from all the hard work as she lay again in the barn, this time alone with the animals. What monstrous changes her life had made.

When Brother Paul returned in a couple of days, he set up chores for each of the children so that he could help Hanna get the small cabin as livable as possible. He built a bed, table and chairs for her. He assured her that on all his trips up the mountain, he would bring her things to make it a home. The Parkers had given her necessities to begin living in the little cabin. At the Parker's evening meal, Brother Paul announced that since every thing seemed to be running fairly smoothly, he had another family that needed his help. The Parkers thanked him for his wonderful expression of God's love and grace and insisted it was OK for him to do God's bidding. This meant he might not come back as often. Hanna's heart sank. She did not know whether to be glad or mad. It really didn't make any difference whether she wanted him to stay or go. He would do "God's bidding" anyway. What was she thinking! This was a man of God, not a normal man for marriage or any kind of intimate relationships. How ironic her life had become -- that she had hated anything to do with sexual attachments, then found the greatest joy in it with a man she accidentally killed, and now desiring the unattainable. He could not even consider the kind of relationship that she might be desiring.

As he mounted his horse, he took a long look at Hanna and for a brief moment, she saw in his eyes a look that could only come from a man that deeply loved a woman. He quickly reoriented his attention to the Parker family. He waved "God be with you all." "Hanna, I will bring you more supplies in a week or 10 days." She could feel the blood pulsating through her body as she watched him ride away until he was out of sight. He never looked back. "What is wrong with me." she thought, knowing well that she had bible teachings and so much religion as a child and knew to respect "a man of the cloth." But with so much heartbreaks and chaos she had experienced, her belief in God seemed sorely missing. His devotion made her think again about her childhood with her father's reading the bible to the family and the slaves.

Hanna was very happy to have a place to be settled in but there was so much hard work to get the cabin ready for the cold winter weather. True to his word, Paul made regular visits every ten days to two weeks to the families living in the mountain area. He always brought something special for Hanna. On rare occasions he would spend the night in Hanna's little cabin. Hanna had made sure she had an extra bed in case he needed shelter from the weather. While they had wonderful conversations, Paul grew more and more distance even with a bond between them that neither could understand, discuss or admit their feelings.

Hanna had never told anyone about her life on the plantation. She had grown so close to Paul, while she would never tell him about life on the plantation, one evening they got into a conversation about her childhood. "We did chores as well as, still we remained Southern ladies.

Northern Yankee ladies did not possess the gentle qualities we had. We had a sisterly quality toward each other that the Northern ladies did not have. When the war came heavily upon us, I was myself in much need of a simple overcoat. There was none around. "Tender Mercy" was my name amount the fighting men. We took care of the sick at the plantations that still stood. Some became a hospital. Mothers, daughters all the women and young and old came to help the injured. We did so much good for all those men - so many killed and dying every day. They kept coming. We had no place to put them. There was no kindness any more. All the kindliness had been drained out of the South when we were all hungry and suffering. No one knows how we suffered. Unless they were there, it is impossible for people to understand." (IF they lived at that time, then that suffering is still deep in their spirit/soul.)

"Almost 20 years of sweet innocent life on my parent's plantation when our beautiful world came to an end -- if it could only have lasted. I was always closer to my father than my mother. The things he taught me as a child has helped me here in the mountain. In the South, we were making changes - the war only made prejudice worst and also, it took longer to conquer slavery. We are all slaves - only most of us don't realize it. After that war, we were all enslaved in one way or another. I saw more horrors in so called "freedom" than I ever did under our so called "slavery". WE called them "neggaras" but it was not demeaning, just the difference color of our skin. In the hot, humid weather of the South, there were many words that got drawn out and spoken incorrectly. We had been such honorable people - integrity - honesty and truthfulness. There may have been bad people but I never saw any of them in my youth. The old people starved to death of their own accord during the war. They left what little food they had for the young people. We cared for our blacks the same as we did the whites, just as we always had done. The South was good place to live before the war. They took everything from us, not only our honor, our pride but our food, our clothes, burned homes of innocent people who had nothing to do with the war. They burned our home with my mother sick in bed. Everything was taken or stolen. It was so dreary that John was willing to marry me and go west to Texas, where my sister lived with her family, maybe then on to California. There wasn't anything left to hold me there. As for marrying him, I was void of any emotions, especially love after what I had seen.

All those years of planning my wedding and what did I have, a shabby one, in an old brown dress. I wanted a ruffled collar and couldn't even find that. I never wanted to wear brown again. My life was never sweet after that. John and I had no real feelings for each other. We both just needed someone that seemed familiar to us. He wasn't in the war. He seemed insensitive to what I had been through. He had been so sweet and gentle before the war. There were no more parties, laughter, gayety and fun. That's enough of my story for one evening." Hanna realized she must not continue with her life's story. With that she bid Paul goodnight.

The months grew into years. Almost every visit Paul brought Hanna supplies, always another book for her to read. She ordered from catalogues and rarely went down the mountain, still fearing she would be seen and reported to the Sheriff in Northern California. As the years passed, she became less and less fearful. Hanna kept an old skirt hanging on the wall in case she ever felt the need to feel more womanly, however that seemed very unimportant in her mountaineer life. She surprised her self with her efficiency and adaptability to be able to physically do things she never dreamed of doing. The hard life took a toll on her beauty and her body! She did not socialize with anyone and had no close friends. Her only friend was Paul and always looked forward to his visits. Her passionate desires for him had long since died away. She enjoyed his companionship and discussions about the books she read. Now and then, he would try to "save Hanna's soul" but each time she would close off to his attempts. She had told him only fragments of the emotional pain she has suffered and the death of her husband but pointedly left out the part of her life in Northern California. He often wondered about the missing years but never insisted that she tell him. She kept most of her heartaches bottled up inside.

When he encouraged her to join in with women living in the mountains, she shot a look at him that he knew he was fighting a loosing battle. When she talked to people, with her hard work, she had more in common with the men than the women. The women resented her attire as they would not wear men's pants. The Parker children grew up and left the mountains. When they visited their parents, they often looked in on Hanna to see if she needed anything. Hanna had dared not love the Parker children having known the pain of loosing her only son. Regardless of how he was conceived, she had carried him in her body for nine long months and had a very hard birth delivery with him. She had bundled a tremendous amount of love into that little boy. Love was so painful for her. She loved her parents and her happy childhood but both childhood and parents were all dead and gone. Just when she began to feel deeper love for John, he was dead and gone. Even though Mr. Huntington had made advances toward her and made her very uncomfortable, still he was very good to her and given her not only financial security but later she realized his love for her had made her feel secure. How could she ever see him again? She knew she could never let him know where she was - that part of her life was dead and gone. She had felt love even for Simeon in a fatherly sort of way, then because of his distorted sexual lust for her; she had been forced to kill him with his physical attack on her. No one would understand how she could have killed both men! And there was Pan, a man she took all of her hate for Indians out on -- Poor Pan, so simple, so close to nature, so close to his feelings and his fantastic passion had introduced her to a joy in sex she could not even imagine, yet because of her, he too was dead and gone.

Summers came and went. Winters were cold and long. As Hanna grew older, winters seemed to grow longer and longer. As the years passed, she had nothing but the memories of times gone by. She realized the most important event that repeated in memory had been that one happy day on the beach with romance, sex and nature - their repeated sex under the huge oak tree -- that oak tree became indelibly printed in her subconscious mind. For that one day in her life Hanna had truly enjoyed the pleasure of her body. For that one day she had some how permitted herself to be free and to feel happiness. Hanna had killed the one man that supplied that happy memory.

Hanna had "killed to survive -- one must kill to survive!" became her motto. Her father had prepared her well for the use of fire arms. How ironic that fire arms had placed her in her hermitage life and she must depend on firearms for her survival. She hated killing animals yet, this was part of her survival -- "if you kill to survive, it is permissible" her father had told her many times in her childhood. She had to kill deer, fowl and rabbits for survival foods. She had to learn to can fruits and vegetables in the summer months to survive the winters. When she first came to the mountains, Mr. Parker and some of the men he knew helped her clean and cure the meats. As time passed, they helped her less and less or they died. She never got used to cutting the guts out of an animal. She would clean and cry. In the beginning she would throw up when she had to cut open an animal she had killed. "Kill to survive!" she would repeat to herself.

On rare occasions, Hanna ventured down the mountain for supplies. She grew hardened in all obvious exteriors ways. People feared her strangeness and always stunned by her sharp mind even as she grew old. Her childhood education was far better than most of the people she dealt with. If anyone tried to take advantage of her, they were in for a surprise as she could always out think them and knew what they were up to. In many ways, she seemed hard on the outside but still there was something about an inner beauty she exuded that was very strange to most people.

There were times, especially in the cold of winter, when she considered leaving the mountains and always planned to leave one day but where would she go. How could she leave the one lasting friendship she had with Paul. If she left the mountains, it meant leaving him and he was the one and only person that had brought her back to life, had cared for her, helped her all through the years.

She knew she could not leave him. Through her books and visions, she traveled all over the world and longed to be in those places in person -- ah, Paris, London, Rome, et al.

When Paul came to read the bible to her, she would read her books, especially the travel ones to him. More and more Paul's beliefs became more like Hanna's. He could see her good acts of caring and kindness had greater validity than many of the pious acts of his fellow monks. Even Paul could not know the fantasy lives she lived with her books. While reading, Hanna would often drift off in dreamland living the life of a beautiful girl in the English courts, a member of a royal family in France, now and then the repetitious dream of the priest and nun making love in the barn during a lightening storm. Even when she did not see Paul for weeks at a time, she knew they shared a special kind of love for each other. No one but Paul dared to visit Hanna's cabin unless she invited them, which was rare. She adapted to her hermit's life and didn't want interruptions.

Hanna had been able to support her self with making these items out of various things she found in nature. She was always creative and artistic. At times, she also taught children various crafts and lessons in math, English and told of her wonderful travels all over the world. Perhaps it was her aloneness and communion with nature that developed her intuition. She knew when someone needed help and would show up without anyone informing her to whatever was needed. In turn, they would give her supplies, even money when they had it. She saved and saved. Her little savings grew and grew. She had greater faith in being able to supply her own needs than depending on God for supplying them. Paul was the one person that saw through her cold, aloofness into seeing her loving nature.

Hanna took pleasure in attacking people's piety, even Paul's. She would make up stories about her own life so that no one ever knew any truths about her. She loved to make up stories about all the men she had sexual involvements with since there was so much piety regarding sexuality. Paul would gently ask her not to make up these tales for the young people, even thought he knew his efforts were in vain. "We all live our lives in total lies, Dear Brother Paul, including you!" she would remind him. "Why are my tales any different -- besides is it educational for the young adults." By then it was the turn of the century Hanna was in her sixties. She still rode a horse every where she went but by the time automobiles began appearing, Hanna was always in favor of anything mechanical and had invented many ways that made it possible for a woman to do a man's work. She eventually dared to drive a car while everyone else was still traveling by horse and buggy. Her body ached so much when she rode a horse; a car seemed to be the answer for her needs. By the time she was able to buy a car, she had saved enough money to pay cash.

As a seer, as she became known, Hanna made many predictions. She kept telling people of a big war that would include the United States fighting in Europe "American men will die on foreign soil." she warned. That war did come and went. She was a sturdy old woman. She still got around OK. By now there were stores in the mountains and while shopping one day she heard some men talking about Brother Paul visiting a family. One of the men shot him while he was trying to stop an argument between brothers. They said he was dead. Paul dead?

It could not be! Hanna always assumed she would die long before him. She could not face another death of someone she loved.

Her rickety old car would hardly make it up and down the hills. One of the men had worked on the right front wheel for her. With her eyes filled with tears as she neared her home, she headed down the embankment toward the cabin. The wheel came off and her car crashed against a tree. Hanna was thrown out on the ground with the car on top of her. Her hip and leg were broken and she was in unbearable pain. How was she to get help? No one was even in gun shot sound distance. In the past when she needed help, someone seemed always to be close by but this time she was all alone. She struggled and wiggled herself from the wrecked car, crawled into the cabin and managed to lie on the bed.

Winter was near and had become so hard on Hanna. Her cabin door was open as the cold air began blowing in. She grew so cold and in indescribable pain, plus the unbearable painful thought that Paul could be dead. Paul was life itself - he was indestructible - he was a God to Hanna. She could not get up to close the door or light a fire. How could she manage? How could she go on? The pain only grew worse. The hours drug by. It was almost dark when she saw the silhouette of a bear beginning to walk in the door. Would she now face the horrible death by the bear or could she end it right then and there! She struggled to reach for her rifle under the bed. She propped it quickly on the pillow so she could get to the trigger. Hanna closed her eyes, took a deep breathe and began remembering pleasant memories of her years with Paul, now no more fears, she would follow after Paul, now both would be free. As the bear was at the foot of the bed, with her eyes closed, she could hear and feel the bear's breath, she gently squeezed the trigger with the thought of Paul. Hanna's pain ended!

Paul's gunshot wound healed. He had not heard from Hanna in weeks. He asked a younger Monk, who now visited the families in the mountains, to take him to Hanna's cabin. When they arrived in the small mountain community, no one had seen Hanna for weeks either. When Paul and the young monk reached Hanna's cabin, they saw the door standing open. They rushed in the cabin and there they found Hanna's gun with dried blood stains on it and everywhere but no sign of Hanna. Men searched the mountain but found no remains of Hanna.

Was she murdered? What happened to her? Had a wild animal carried her body off into the woods? It was later that their answer came when they found bear hair stuck to the sides of the cabin door.

As time passed there were stories about an old woman ghost in the woods coming to the aid of those needing help. These tales went on for many years. A glowing light was sometimes seen. About ten years after Hanna's death, Paul slipped into a deep sleep and never awoke. From that time on there were never any tales of the old woman ghost roaming the mountains. Old timers swore on the night of Brother Paul's death the wind whispered "Oh Paul – I am here, I am here...come.. come with me."

My second husband, Bob, grew up in Belgium; however, he told me that his father was a Chiricahua Indian. The Chiricahua men are well built, muscular, with well-developed chests, sound and regular teeth, and abundant hair. This described Pan as well as Bob. Later, Bob's mother told me that he was not a Native American, that his father was Belgium and lived in the South of Africa. Bob convinced himself he was part Chiricahua Indian. Hanna's greatest joy and memory was the day of love making with Pan. Bob introduced me to great love making and sex! Bob also was detrimental to my career as we had to focus on HIS acting career, not mine. Pan's constant focus was on Hanna so in this life, I unknowingly was obligated to focus on Bob's career and his happiness. The man Hanna continually refused to have sex with was Mr. Huntington who provide her with a lot of security, which she had to leave behind. In this life he was the executive of a TV network whom I did have sex with and never helped with anything that was helpful for my career or income.

Often I have found connections with "Richard" in past lives with repeated lives as a Priest or Monk. Leanne's seduction of Jonathan (Richard) was abdominal manipulation that caused him to go into the Priesthood. The repetitious connections are phenomenal and mysterious as well.

CHAPTER 16

ANNA THE BALLERINA - NYC

GALLERY OLDHAM – UK – Finishing Touches – George Wimpenny

During a visit to my friend Arlene who lived in Connecticut, Arlene, suggested I take her car instead of renting one for a littler circle from her home in Bridgeport, CT up through Massachusetts to Boston, Salem, Marblehead, Plymouth, Cape Cod, Newport, Rhode Island, back to Bridgeport via the coastline. I didn't feel any particular connection to the witches of Salem but felt a great deal of sympathy for how they were treated and murdered.

All through the areas I traveled, I saw the name "Palmer" often. Seeing red brick two story homes recalled my repetitious dream I had as a child. In the dream, I lived in a red brick house with a red brick playhouse in the back yard. These East Coast houses seemed more familiar than any houses of the description that I had seen anywhere. They were like the one in my childhood dream.

Newport, R.I. was so charming. What a quaint old town it was. I stayed in a Bed and Breakfast, which was related to the story of Lizzie Bourdon. The next day I took a tour through the stately homes on Bellevue Avenue. It was a thrilling experience to go from one magnificent mansion to another and had a strange familiarity about them. I could even visualize the parties in them. The last was The Elms, designed by architect Horace Trumbauer modeled after the mid-18th century French chateau d'Asnieres (c.1750) outside Paris. The elaborate Classical Revival gardens on the grounds were developed between 1907 and 1914 includes terraces displaying marble and bronze sculpture, lavish lower garden featuring marble pavilions, fountains and a sunken garden. As I sat in the garden looking back at the mansion, the familiar feeling was so strong that I felt tears flowing as though I was home or at least a very familiar place. Had I been there before -- had I danced at parties in those mansions? Or was Chateau d'Asnieres so similar to the one in Anne Marie's life! While I don't believe it is the one - searching through photographs of places and chateaus, it was similar but lacked the U shape gardens or the right semi-circle stairs, etc.

As I was leaving the area, I stopped to admire the fabulous array of yachts -- so many beautiful boats. What a grand life style. Then I stopped and said to myself "Ann, this is not your life style in this life. Wishing or longing for it would not make it happen." I decided it was a form of self punishment that I did not need.

I had always loved to dance. As a young child and into my teen years, I danced so gracefully, people were convinced I studied ballet. Even in the High School annual, the senior predictions were that in the future I was seen as a ballerina on the New York Stage. I wanted desperately to take ballet but it wasn't in my family's budget. In movies, I would take in the graceful movements, even with my hands, then mimics them. Later, in my career years, I was asked to try out as a dancer for a TV show. When I tried to do the routine, the choreographer told me I wasn't a "dancer." Of course not! I had never had one dance lesson in my life. I had not pursued the job, I had been asked to try out for it. Apparent there was a misunderstanding with the choreographer. I was there to try out as a costumed model in the production. I was too shy to tell him that was what I should have been considered for. I went away feeling very defeated, which seemed the easier choice for me. I never want to think of trying out for anything involving dancing or appear on a stage dancing.

I had a friend that was a New Yorker and retired from the NYC police force. An injury had provided him with early retirement. We decided to trade apartments. He stayed in mine in Beverly Hills and I stayed in his in NYC when I was there as a speaker for a Whole Life Expo. One morning I was going to take a shower and turned on the water to get the hot water started. It never got hot, so I turned it off. Unfortunately, the faucet was one of those round ones that didn't show which was hot and cold. When I retuned after being gone all day, the front door was hot to the touch. When I carefully opened it, I was flooded with hot steam! The entire apartment was filled with steam and dampness. I was horrified and quickly opened windows and the door. I got every towel and anything that I could mop up the water that was everywhere and on everything. I was scared and heart sick for this to happen to my friend's apartment. It took hours to clean everything up and laundry the towels, etc. When I noticed that the surface of his beautiful antique desk was affected with a milky look, I was really sick. I didn't know what to do. Early the next morning, I began calling antique refinishers. One of them told me to just leave it alone and it would probably return to its natural state. I was filled with so much guilt.

As things worked out, when I returned to Beverly Hills, he had dented my van - tit for tat! It was during this time when we were communicating back and forth as well as my recent experience in Newport, that a scene appeared before me.

I had an inkling that something was missing in my past life scenario. The scene was in the mid 1920s. This same friend was a buddy in a former life as well as this one and was also a NYC policeman in that life. We lived in the same apartment building. I was in a dance school studying ballet. I was from a wealthy family living in Newport and had moved to NYC to pursue a dancing career.

I was in the last semester of my training and as much as I loved dancing, I had a terrible fear of ever appearing on stage or dancing in public. He tried to help me overcome my fears and was always there when I needed any kind of help. For whatever reason, I was acquainted with a very influential man that was involved with the Mafia. He was always trying to date me. My policeman friend told me I had a very important role to play and it could really help him in his job. Why not, he was always helping me! It would even benefit the whole city. All I had to do was to accept a date with this guy and let him know which restaurant he would be taking me. I was in my early twenties and still quite naive. It seemed like a harmless favor to do for my buddy. When the date event was set, I told him the time and place. That was all I needed to do. I would have a nice dinner and that was the end of it. When the black limousine we were riding in pulled up and stopped at the restaurant, before we could depart, bullets rang out and were flying all around us. In a brief moment, I lay dead with my ballet and whole future wiped out in those brief moments! My buddy had no idea that this would happen. He had no intention for me to be killed.

I worked in the movie, "Bonnie and Clyde" -- later when I saw it, when Bonnie and Clyde were shot, and the way the bullets struck Bonnie struck a cord within me. Again, a familiar feeling! A year or so later in Hollywood, Fay Dunaway was shooting "The Thomas Crown Affair" on the lot where I went on an interview.

I visited the set and she invited me to her dressing room. I told her how impressed I was with the death scene and bullets pounding her. I told her that it really affected me and asked how she did it so convincingly real. She told me the dress was rigged with small fake blood containers connected to electricity and each time one went off, she received a small shock and reacted to each one. Skeptics would say that is what caused me to make up the story about being shot in NYC; however it all fit -- the feeling of familiarity in the 1920s to the social life in Newport -- the brick house with the brick playhouse -- seeing my last name in this life all over that area near Newport and my lust for ballet. My friend in this life and in that more recent past life, he was a same NYC policeman plus my vivid picture of sitting in the back seat of that limo, looking at the man I was with and no other memories beyond that.

It was only after that visit to my friend in Connecticut that my memory of that short life appeared. Before that, I had believed that the life of Hanna during the Civil War was my last life before the present one. Perhaps, through the years, more past lives will open up. The pieces of the puzzles drop in place at any and odd times. In my present life, I have always had mixed emotions about pursuing my career in NYC where I probably would have had more success but remained in California. This is one of my poems that I wrote a few years ago.

I AM A DANCER
I am a dancer, so let me dance!
I *whirl and dance*, reaching for a star,
Then, ever so lightly a star reaches down to touch my brow,
And perhaps, steal a bit of my soul.
Then, I whirl with glee, filled with hope and possibilities.
But as I *whirl and dance* in the warmth of that star,
Suddenly it's gone, and darkness surrounds me.
Yet, remembering the warmth of that star,
I blindly reach through the darkness believing I'll find it again.
Whirl and dance in darkness,
Ahh, there's another, *whirl and dance* in its light.
Again, I'm touched ever so lightly, *whirl and dance*.
Again, as I whirl darkness befalls my dance.
I know it is yet to shine, years double, triple,
a decade then another.
Light my way to find my place,
I cannot find it without the light
And love of that special star –
Whirl and dance - whirl and dance –

239

W-h-i-r-l and d-a-n-c-e – w-h-i-r-l and d-a-n-c-e
I am a dancer, so let me dance....
I am a dancer, so let me LIVE,
Let me live LIFE filled with joy,
No cancerous experiences that
Invade my body's delicate cells,
"Why me, God" is my prayer,
Haven't I had enough battle scars?
I stood strong and said,
"I will SURVIVE!"
Has it all been in vane?
Only now to succumb to this,
Wasn't there supposed to be joy,
Fulfillment for accomplishments?
And Jobs well done?
There's so much dancing yet to do,
Would I cease to whirl and dance?
Over and over, I stood tall,
Again and again, I said,
I am a dancer, so let me dance,
Whirl and dance, whirl and dance,
And in that vortex of dance, again
I win, I survived another,
And another, another and another,
Gods and Goddesses, don't you know,
I haven't finished the dance?
There is so much more to do..
I must yet whirl and dance,
Whirl and dance--- whirl and d-a-n-c-e....

No doubt there are other connections in that life with people in this one. I feel sure that my friend Diane was my friend then, too. Possibly my friend, Patti, who has lived in Spain for many years because she spent a number of years modeling in NYC where she met her husband that moved them to Spain. When we both lived in Dallas, Patti introduced me to my modeling career. If it had not been for her, I may never have pursued modeling and acting. With the retired policeman in NYC, once I gleaned this knowledge of that past life, we seemed to loose contact from that time on. The connection was made and apparently the Karma was released.

Had it not been for my daughter to raise, I probably would have headed for NYC to pursue a career. I felt I would have been more successful as my forte' seemed to be as a commentator. There were more of those jobs in NYC than in Hollywood, CA.

CHAPTER 17

RICK JASON AND OTHERS

Memories flash across my mind unexpectedly. As I was flipping around the TV dial, I saw an old "Combat!" TV series and there he was, the star, Rick Jason. My friend, Simon, usually had interesting guests for his pool gatherings on Sunday afternoon. For me the most interesting guest was Rick Jason, who lived just down the street from Simon. Simon, an attorney, was handling Rick's long drawn out divorce settlement. Some of the interesting celebrities I met were through Simon's connects with handling their divorces. He was well known for divorce cases. After Rick and I became romantically involved, I remember Simon's cold warning - ""Enjoy the relationship but don't plan on any future. Rick will never marry you - you don't have enough money!" Never mind his pessimistic attitude, I knew our LOVE would win out --- I thought!

That day I met Rick in mid 1965, he invited me to stop by his house on my way home to see his house and the work he had done on it, knowing I did interior decorating part time. He and his wife were still living in separate parts of the house during their divorce proceedings but she was out of town. I remember a huge old dining table and chairs that was lovely. I loved his taste. In the back yard he had terraced the hillside with railroad ties and did it all himself.

At the time "Combat!" was one of the most successful series on TV. He was easily recognized and with the divorce pending, he really could not be seen on a date with a woman so our times together had to be at my house. Right or wrong in people's minds, I didn't care if we had to have a clandestine relationship because he was about the most exciting man I had ever been involved with.

That first date remains as one of my very special memories. He appeared at my front door with a big smile, a big sack and came dashing in, heading for the kitchen. He planned to prepare our dinner with great gusto. With his great sense of humor, he kept me laughing. I felt such joy in my heart. He described himself as a walking encyclopedia of unimportant knowledge. He was that! Seems sad that we can't bottle up those wonderful feelings to savor later in life when youthful exciting years fad away.

I had never tasted caviar and didn't think I would like to eat fish eggs! To watch Rick's ceremonial actions of boiling eggs, finely chopping onion, then serving the caviar on a small piece of toast, sour cream, finely chopped onion and egg with the right amount of lemon was such a treat and I loved it. Wine and caviar - what a fantastic beginning - then steak and salad followed. Suave - debonair - intelligent - great sense of humor - very handsome AND an extraordinarily great lover! How could any woman NOT fall in love with him? He has always remained one of the greatest loves of my life. We continued this private romance for many months.

I worked with Interior Designers on a part time basis and knew that red was not a color for bedrooms because it wasn't considered restful, however, I had used America Beauty red that has a bit of blue giving it a much softer, even romantic vibration. It was like sleeping and romancing in a huge valentine with flocked red walls - red deep pile rug, red bedspread and red drapes.

That was in the mid 1960's when LSD was all the rage and <u>not</u> illegal. I remember a scientist friend had invited me to try it at his house, which I did and had a very interesting revelation. I took it only twice and both times I had no problem being in control of myself and was mystified at how our inner being can be so limited when with something like LSD, our senses are extremely heightened. We can hear, feel, taste so much more; at least that was my experiences. When any thing appeared as hallucination, my conscious mind could take over and change it back. After the effects had worn off and I was home in bed, Rick had spent the night with me the night before and as I rubbed my hand across the sheet where he slept, I could still feel the oil from his body.

The next morning I could no longer feel it. My experience with LSD was not radical but proved that our five senses can be heightened tremendously, which was not hallucination but reality. There was good research on LSD that began with Timothy Leary and Richard Alper who became "Ram Dass," ("Ram Dass," which means "servant of God") and was as a wonderful spiritual leader and author. Having listened to his lectures and meeting him, I saw in him an unconditional love few people exude. A lot of very vivid colors and designs came out of those experiences and seemed to be a way to go deeper into our inner selves. Timothy Leary died in 1996. Ram Dass suffered a devastating stroke in 1997 but made a positive conclusion out of that experience as it did with all of them! I have always believed that a lot of good things and research could have come out of LSD if the younger generation hadn't discovered and abused it so radically.

That was the era when I was determined to "beat the odds" and become a female producer when there were almost none. I worked as Executive Assistant to the Vice President of Selmur Productions, an in-house production company for ABC-TV shows that included "Combat!" Huge photos of the actors of the various company productions lined the hallway to my office. As I passed Rick's photo, my heart always skipped a beat. I couldn't wait for the evenings when he would come to my house for our dates. I had fallen so deeply in love with Rick; I didn't want us to go out on dates. I was so mesmerized with him -- I wanted him all to myself.

The one time we were more or less out in the open was a day that I had a job as a model to do publicity for "Magnificent Men In Their Flying Machines" – Part of the day was at an airport, then for the premier at the theatre across the street from the Beverly Wilshire Hotel where they rented a room for us to use as a dressing room since we were wearing period costumes. When we were finished, I headed for the hotel to change clothes. There on the elevator was Warren Beaty. He asked about my costume and as the elevator headed up we chatted about my apparel, he then asked me to just stop in his room for one drink before I changed clothes. Being curious, I got off on his floor. He was easy to talk to and our conversation flowed. We continued chatting and went to my room where I changed clothes in the bathroom. Warren asked me to have dinner with him but I told him I had a previous engagement. I told him I would love to have dinner with him later and gave him my phone number. He never called. Today it seems impossible to believe I turned down a date with Warren Beaty! Later, I worked with him on "Bonnie and Clyde" but I don't think he remembered meeting me that night at the Beverly Wilshire Hotel.

My previous engagement was a dinner date with Rick at M.G.M. studios where he was shooting "Combat!" on the back lot, which meant that he had a small travel trailer for a dressing room. When I arrived, they were shooting at a Railway Station shortly before the dinner break. Rick seemed very happy to see me. As the break came, he grabbed a couple of dinners and said "Let's eat in my dressing room." For desert, he wanted to make love. Rick was a very passionate man and our energies were unbelievably harmonious. So the little trailer "rocked and rolled" and I was horribly embarrassed afterwards with the crew teasing Rick.

About the time I was feeling quite secure in our relationship, he announced that he would not be able to see me for awhile. Simon had warned him that his wife might have spies out checking on him and he had to be extra careful until the divorce was finalized in court and all settlements secured. Weeks or months afterwards I was so devastated that I decided to move back to Texas to my parent's home and shipped furniture and all my things back as well. I felt that my daughter being around male family members would substitute for a father image. She could also see her father in Dallas. I believed that with some productions going on in Texas, maybe I could get production of my own started there.

I could never last long being away from California no matter how determined I was to not return. I had found a film production in Dallas and we went to Los Angeles to cast the film. When I saw that the money man producer was using it as an excuse to find girls, I quit right then and there. My friend, Arte Johnson was leaving for a film to be shot in Europe and loaned me his apartment until I found a place of my own. It was a year or so later after I had left California that I saw Rick once again. He was divorced and could take me out on a date now. I was overjoyed! He came over to my apartment and said he had a public appearance. I was delighted when he wanted me to go with him. Unfortunately he stood me up and I never saw or heard from him again. I think it was around the time he started dating the woman he later married.

I was saddened to know that Rick committed suicide by a self-inflicted gunshot to his head. He had been despondent over personal matters after he and fellow cast members of "Combat!" had a three day reunion in Las Vegas. What a loss! The saying "Old age is not for sissies" comes to mind when I think of him. He apparently had no health problems so I surmised that it might have been reminiscing over his successful career that could have left him feeling very empty after their reunion.

Rick had written a book about the loves and wives in his life but no mention of our affair leading me to wonder why and how it could have been so meaningful to me and nothing worth mentioning for him. With such an enormous memory left in my life for so many years, I know that we have been together more than in one life. Even now, I think of his often as though he is contacting me from beyond. I saved photos of him off the Internet. I have had to search within to find out when we were together in our past lives, however, no matter how much I have searched, I still don't know for sure. When the time is right, the pieces will come together. I feel sure that he was in the Anne Boleyn scenario as well as Anne Marie's French life. Since he was from New York City in this life, maybe I knew him in my life as a ballerina in NYC. He might have been the man I was with when we both were killed. Perhaps in other lives, too, since he had such a strong force in my current life.

I was single more than I was married and dated men that I don't even remember now but those few that stand out even more than the three men I was married to were Rick, Richard, Burt and Tom. Ironically, as much as I may have cared for each one of them, my downfall was their rejections. Yet, when they remain so strong in my memory, I feel they have each had a very important part of past incarnations. I know that Burt was my father in Anne Marie's life. We had time in France together, too. We had started dating in the early 1960's and I fell madly in love with him. He had left for Italy to produce two films with Carlo Ponte and expected to be there for months. I was so sure that if I went to Rome, he would decide to marry me. Instead, after much effort saving money, along with a friend, we took off for Paris. When I called him in Rome from Paris, he was headed for Paris the next day. Silly me, I thought he was coming there to see ME! Instead, his Rome deal fell through and he was on his way back the Hollywood. What a shock! He stayed in Paris for a week to help edit a film for Leo Lax so we had that week together. We visited Versailles and afterwards, we sat in the car in the parking lot, just talking for hours. With my artistic appreciation, I was appalled when he remarked about all the wasted real estate of the garden and how many homes could be built there. We visited other places, dined with our host Leo in very exciting places in Paris. Leo took us to his charming small country home. Just outside the window, a cow walked by.

It was like being in a movie. We dined in an old Abby that was made into a restaurant. Who should be at the next table but Louis Jourdan and his date! What a perfect setting!

It was bad enough that I had traveled from Hollywood to Paris to be with Burt and he was on his way back to the states but even worse, I discovered in a letter that he was returning home expecting to marry someone else. What a fool I was! There is no way that I could every imagine spending the next twenty or more years with an off and on relationship with him! How odd the ties of our past - a father I dearly loved in a French life and a lover in the present one with years of hope and rejections. We must have been together many times to warrant so many rejections! Trying to understand my devotion to him and his constant rejection of me even thought with so many years of involvement, I knew that he had to love me. I have wondered, if in my French life, with him leaving me with friends away from the palace, then getting in a fight and killed, if that could have been his guilt that kept him from making any marriage commitment in this life -- or if buried deep in his subconscious that it was as though he would be marrying his own daughter. Burt was the most difficult of any relationship in my life. He was the Indian that killed John, Hanna's husband and created extreme hate within Hanna. If I had karmic indebtedness toward him it was to really love him in this life. I hope the Akashic records are balanced so we finished whatever was needed. In all those years, he never used me in one of his films, nor every helped me in any way. It was the opposite for me, as I often went to his boat at the Marina and helped him work on it. The only gift he ever gave me was a small hair dryer that I still have.

I feel sure that Tom, the TV executive was Mr. Huntington in Hanna's life as well as an important man in Anne Boleyn's life and lost his life because of Anne. His attitude toward me in this life was so much like Mr. Huntington in that life but in this life he did get me in bed and gave me no kind of security!

I have explained the numerous lives that I feel Richard and I have shared. The one important life shared with Manrique, the handsome Mexican man – and of course the three men I married had to be connected in past lives that seem minor connections except for Bob. Bob, my second husband, was born in Belgium and claimed to be part Native American was Pam in Hanna's life. I have only described family members in this life lightly, as with friends; I have not described many of those connections as I have trusted that my intuition has given me what was needed for this book.

CHAPTER 18

THE WINDUP

In my present life, not only have I had a lot of experiences involved with RV travel all over the USA, but as a young child, I was always drawn to covered wagon movies. I seemed to identify with the hardships of the covered wagons travels and the Indian attacks. Recognizing these attachments are so important in uncovering our past experiences. It may be quite logical that many people involved in RV travel all over the country now could have been wagon train travelers in a past life.

It is important to allow what may seem like our imagination to run free no matter how outrageous they might appear. One example of what could seem utterly ridiculous to anyone, especially coming from a former motorcycle cop in California, (CHP) the knee high boots, macho man, et al. It was probably the most unusual regressions that I ever did! In his regression, he went into outer space, which just "blew me away." I didn't know if he was just "putting me on" or if he was really getting a very unusual past life. Even so, I moved along with him – He said they lived inside a planet. The people or "beings" were aware that their planet was going to destroy, so they had to get out and away from it. They had some form of transportation and seemed to have choices as to where they might go. He chose to come to this planet. Upon arrival they seemed to be able to morph into whatever life form they chose.

That got me to thinking about extraterrestrial beings that look very different from human beings on Earth. In the 1980's I was very actively doing psychic readings at fairs and in my office. I "got it" that extraterrestrials could not communicate with masses because we could not accept any being that did not look like us. They had to be incarnating in physical bodies. Since the 1980s we have made remarkable progress in the fields of electronics and communications. As I understand, phenomenal advances have been made in war aircraft as well, so that I wondered if that could be because of extraterrestrial influences. Perhaps we've had more of an abundance of them entering our Earth and probably have had since the beginning of time, especially when we Earthlings seem to be screwing up our own planet! Can you just imagine being from another planet observing people on Earth's activities of war after war, killing each other with bombs, guns, even with so called "love" that strangulates another person. Such things as possessiveness, demands, jealousy, accusations and especially religions that keep preaching "hell fire and damnation" and the end is coming -- the end is coming! I can't count the times in my life that there were world wide predictions of the earth ENDING.

We are constantly confronted with these "the world is ending" cries and predictions, now TV shows and movies! In one of my channeling, I was told that there were "Sentinels watching over Earth" and that they would not let any major atomic or hydrogen bomb explode as it would affect other areas of the Universe. Higher Intelligences must get very impatient with Earthlings. In my life time our Universe has been expanded by leaps and bounds. I cannot imagine that we could be the only seemingly "intelligent" beings in the entire Universe! To me there is ample proof in ancient drawings and writings that Earth has always been visited by beings from other planets, maybe even different dimensions. We think we are so intelligent, yet we don't even know what electricity is and we can't live without it. A magician can move an object quicker than our eyes can follow. One of the greatest gifts is the opportunity to have an open mind and consider any and all possibilities. I can't say that getting to the down hill run in life is fun; however, it is so good to get to the place of wisdom, which is something no one can buy or read books to get! It is inborn and it GROWS with AGE!

We ARE energy --energy does not die, it may change forms. When a small molecule of energy is isolated in a cloud chamber and photographed on ultra sensitive film, the molecule has a particular size, weight, pattern and speed. It continues to move in the cloud chamber until it finally falls to the bottom, apparently dead. Yet soon the molecule is back, it now exhibits a new size, weight, pattern and speed. The process continues endlessly. That seems to support that reincarnation gives the opportunity to evolve back to what we call God. Born with level of vibrations earned in past lives, how you live determines if you raise or lower those vibrations. It is our resistance to life that causes our pain. Embracing this life and other lives without resistance allows one to experience far deeper aspects of love. Problems are opportunities for growth. Rising about painful situations we gain soul growth. A master detaches from illusion, recognizes it exist only as experiences, which can be hostile separateness or tranquil oneness.

"Let your conscious be your guide" is good to remember (and your only guide - as it knows where you need to go for your spiritual evolution). If anyone tells you what you must do but you feel a bump -- an uneasy feeling -- repulsed, then that is your subconscious yelling "Hey, wait a minute! I'm here to guide you!" There is another saying worth heeding "When the student is ready, the teacher will come." As I have researched spirituality for many decades, it seems to me most devoted religionists become Automatons, never reaching out of their cocoon to find their own individualized path to their earth completion. They never become a beautiful butterfly that can soar and fly freely. They may be very well educated and hold many degrees – but still, they are Automatons! (I hear them all the time on TV). I have had many years fighting the battle of the word "psychic" - so often criticized for my work in helping others. What is "psychic" but a word, like "intuition" - "gut level feeling"! We accept our five physical senses denying those beyond. Religions "sell" the idea that you must go through their particular religion to reach "God" or what ever name they call "that that is"!

Are we materializing thought forms of earlier fragments of the over soul? With years of word implants in the human brain, as "evil" and "devil" in the most negative way, isn't it time to reverse those to "live" and "lived"? Light and dark appear in the same space. A light switch proves that. We must flip on the "light" to erase the darkness in our lives. I hope I might inspire you to flip on your own inner light! I believe we can go back into what appears to be a past life that may reveal a part of our over-all-self (over soul) that has experienced an unfortunate event that, in our present incarnation may appear as evil, cruel; some terrible action that we perceive is a choice we made. By "rewriting that script" we can immediately change the event that appears to be bad "karma" in our present life. "God is LOVE" therefore, when we work with love, it can only have positive results. We can identify these past experiences unemotionally and RELEASE them by SELF forgiveness, realizing that at the previous time, you did what was expected. Whatever caused you to make what appears today as a "bad choice" makes no difference. Just know that you CAN forgive any past experiences in other lives, dimensions or in your present life! I have come to the conclusion that we are here on earth to learn through our emotions – to experience many, maybe all emotional reactions. What do we do with them? Do we just sink into them and accept that we can do nothing about them? As I stated, I feel I was born with a terrible temper. I have always had frown marks between my eyes. It took years of work to overcome it. My seeming last and hardest emotion to overcome was always wanting a man in my life and wanting to be deeply loved. I finally conquered it but it took getting to the senior years to make it.

Just to briefly inject "de-possession" as an example. This was not in a past life session but in a psychic reading I was doing. In a client's vibrations, there appeared to be a 16 year old boy who seemed to have fits. In my vision, I held him firmly with both arms around him explaining to him that love conquers fear and that I loved both he and that which appeared "evil" as well as the physical boy. "It" merged or left. We can transform "evil" thought forms with love. When we work in love and light we never need to fear darkness.

I have contemplated the whole idea of ghost, disincarnate spirits, possessive entities, etc. There are many different theories and methods of getting rid of them. My theory will sound absurd to most people. Is it possible that these entities appear to certain individuals because it could a part of THAT particular person from a past life and is simply lost or confined to a certain place in time? I feel that it may need to be lovingly integrated into the person that must be stronger than the lost part of the soul. Instead of attempted to "send the entity to hell" as I heard a priest do on TV, I believe they should be thought of as scared, confused, don't know how to leave the Earth realm and may appear to be evil -- but that evil is a reaction of fear of others, trying to be equal or predominant over others. Instead of sending the disincarnate spirit off to hell or white light, first maybe it should be asked to rejoin the part that is now the living physical body. Then if it is not a part of that physical body, it should be encouraged and invited to go into the white light by supporting it with love.

I had one unusual experience of getting rid of a feared ghost. It was a man that seemed to be psychically raping females in an apartment building in their sleep. When I tuned into him, he was a middle age man, not too intelligent nor an upstanding person. He had lived on that property before the apartment building was built.

When I asked him to go into the white light, he gruffly refused! No matter what I said, he would not go. Finally, the scene in my head appeared to be a stage with two attendants emerged from behind a center partition, they knocked him out, carried him off on a stretcher. I had not asked for helpers but they came anyway. The women ceased having problems. My client could once again sleep in her bedroom and apparently other women in the apartment building stopped feeling psychically raped.

Another difficult one was a man's wife that had died several years past. He felt that somehow she was stopping him from having any romance or sexual experiences in his life. As I visually confronted her, she was a very possessive red head and she had no intentions of leaving. It took a lot of persuasion to get her to leave him alone and go forward in her own existence in the after life. I never heard if she stayed away.

Many people deny reincarnation because there are more people on earth today than in the past, as far as we know our past. I have stressed the lack of balance of our <u>physical</u>, <u>emotion</u> and <u>mental</u> bodies. Our physical incarnate body is the "glue" that holds all others together until they can realign with the wholeness of the soul. I don't know that anyone agrees with my conclusion concept and I don't care, it makes sense to me. Our basics are physical body, mind and "soul" (which seem to have many definitions to different people and religions!) – Most of us do not strive to balance these three. I suggest that upon death, the vibrations of each goes into a like vibration of our Over Soul, so when out of balance – for example – we have not taken care of our physical body, then we go into that vibration of needing to improve the physical vibration. Thus, we next incarnate in a body that we focus on physical improvement, the same for the mental and spiritual. My own example is that I seemed to abuse power when born in royalty or wealth, thus, in this life, apparently I said "sock it to me" – "I will do it WITHOUT money!" (Yes, I am not sure that was a wise vow!) This entire life has been devoted to spiritual evolution. As stated earlier, I began feeling that at the moment of climax with certain lovers, that I could dedicate them to higher spiritual evolution. Crazy? Maybe! As I worked in TV and films and since they are electronic energy, I put my hands or parts of a set and meditated on sending out positive spiritual vibrations to masses. Judging from the extreme greed in this nation, I'm not sure that it helped. I DO know that through association with influential people in the industries and making suggestions, then later seeing them on TV, I had to know that my concepts were NOT worthless after all. It would have been nice to make money off of them.

*****

Always think of your individualized finger print - like NO other in the world - thus, why wouldn't your spiritual journey also be INDIVIDUALIZED? If you read Astrology's definition of each month's basic personality traits as well as varied combinations of traits that describe you, why isn't your journey *your own individualized path* that only YOU can discover for yourself? If you don't want to recognize your responsibility for yourself, then you path may be easier to follow the long established various organized religions. You can choose to keep going round and round on the wheel of reincarnation and it may be necessary for your evolution as you may not ready to move on into Universal ONENESS. You are in your perfect body even if it does not seem to be perfect - and few are! This means that in this particular body that you wear in this incarnation is what it is for your learning. Like millions of others, I battle the weight problem! No matter what I do, it doesn't come off. Am I forced to carry this excess weight because of karmic decisions I made, even in this life? Most of my life I disapproved of my mother's weight. Did that set up a karmic experience for me now? I am by no means perfect in any way, yet, in God, I AM that I AM and God sees perfection in me. When I think of my life's journey up to now, I know that the path I chose was the right path for me. There are many things I wish I had understood better in you younger adult years. Free will maybe God's greatest gift to us. Most of us fail to appreciate and use our gift of free will when it comes to religions or spiritual researching to our individualized path.

In the chart that shows the division of body, mind and spirit at death, which is my own concept, I have recently awakened to the thought that perhaps in past lives we have worked through one or the other. What may appear to be lacking, especially in judgments of other people, may have been accomplished in a past incarnation. People are so quick to judge us. It makes them feel stronger if they can see fault in someone else, under the guise of "constructive criticism." Some criticism may be worth consideration but much of it should be disregarded and just listen to your OWN inner voice. If in this physical body you are dedicated to improving your emotional reactions, perhaps you have found balance in the physical or mental bodies.

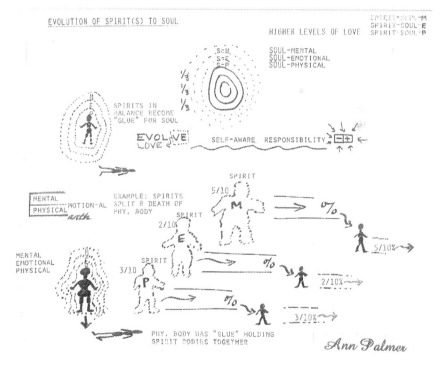

For those of us adapted to a "Christian" faith that incorporate Jesus and the teachings said to be his, there is so much misinterpretation! Firstly, how do people miss the whole point that Jesus NEVER wanted to be WORSHIPED, put on a pedestal, images made and worshipped, calling him "God", et al. He was born into a physical body to show simplicity - not royal birthing - not wealth - not super intellectual ability or training - but showed a way for anyone to reach the Christ consciousness -- "CHRIST" was not his last name but a place to unite with the allness of what we call "God." His ability to merge in total love, non-judgments, compassion, understanding showed how we could also create the same miracles he displayed if we simply understood that he was HERE to show us the way. Miracles are created daily in our lives if we just look at them. Medical developments are miracles, money or help coming just at the right moment, a friend or family member showing up at the right moment, on and on. Every day things like telephones, televisions, etc. that we take for granted would have been unbelievable miracles in Jesus time and beyond.

Regardless of what people say about "creating your own reality" and believing you can do anything, I was always aware that I did not have the intellectual capacity of others. Accentuating that was when schools added the 12th grade; I skipped an important year that probably affected the rest of my school years. In those days we didn't have the descriptions of "disabilities" -- that might be called a learning disability today. I was an artist, a creative person, not great at "book learning." In present day, we accept that there are different forms of learning. I learned through touch and feel. I have struggled to understand things I read, plus I have never been able to recall what I have just read and hope that somewhere in my brain or mind it is stored away. This is a real handicap when writing books! What I DID see later was that I had an innate ability to know things -- inner wisdom -- knowing how to do things where I had no training. In my older age, I now realize for me, it pushed me on to strive harder to understand the complexities or behind the "trained way" of doing things. I often felt guilt as though I was cheating because I had not had the accept method of learning; as when I was in an organization of highly educated PhDs, M.F.C.C.s, Psychologists, Psychiatrists focusing on past life research. I saw that as a rule they followed a set form and time. When I did regressions, I "went with the flow" that included utilizing my own intuition regarding how I lead the client. "Leading a client" was not recommended, but for me it was a far better way. An example was at a conference when we were doing regressions on each other. A hypnotherapist was regressing me. When she saw that I was veering off the subject that we agreed to pursue.

She kept trying jerking me back onto that event. My subconscious knew where I needed to go and was leading me there. As a result, I had a terrible headache that day and all night. It is important for the regressionists to be flexible and move with the client no matter how far from the original goal they may go.

SEEDS PLANTED IN PAST LIVES

I have attempted to analyze what I call "seeds" planted in past lives that I recognize in my present life. Here are just a few examples:

Atlantis - Male – pilot, slave to political system - opposed to killing (seed: male kills, repeated incarnations as a woman.)

Atlantis - Female - priestess - created energy – dedicated to spirituality

Egyptian - Male - artist - became advisor to Pharos (seed: guilt, causing brother to be killed, also defying expected career.)

Egyptian - Female - educated - abducted - enslaved by male (seed: at death -- "never leave him" – as demonstrated in my relationship with Richard)

Rome - Female - Helpless (seed: fear, helpless, must obey, entrapment by a male)

Anne Boleyn - (seed: manipulation, devotion, determined to change religion, influence daughter, Elizabeth's rein)

Anne Marie - France - duty to King and family (seed: escape, deception, pride, hatred, using the body for monetary gains, accepting responsibly)

Leanne - Belgium (seed: extreme manipulation, using female body, overly possessive)

Ann - Nun (seed: forced into religion, resentment and stripped of self confidence, lost child)

Hanna - America (Seed: after affluent life, learned hard man's work, more guilt from taking 2 men's lives - fear of future motherhood, always loosing a child in past lives, including present – I fail to understand why I never had more than one child and either the child or I died before they reached adulthood)

Ann - Ballerina (seed: wrong companions create death, next time overcome fears, avoid any form of criminal behavior).

What has connecting to my own PAST LIVES revealed to me? In many ways they have revealed how my childhood discomforts with family and religions created rebellion within me. It has given some consolation and answers for the whys in this life I have never been able to attain financial success, yet abundant spiritual success, which was a necessity for this soul, called me. While my intent was one husband, possibly three children and live a "normal" life; yet in my teens, I chose the unknown path that has taken me to many of the highs but also many of the lows in life, never achieving my original goals.

I was possessed with the need of a life partner and with the romantic idea of my own Prince Charming. None of three marriages came any where close to a Prince of any kind! With each marriage, it seemed that each was a forced situation. First, I very accidentally got pregnant and had to get married. Second, Bob was a great lover but we had a lot of fights and if he had not told me a major lie -- that he had only five years to live, I might never have married him. Number three was a some what desperation to be loved and cared for after going through over a year of the most horrendous grief of my life over my daughter's disappearance. He seemed to be a man who wanted to take care of me and my needs, never showing his obsession with alcohol until after we were married. Also, at that point in my life, I had so many unfilled romances, I was willing to settle for a man that seemed to want to be with me for life and make the commitment of marriage! In earlier years, I regret that I did not understand the first thing about reincarnation and if I had, perhaps I could have resolved many of these repeated confrontations with the men in my life. Whatever circumstances arose, I traveled to many places and was with people that I had past life experiences with. I was put into circumstances where I had to made responsible decisions without anyone to lean on for help. It has been a very solo journey!

The one thing that I do not understand is being a woman in most lives, yet, never having the satisfaction of having children that lived longer than me and grew into adulthood with children of their own providing me with grandchildren. In not one life have I found any grandchildren. In Anne's life, Elizabeth lived out a full life but no children. I don't know if there is any proof that Elizabeth had a child out of wedlock that could have been with Robert Dudley, whom she dearly loved and kept raising him to higher offices. She made him Earl of Leicester. Two other prominent men in her life were Sir Francis Drake and Sir Walter Raleigh. I have thought that she may have had a child that was later sent to America and could have been a part of my Montague heritage that was also related to Henry VIII. The reason I mention this is because, my past live memories related to Anne Boleyn could also be genetic memories!

As I have stated, I felt a youthful rebellion against organized religions as early as five years of age, culminating with leaving the church by age thirteen in the one where I was baptized. For many years I searched trying to find one religion with which I felt synchronicity. Studying various world religions, I realized all seemed to start with just ONE man and his followers. As it began to happen in the mid 1960's as I stumbled into Metaphysics and drifting into my own psychic ability. As unseen forces began communications through instincts, meditation, channeling and spiritual writings, more questions stirred in my head. Why would God speak to or inspire one man and not continue to speak to others throughout history? And why -- only MEN? Women are the physical producers of human beings and emotional strong hold, why wouldn't women's influence in religious writings been include in various religions?

When I considered the limitations hundreds and thousands of years ago compared with our modern communications and technologies, failure to move these religions forward through the ages just seemed unreliable to me. With my personal Christian background, I remained grounded in it while keeping an open mind to learn all that I could. In the spiritual guidance that came through to me, I was told that I was not meant to be attached to just one religion but seek to understand more and more and more. One problem I had was my insecurity of having the confidence in my own convections, which lengthened and limited my progress. I always seemed to be a salmon swimming upstream with anything related to religions. I always seemed ahead of my time, suffering the guilt and confusion that later seemed "normal" to others. Even in companions, I never sought younger friends but that was where the better communication transpired.

I wondered if there was any religion that had <u>not</u> been based on just one teacher or prophet. Paganism seemed to be a possibility but there was gods and goddess worship, which is over 40,000 years old and was once, practiced everywhere. Related to Paganism is Celtic religion that spread all over Europe into Asia. It became predominate in Spain and

Ireland. Out of Celtic religion became Wicca honoring Mother Earth and spiritual earth beings. Original Witchcraft was based on nature and witches were the original "doctors". Evil sprits were not a part of witchcraft, which was added by the Catholics through the decades. There was NO Beelzebub in witchcraft!

Vedic Hinduism and Zoroastrianism are considered the oldest organized religions. Hinduism was held to be the world's oldest religion. Hindu religious texts, the Vedas, are the oldest known written works on Earth and Sanskrit is the oldest written language. According to the calendar, when Rama appeared it was a million or so years ago. The estimates on just how old range anywhere from 5,000 to 20,000 years old, yet, there are no dates and facts, but its history is thought to be more than 50,000 thousands years old. Krishna, God himself according to the Vedic scriptures, appeared here 5,000 years ago. Buddha, about 500 B.C., Jesus, about 2,000 years ago. The origins of Hindu tradition have been traced as far as the ancient Vedic civilization

3,000 - 1500 BC although there are archaeological indications that strongly suggest such spiritual traditions whether Hinduism or not existed long before that - into pre-history. Australian aboriginal religion began about 6,000 years ago; Christianity, Judaism, and Islam are all Abrahamic religions. Abraham dates back to 1800 BC. I don't know of any religion that even considers the influence of possible Aliens from different planetary systems. There seems to be a lot of art and symbols to indicate those visitors. One book I read indicated the source of different races – i.e. black, brown, yellow and white - were because of inner planetary visitors.

Recent archeological sites reveal 70,000 year old carved statue of a snake in Botswana. Snakes have been religious symbols all over southern Africa. This unifying concept may be the earliest form of organized religious practices. Snakes and serpents played roles in religions everywhere around the world including Adam and Eve. To my own perceptions, the snake represents that in the newness of spring, it sheds its outer skin. It would seem a very painful process as is our processes of letting go of past traumas in this life or in past ones.

A prophet is never known in his own land – or TIME! History tells us that many of these great teachers were not recognized in their own time – crucified Jesus, being the best example. IF one opens their mind just a bit, there ARE many GREAT prophets through out all ages including our present day. It was the same with great artists. Interestingly, some of our greatest artists lived in the same era. Many died poor but today their paintings are worth millions of dollars.

Throughout my life from childhood forward, I have spent a lot of time alone, learning to do things for myself, travel alone, etc. I could say that one of the most enlightening, even spiritual awakenings I had was a very simple one – as great lessons often are! In the mid 1980's I wanted to see the Rose Bowl Prade floats in Pasadena that are displayed for a few days after the Parade. I could not find anyone to go with me. I was living in Newport Beach, CA that was over 50 miles away. I "took the bull by the horns" and decided to go ALONE! I throughly enjoyed moving at my own speed as I observed the many floats – then I decided to visit the Norton Simon Museum. There, too, I moved at my own pace, rested when I wanted. I visited the various parts of the Museum just pleasing myself and not having to go where someone else wanted to go. From that time on, I enjoyed shopping alone, going to the movies alone and always had my own choice. It was that day that I made the choice to go alone that helped me with many decisions from that time forward. It was a good thing, too, since from the mid 1960's forward, I have moved further and further away from any "organized" thinking and followed my own guidance – that wee small voice within.

As for those who participate in organized religions, my one wish would be that they learn to honor people who may not worship as they do and leave them alone! When people begin "preaching" at me or judge me to NOT be as "holy" as they think they are, they have no idea how many years and how my spiritual search has been a major part of my life while they wore theirs only on Sunday, then Monday pursuing growing their bank accounts. I sincerely believed that if you follow your dreams and goals, success will come -- so I wait and wait… From the time I arrived in Hollywood, I positively knew that my goals to produce films and or television with good moral values would eventually come my way. Instead, reaching for those goals was apparently my path to enlightenment -- a path so different than anyone would imagine a spiritual journey to be. My goal for this book is to share those devoted years of searching for answers so that if any of it appeals to the reader to open their mind to unlimited possibilities, I have achieved my goal.

Describing what I believe to be my past lives - be they fact or fiction - may help the reader understand repetitious dreams they may have had deja vue experiences while visiting places where they have never been, repetitious experiences where there seems to be no reason or understanding. So to use a bible quote "He who has ears, let him hear." Over a quarter of people in the United States and over four-fifths of the world believe in reincarnation.

Reaching a point of love, contentment, peace and a certain amount of wisdom within my own nature, yet from outward appearances lack of success when we are continually judged primarily only by financial success! I have realized why I had to have certain connections with various people, situations, places, et al, in my life so that I could end the never ending hold on the wheel of incarnation. It seems an oxymoron that I lived in a very glamorous world of movies and television, yet it has been the source of my greatest spiritual growth. The same could be said for love relationships. While religions teach us that we should have only one person to share sexual relations with, having had many love connections has also forced me into seeing how spiritual sex can be and for some of us, our greatest spiritual growth. It is so sad that it is made to be "dirty" and inspiration for a lot of crime. I learned that I could release the hold that kept me reinventing the same situation over and over through time and space. By my own standards, I feel free and content and I am IN love with the ALLNESS and I hope that I am able to complete whatever part of the OVER soul that was incomplete related to this person known only as Ann Palmer.

Namaste' and I wish you success on your own spiritual awakening journey...

ARTRIST PRAYER
Oh God, give me the ability to create, I pray,
Whether with expressions or words
A brush and paint, whatever I may be.
But please, Oh God, let me create beauty.
Guide my hands to the talents
Of which it is meant to give.
Fill the searching of this soul
That cries out to You
For guidance and for peace of mind.

Let my soul know satisfaction
Of creating beauty and of doing it well.
For this, Oh God, I pray, and
For the patience until your guidance
Will come to me one day.

WHEEL OF LIFE - ACTIVITY - TIME

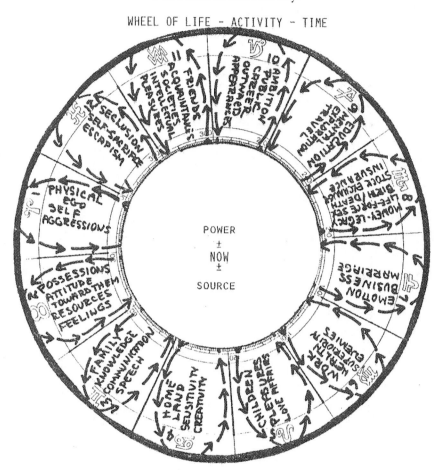

"THE SAGE IS HE WHO HAS ATTAINED THE CENTRAL POINT
OF THE WHEEL IN INDISSOLUBLE UNION WITHTHE ORIGIN,
UNITING IT'S NON-ACTING ACTIVITY"..."HE WHO HAS
REACHED THE HIGHEST DEGREE OF <u>EMPTINESS</u> WILL BE SECURE
IN REPOSE. TO RETURN TO THE ROOT IS TO ENTER INTO
THE STATE OF REPOSE, TO THROW OFF THE BONDS OF THINGS
TRANSITORY."

WHEN WE LIVE <u>NOW</u>, WE HAVE <u>WON</u>! (AND LIVE <u>ONE</u>!)

Thank you for your time in reading my experiences in my personal journey and research in what appears to be the more important experiences in my own past lives -- or genetic memory. I have included these websites to help you on your personal journey toward your spiritual awakening. I can be reached at my website AnnPalmer.net

ANN PALMER – http://www.annpalmer.net/ or
   http://www.WeddingsByAnn.com
Lynn Andrews - http://www.lynnandrews.com/
Jose Arguelles - http://www.lawoftime.org/home.html
Jean Shinoda Bolen - http://www.jeanshinodabolen.com
Gregg Braden - http://www.greggbraden.com/
Page Bryant - http://www.pagebryant.com/
Deepak Chopra - http://www.chopra.com/
Clarissa Pinkola Estes -http://www.wildwolfwomen.com/
Matthew Fox - http://www.matthewfox.org/sys-tmpl/door/
John Gray - http://home.marsvenus.com/
Louise Hay - http://www.louisehay.com/
Jean Houston - http://www.jeanhouston.org/
Shirley MacLaine - http://www.shirleymaclaine.com/
John Randolph Price -http://www.johnrandolphprice.com/
Don Miguel Ruiz - http://www.miguelruiz.com/
BRAD STEIGER - http://www.bradandsherry.com/brad.htm
Eckhart Tolle - http://www.eckharttolle.com/eckharttolle
Marianne Williamson - http://www.marianne.com/
Gary Zukav - http://www.zukav.com/home.html
http://www.newagepride.org/pages/Au --MANY MORE on this website